# What's Fair on the Air?

# What's Fair on the Air?

*Cold War Right-Wing Broadcasting
and the Public Interest*

HEATHER HENDERSHOT

THE UNIVERSITY OF CHICAGO PRESS     CHICAGO AND LONDON

HEATHER HENDERSHOT teaches at Queens College and the City University of New York Graduate Center. She is the author of *Shaking the World for Jesus: Media and Conservative Evangelical Culture* and *Saturday Morning Censors: Television Regulation before the V-chip.* Hendershot is also the editor of *Cinema Journal.*

The University of Chicago Press, Chicago 60637
The University of Chicago Press, Ltd., London
© 2011 by The University of Chicago
All rights reserved. Published 2011
Printed in the United States of America
20 19 18 17 16 15 14 13 12 11    1 2 3 4 5

ISBN-13: 978-0-226-32677-1 (cloth)
ISBN-13: 978-0-226-32678-8 (paper)
ISBN-10: 0-226-32677-2 (cloth)
ISBN-10: 0-226-32678-0 (paper)

Portions of chapters 3 and 4 appeared in "God's Angriest Man: Carl McIntire, Cold War Fundamentalism, and Right-Wing Broadcasting," *American Quarterly* 59, no. 2 (June 2007): 373–96.

Library of Congress Cataloging-in-Publication Data
Hendershot, Heather.
    What's fair on the air? : cold war right-wing broadcasting and the public interest / Heather Hendershot.
        p. cm.
    Includes bibliographical references and index.
    ISBN-13: 978-0-226-32677-1 (cloth : alk. paper)
    ISBN-10: 0-226-32677-2 (cloth : alk. paper)
    ISBN-13: 978-0-226-32678-8 (pbk. : alk. paper)
    ISBN-10: 0-226-32678-0 (pbk. : alk. paper) 1. Right-wing extremists—United States.
2. Radio in politics—United States. 3. Mass media and propaganda—United States.
4. Hunt, H. L. 5. Hargis, Billy James, 1925– 6. Smoot, Dan. 7. McIntire, Carl, 1906–2002.
I. Title.
    E743.5 .H43 2011
    302.23'4097309046—dc22

                                                                                2010052461

FOR MARGARET GAGE

# Contents

# Acknowledgments

This book began in 2001 as a short paper given at the Shelby Cullom Davis Center for Historical Studies at Princeton University; the paper was written in response to an essay by Randall Balmer on Carl McIntire's pirate radio station. So I thank the Davis Center, Balmer, and the Princeton Theological Seminary, where my research began, for getting me jump-started on this project. Later, the book could not have been written without access to documents held at the Columbia University Rare Book and Manuscript Library; the Cushing Memorial Library at Texas A&M; the Texas Tech Southwest Collections/Special Collections; and the National Archives, College Park, Maryland. I thank the librarians and archivists at all of these institutions, particularly the wonderful Texas Tech staff who rushed out to buy me a turntable to listen to phonograph records of *Life Line* and, at Columbia, Tara Craig and her wonderful colleagues.

The bulk of the work on McIntire was developed while I was visiting the Center for Religion and Media at New York University, and many thanks are due to the center for research support. Later, while visiting as the Anschutz Fellow in American Studies at Princeton University, I was able to finish revisions on the Billy James Hargis chapter. At Princeton, Hendrik Hartog was a most gracious host and colleague; I'm so pleased that we agree about *Buffy*, even if we cannot see eye to eye on Klingons. Finally, a John Simon Guggenheim Memorial Foundation Fellowship enabled the completion of the project, and the author expresses appreciation to the Warner Fund at the University Seminars at Columbia University for their help in publication.

Doug Mitchell at the University of Chicago Press was a pleasure to work with at every stage of the process; one simply could not ask for a better editor. The press's anonymous readers provided terrific feedback on the manuscript, and, in the early stages of the project, Peter Walsh provided wonderful technical assistance with images. Kevin Kruse, Rick Perlstein, Kimberly Phillips-Fein, Dan Rodgers, and members of the Columbia University Seminar on Religion in America most graciously read both polished and rough drafts of several chapters. Karen Beckman, Tim Corrigan, Stewart Hoover, Jonathan Kirshner, Sarah Kozloff, David Morgan, John MacKay, Ellen Seiter, the German Association for American Studies, and the Annenberg School for Communication at the University of Pennsylvania most kindly invited me to give presentations of the work-in-progress, and Jeff Turentine was not merely willing but actually excited to talk about H. L. Hunt with me. Allison McCracken provided shelter (and DVDs) during innumerable research trips to Chicago. Barbara Abrash encouraged my oenophilia; Mark Betz, Chris Sharrett, Brooks Hefner, and Kevin Maher my cinephilia; Derek Kompare, Eric Freedman, and Julie Lavelle my telephilia. An additional huge thanks goes to Frank Episale, who was my right-hand man during the last two years I worked on the book and who provided invaluable assistance when I was in the home stretch, as did the ever-vigilant Erin Lee Mock. I doubt the book would have ever materialized if not for J. Fred MacDonald, who shared his wonderful archive so generously, and who introduced me to so much terrific material. Both Fred and his 16mm films are invaluable treasures. Finally, the stupendous J. P. kept everything afloat, as always.

*What's Fair on the Air?* is dedicated to my high school history teacher, Margaret Gage, a woman of conviction, with gravitas and a sense of purpose. She also had a wonderful sense of humor, and how else could one approach the study of history, in the 1980s, in Birmingham, Alabama? The star of *Bedtime for Bonzo* was in the White House, and—impossibly, incredibly, ridiculously—George Wallace was back in the gubernatorial mansion in Montgomery. You had to laugh or cry. Mrs. Gage demonstrated through example how to take history seriously without losing sight of the comic absurdities of the human condition.

# Right-Wing Media vs.
# Cold War America

*"Lace, Luncheons, and Frying Pans" Collapse*
*into a "Nightmare of Raw Violence and Brutality"*

In the early 1960s, before infomercials, YouTube, and blogs, there was 16mm film. And Robert Welch, founder of the John Birch Society (JBS), had a plan for how to use it to increase the member rolls of his right-wing organization. Welch instructed his followers to invite their patriotic neighbors over for a night at the movies—a night of *serious* movies. Popcorn? Probably too frivolous, though pie and coffee might have been on hand to take the edge off of sitting through Welch's long, dry lectures.[1] One historian aptly describes the JBS as "a kind of matchmaker, where lone individuals with broad visions could join each other and help turn an ideology into a movement."[2] If the society was indeed a matchmaker, these slowly paced 16mm offerings were perhaps not the most exciting way to kickstart a first date. After circulating the talking-head films for a few years, the JBS created a new recruitment film with a bit more pizzazz. So let's start with this film as an introduction to cold war right-wing media.

Picture a soft-spoken man in a suit standing in a nondescript chapel with a cross mounted on the wall behind him. He quietly and rationally explains why he's joined the Birchers:

> I've been a minister now for about eighteen years, and though I've been alarmed at the drift away from fundamental church doctrine, it wasn't until I had read the John Birch Society material that I saw the parallel between the spiritual liberal takeover of the church and the liberal political takeover of our country.

Yet because of my own fundamentalist background, I hesitated to become a part of the John Birch Society, because I didn't want to mix religion and politics. But the more I meditated the more clear it became that the society's fight against communism was far more than just politics. Suddenly I realized that if we don't stop the advance of communism, none of us will be free to preach the gospel. Neither I nor any of my fundamentalist brethren hesitated during World War II to volunteer for the armed services, so why should we hesitate now? . . . I couldn't live with myself today unless I had joined the only nonreligious organization that has any chance of turning back the greatest enemy our country has ever faced.

It all sounds so logical. This pastor isn't the kind of Bible-thumping lunatic one might stereotypically associate with an ultraconservative group like the JBS. But most people watching this 16mm black-and-white recruitment film probably didn't consider themselves lunatics either. They were professional, white, middle- or upper-class suburbanites, living in California or elsewhere in Sunbelt America, where support for Barry Goldwater's candidacy was gaining momentum. There was surely also an audience for the film in Belmont, Massachusetts, where the JBS home office was based. Viewers were a self-selected group who felt a conservative grassroots movement fomenting all around them and were considering jumping in. They didn't know yet that Goldwater was going to lose and that the movement wouldn't fully crest until Ronald Reagan's ascension to office in 1980. And they had probably never seen this unidentified pastor before, wouldn't have even recognized his name—Tim LaHaye—if it had been given. Almost twenty years later, LaHaye would cofound the Moral Majority, and over thirty years later he would become world famous as coauthor of the bestselling *Left Behind* apocalyptic Christian book series (figure 1). But in the early 1960s LaHaye was nobody, just a minister in a recruitment film full of various *types*, designed to show the *averageness* of the JBS. The society, the film insisted, was not dominated by little old ladies in tennis shoes (the condescending caricature of Goldwater supporters) but, rather, by housewives, plumbers, doctors, even society matrons. The JBS drew members from every respectable walk of life, the film insisted with its casting choices (figures 2–5).

Some forty years later, I didn't immediately recognize Reverend LaHaye myself. I was at MacDonald & Associates, an archive in Chicago, drinking some gruesome instant coffee in a chilly storage room and watching the old 16mm JBS film piped into a TV monitor. On break from hunting down interesting films on eBay, the curator, broadcast historian J. Fred

FIGURE 1. Tim LaHaye, coauthor of the *Left Behind* book series and cofounder of the Moral Majority, appears in a John Birch Society film in the early 1960s to explain why religious people should be involved in politics. *John Birch Society Film II*, MacDonald & Associates.

FIGURE 2. A housewife makes a hard sell for the John Birch Society, warning viewers that "unless the present trend away from public morality and law and order is reversed, the women of this country will wake up some night to find that their little protected world of lace, luncheons, and frying pans has suddenly collapsed into a nightmare of raw violence and brutality." *John Birch Society Film II*, MacDonald & Associates.

FIGURE 3. Another housewife makes a more emotional appeal to explain why she joined the Birchers: "I guess it was my mother hen instinct that finally came out." *John Birch Society Film II*, MacDonald & Associates.

MacDonald, wandered through the room and noted, "Oh, there's Tim LaHaye," adding a few colorful pejoratives to express his contempt. What a "eureka" moment! Tim LaHaye in a John Birch Society recruitment film! Here was one of the men behind the New Christian Right explaining that religion and politics were not incommensurate, as many fundamentalists of the 1960s still believed, and admonishing concerned citizens to take action against communism by joining an organization that was widely understood, at the time, as part of the lunatic fringe, but which he contended was simply a group for rational, concerned anticommunists.

Later, LaHaye would be part of a movement that brought formerly separatist born-again Christians into politics. With Jerry Falwell and others, he helped, in effect, to convert fundamentalists into "conservative evangelicals," then into "conservative Christians." And today, this group sometimes even refers to itself as "people of faith," in a move that seems to mask any kind of specific political allegiance. (Some leaders of conservative Christian organizations contend, for example, that "people of faith" oppose gay marriage, when only a very specific kind of "faithful" person feels this way.) The *Left Behind* books and the Moral Majority, along with later groups like the Christian Coalition and the Family Research Council, may still seem

pretty "out there" to a lot of people, but there's no denying that many notions that used to be widely perceived as "extremist," such as the elimination
of welfare, huge tax breaks for the wealthy, or the eradication of reproduc-
tive choice, have shifted closer to the center of American political life.

In fact, conservative evangelicals have been so successful at making in-
roads into mainstream politics that when new extremists appear, like the
Tea Partiers attacking President Obama and comparing him to Hitler, veteran conservative activists like James Dobson and Gary Bauer seem almost balanced by comparison. A gun-toting libertarian featured on CNN
explaining that the "tree of liberty must be refreshed from time to time
by the blood of tyrants and patriots"[3] really does come across as more unhinged than Pat Robertson. With his occasional calls for assassination or
proclamations that Haitians made a "pact with the Devil," Robertson does
disturb, but he's generally canny enough to deliver his proclamations in a
low-key, rational-sounding manner. In any case, neither Robertson nor
the CNN libertarian sees himself as abnormal. And, indeed, right-wing
rage is not a deviation from the norm: it's America's default setting. As

FIGURE 4. A doctor is included in a John Birch Society film to illustrate the organization's appeal to upscale professionals. He compares communism to polio and expresses concerns about
socialized medicine. *John Birch Society Film II*, MacDonald & Associates.

FIGURE 5. A plumber breaks from his labor to explain the appeal of the John Birch Society to the average Joe. *John Birch Society Film II*, MacDonald & Associates.

Rick Perlstein explains so well, "the crazy tree blooms in every moment of liberal ascendancy, and . . . elites exploit the crazy for their own narrow interests."[4]

Some crazy trees bloom and die, while others put down roots for the long term. The JBS technically still exists, but it's a shell of its former self, its National Council peopled mostly by septuagenarians and octogenarians, including Nelson Bunker Hunt, a bit player in chapter 1 of this volume. But in the heady days of the emerging conservative movement of the early 1960s, who knew how bright the future of the JBS might be? The future of conservatism in general was still up for grabs, and few even saw the big picture of what was happening at the time. It was sometimes hard to disentangle the differences between the "extremism" of the JBS and the apparently more respectable conservatism of William F. Buckley, Russell Kirk, or Young Americans for Freedom. After all, in the 1950s fervent anticommunism was the norm; by the 1960s strong anticommunist language began to sound excessive to some, but certainly not to everybody. When did one cross the line from extreme conservatism to just plain extremism? Certainly, all virulent anticommunists could not reasonably be lumped together as extremists. Buckley's *National Review* repudiated the JBS in 1965, but the magazine was still anticommunist and opposed to federal action on civil rights, just like the JBS. Was this extremist? It was a label Buckley rejected, though he had no problem with "right-wing."

In fact, he and Welch had at one point been very much aligned in their thinking. In his history of modern American conservatism, Jonathan Schoenwald observes that in the mid-1950s, "Welch and Buckley seemed to be in total agreement in regard to what direction the [conservative] movement should go," and that "long before the creation of the John Birch Society, Welch was undeniably one of the best known—and well-respected—conservatives in the United States. The fact that the 1950s conservative community embraced Welch so warmly makes his later ostracization that much more telling." Schoenwald further argues that "Welch's acceptance and expulsion is, in some ways, a metaphor for the entire conservative movement from the late 1950s to the early 1970s."[5] The four key figures examined in this book would also be ostracized by the early 1970s, making room for more "legitimate" conservative forces. The difference from Welch, though, was that they had never been embraced by upright conservatives like Buckley. Welch was an articulate, successful businessman with deep ties to the National Association of Manufacturers; the broadcast extremists were, by comparison, mostly outsiders—freelance right-wingers, if you will. They agreed with Welch on many points, but they were louder and angrier in their self-presentation. There is no polite way to put it: they were tacky. This would forever limit their ability to directly impact "mainstream" politics, though they obviously fostered right-wing thinking among their millions of listeners and viewers, tilling the ground for the electoral rejection of the Great Society and the eventual triumph of Reagan.

Schoenwald argues that the JBS acted "much like a third party" insofar as it pushed Republicans to pay attention to certain issues the JBS held dear; the GOP gradually made adjustments that appealed to those "on the fringes" of the party.[6] Welch's organization would not thrive for long—and it would be an overstatement to imply that the society alone was responsible for the Republican Party's ultimate shift right—but, in pushing the party to appeal to its more conservative constituents, Welch's work did pay off over the long term. The extremist broadcasters pulled for many of the same issues that the JBS did, but they lacked Welch's organizational, top-down management skills. Instead of creating "cells" (purposely imitative of communist tactics) and promoting direct action (the campaign to impeach Supreme Court justice Earl Warren, most famously), the broadcast ultras created an alternative universe of words alone, of political coverage and pontification, where millions could hear—and in a few cases watch—right-wing news coverage. It was a primordial version of Fox News, lacking national sponsorship, centralized funding and distribution, and whatever legitimacy Fox News may now possess.[7]

Of course, no one could have foreseen a phenomenon like Fox News, and to politically moderate Americans in the cold war years, the differences that we can now discern between the JBS and other extremist groups were hardly visible. Though the pieces of the puzzle were hard to sort out at the time, some liberal commentators did think that they had a perfectly clear picture of what was happening in the early 1960s: there was a growing extremist movement, full of ignorant, anti-intellectual yahoos, and they could all pretty much be lumped together. In 1966 Richard Hofstadter famously described "the paranoid style" as a way of understanding the world based upon "heated exaggeration, suspiciousness, and conspiratorial fantasy."[8] History, the extremists of the 1950s and 1960s would have had us believe, was the product of a series of conscious decisions made by duplicitous politicians—all communists, or dupes of the Communist Party. McCarthy was emblematic of this worldview in the 1950s, but, Hofstadter observed, "today, the mantle of McCarthy has fallen on a retired candy manufacturer, Robert H. Welch, Jr., who is less strategically placed but whose well-organized following in the John Birch Society has had a strong influence."[9] Other cold war intellectual critics of right-wing extremism would also single out Welch and his society as the centerpiece of the extremist surge. The JBS was, indeed, one of the major right-wing groups of that era, but there were many others, some holdovers from the McCarthy years, others formed in the wake of the Goldwater campaign.

These ultraconservatives, or "ultras," as they were often called by their opponents, were not a coherent movement but rather a large number of fractured groups with fiercely individualist leaders at the helm. One of the things that these figures have in common is their unequivocal rejection of the "extremist" label. They weren't much more pleased with labels like "superpatriot." (FBI director J. Edgar Hoover disparaged them as irresponsible, "self-styled experts on communism" who made "more difficult the task of the professional investigator," and an FBI chief inspector referred to JBS members as "fanatics."[10]) "Extremist" is, admittedly, an insulting label that few actually embrace for themselves. Further, a broad adjective like "right-wing" implies a homogeneous and coherent philosophy and ideological purpose that didn't really fit across the board for these staunchly individualistic and idiosyncratic characters. It's the same problem one encounters today with "Christian Right," an awkward descriptor for a wide range of groups, and not a label that many people choose for self-designation. H. L. Hunt, Dan Smoot, Carl McIntire, Billy James Hargis, and the other characters of the cold war right were a disunified bunch, but they can be loosely grouped together as ultras, superpatriots, and extremists. Such labels are certainly dated—and usefully so. Such datedness reminds us that there was a moment when vilifying taxation and federal spending across the board was most typical of fringe conservatism.

The general consensus today is that Hofstadter went too far in psychologizing and pathologizing the "paranoid style" of extremists, but his impulse that there were some coherent elements to be found across this motley crew was a good one. As a group, the cold war right-wing extremists saw hidden agendas everywhere. They were incapable of compromise and demanded ideological purity. They were obsessive fact collectors who saw their point of view as objectively true, and their obsessive fact collection was frequently coupled with anti-intellectualism. Collating facts to make arguments (e.g., all foreign aid advances the cause of communism in the US and abroad) was considered rational and logical; such "research" did not make you an intellectual, for intellectuals were an elitist Ivy League cabal irredeemably tainted by liberalism. And there was no such thing as true liberalism. All liberals were actually communists or fellow travelers. Although not all of the right-wing extremists of the 1950s and 1960s were Christian fundamentalists, there was a kind of fundamentalist logic that united their thinking: there was no room for compromise, and certain inviolable texts—the Bible, the Constitution—could be read literally and referenced to prove the veracity of the extremists' positions. The ultras argued that they were not extreme at all. Only the Left was extreme: conservatives were just true patriots (figure 6).

Notwithstanding the many subtle differences among these individuals, they did come together in one concrete way: the right-wingers were programmed one right after the next on independent radio stations owned by ultras (mostly Christian fundamentalists) in the 1960s. There was a moment when you could sit in your home or car, in downtown Dallas or suburban Philadelphia, tune in a single spot on the radio dial, and listen to anticommunist, anti–civil rights, anti–United Nations, anti-fluoridation, anti-Halloween (pagan holiday!), anti–mainline Protestant, anti–Earl Warren, anti–federal income tax, anti–Social Security, anti-JFK (or LBJ or Nixon), pro-Goldwater, and pro-Jesus programming all day long. If the right-wingers did not constitute a single united movement, their ideas did

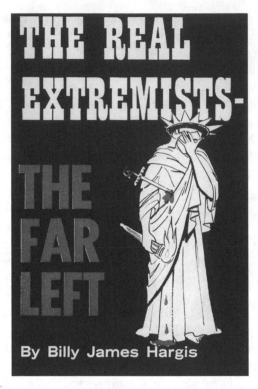

FIGURE 6. The cover of Billy James Hargis's book *The Real Extremists: The Far Left* graphically illustrates the rejection of the "extremist" label by the cold war right. Christian Crusade, 1964.

circle each other and overlap quite frequently, nowhere more so than on the radio.

Many of the extremist groups did not include broadcasting in their activities, but the ones that did were those with the greatest longevity, and the largest operating budgets. *What's Fair on the Air?* charts the rise and fall of four of the era's most prominent extremist broadcasters: H. L. Hunt, Dan Smoot, Carl McIntire, and Billy James Hargis.[11] All thrived on radio, with McIntire finding the largest audience of all of the extremists, and Smoot being the only one also to find a significant home on television. These four maintained their organizations and programs longer than most. Table 1 lists the incomes of the major right-wing organizations of the era. Though no indicator of financial success—*National Review* (not exactly ultra, but useful as a point of reference) was in the red for years—the figures do give

TABLE I **Annual Income of Selected Cold War Conservative Organizations**

| | 1958 | 1959 | 1960 | 1961 | 1962 | 1963 |
|---|---|---|---|---|---|---|
| *Twentieth Century Reformation Hour* (Rev. Carl McIntire) * # | 62 | 177.5 | 382.5 | 635.5 | 1,163 | 1,718 |
| *Human Events* # | 329.1 | 390.4 | 594.6 | 918.5 | 1,005.9 | 927.5 |
| *Life Line* * + # (H. L. Hunt) | 50.2 | 295.4 | 439.9 | 606.5 | 994.3 | 1,088 |
| John Birch Society @ % & # (Robert Welch) | N/A | 129.8 | 198.7 | 595.9 | 826.1 | 1,092.3 |
| Christian Crusade * # @ { (Rev. Billy James Hargis) | 275.3 | 373.2 | 595.5 | 817.2 | 775.4 | 677.2 |
| Christian Anti-Communist Crusade @ & (Dr. Fred C. Schwarz) | 104.9 | 207.7 | 366.5 | 1,209 | 725.5 | UA |
| Freedoms Foundation at Valley Forge | 327.5 | 333.4 | 633.3 | 817.3 | 706.2 | 711.8 |
| *National Review* # (William F. Buckley) | 390 | 287 | 370 | 563 | 704 | UA |
| *Manion Forum* * (Clarence Manion) | 305.6 | 385.3 | 405 | 472.5 | 600 | UA |
| American Economic Foundation | 320 | 443.5 | 481.3 | 562.2 | 538.3 | 953.1 |
| Dan Smoot * # | 186 | 206 | 242 | 320 | 384 | 455 |
| National Education Program % { (Harding College) | 151.3 | 182.1 | 232.9 | 293.4 | 240.7 | UA |
| Christian Nationalist Crusade # & (Gerald L. K. Smith) | 172.7 | 168.7 | 181.9 | 210.7 | 229.1 | 288.7 |
| Church League of America (Edgar C. Bundy) & # { | 49.9 | 50.2 | 78.2 | 196 | 200.4 | 235.1 |
| Citizens' Councils of America * # | 200 | 192 | 186 | 184 | 200 | UA |
| *Common Sense* # | 146 | 156 | 168 | 179 | 182 | 160 |
| Americans for Constitutional Action | 5.7 | 197.7 | 126.8 | 61.2 | 145.7 | 84.9 |
| Citizens Foreign Aid Committee for America | 37.5 | 40.9 | 49.7 | 60.1 | 62.5 | 72.3 |
| Liberty Lobby # | 20 | 30 | 40 | 50.2 | 58.7 | 60.5 |

*Source*: Income numbers are from several charts in Group Research Directory, "Special Reports Nos. 10–20" folder, report #16, Columbia Rare Books and Manuscripts Collection.

*Note*: Numbers represent thousands of dollars.

\* heavy involvement in broadcasting

& moderate involvement in broadcasting

# producer of print publications

% producer of 16mm films

{ distributor of 16mm films

@ producer of phonograph records

+ heavy producer of newspaper columns/editorials

UA figures unavailable.

a sense of the relative scope of each operation, showing that the media producers were clearly the biggest operators. It's impossible to clearly trace the circulation of all the record albums, pamphlets, books, 16mm films, and reel-to-reel tapes produced by ultraconservatives throughout the 1960s, as the distribution of such media was so completely decentralized. But there is a clear link between the amount of media produced, the amount of money that came in, and the longevity of each group. One might conjecture that Hunt, Smoot, McIntire, and Hargis were the most powerful of the right-wing broadcasters, but having a considerable cash flow did not necessarily translate directly into political power. These four were, at least, the most *heard* of the many competing cold war ultraconservatives.

Hunt and Smoot did not deal in religion, and we can tentatively refer to them as examples of the "secular right," though such terminology is tricky. Virtually all of the extremist groups of this era (along with most middle Americans) acknowledged that faith in God was one thing that made Americans better than communists. Smoot himself was a church-goer, yet he only emphasized religion in his annual Christmas broadcasts. Hunt was apparently not religious at all, though he experienced a curious conversion to "creeping" (an exercise that included elements of yoga but mainly consisted of crawling on all fours) and vegetarianism in his twilight years and announced his belief in physical (as opposed to spiritual) immortality.

McIntire and Hargis, on the other hand, can clearly be identified as fundamentalist Christians. Secular and religious American conservatives are often thought of as separate historical contingencies, but these four, though unable to join forces and actually get things done, shared a number of assumptions and tactics, and also sat next to each other on the radio (and occasionally TV) dial. Understanding right-wing broadcasting complicates our history, then, of not only the Republican Party's shift to the hard right but also the roots of the Christian Right. If secular and evangelical conservatives have had an on-again, off-again love affair since Reagan's election, the cold war secular and religious conservatives had a more stable—if largely unconsummated—relationship.

\*   \*   \*

In recent years there has been a surge in historical scholarship on American conservatism, with books examining it as both a bottom-up grassroots movement and a top-down expression of resentment against sixties leftism and the New Deal. Prominent studies include Rick Perlstein's *Before the Storm*, Kevin Kruse's *White Flight*, Dan Carter's *The Politics of Rage*, Lisa McGirr's *Suburban Warriors*, and Kim Phillips-Fein's *Invisible Hands*, to name just a few.[12] While it is commonly acknowledged that extremists like the White Citizens' Council and the JBS were forces to be reckoned with in the fifties and sixties, there has been no lengthy study to date of the ultras who ultimately had to be swept aside for the conservative movement to shift into the mainstream.[13] The present study, then, is an effort in this direction. With its central focus on four figures, it is hardly a comprehensive history of cold war extremism, yet these figures are considered not in isolation but rather in relationship to fellow extremists, such as the JBS, and in relationship to those who sought to remove the taint of extremism from conservatism, such as Barry Goldwater and Ronald Reagan. Classics such as Daniel Bell's 1963 anthology *The Radical Right* and Arnold Forster and Benjamin R. Epstein's 1964 *Danger on the Right* remain valuable, but they do not consider the extremists as media producers but, more flatly, simply as propagandists. And, of course, these authors had no crystal ball. They didn't know what was coming, and they assumed that exposing the ideas of people like Hargis, Smoot, Hunt, and McIntire would naturally defuse them. The right-wing movement was dangerous, but doomed to failure once exposed to the light, in theory. Ironically, the broadcast ultras similarly assumed that simply revealing liberal-communist villainy would inevitably destroy it.

Looking back, it's impossible to pick one moment when it was clear that the Republican Party was going to veer right, pulling along Democrats in its wake. Who knew that the War on Poverty, the brainchild of a Democratic president, would be dismantled by welfare reform, also the product of a Democratic president? Or that the communications deregulation begun by Reagan, with roots in the hard Right, would find its ultimate manifestation in The Telecommunications Act of 1996, under Clinton, the same "liberal" president who gave America welfare reform? As scholarship on the postwar conservative movement continues to grow, historians are beginning to have a clearer picture of America's political shift toward conservatism. Similarly, media studies scholars have charted the shifts in policy that have accompanied the rightward political tilt. Although historians have sorted out many of the details of the conservative shift, and media scholars have charted the changes in telecommunications policy that resulted from that shift, we don't yet have a clear understanding of where the historians' narratives and the media scholars' narratives converge.

This book, then, seeks to sort out the details of the cold war explosion of right-wing broadcasting that has been all but forgotten today.

Indeed, researching this book I sometimes wondered if some accounts of conservatism I'd read had been gaslighting me. The proof of widespread extremist groups—above and beyond the usual suspects such as the White Citizens' Councils and the Ku Klux Klan—was right in front of me, in archival documents neatly stacked in manila folders: there were hundreds of groups with names like We, The People!, The National Indignation Convention (a JBS front group), Liberty Lobby, the American Economic Foundation, and Freedoms Foundation at Valley Forge. The John Birch Society was only the tip of the iceberg. Further, these were hardly underground groups: many were broadcasting on radio and TV all over America. In 1962, the *Nation* published an entire special issue devoted to the radical Right, and in 1964 the magazine released a widely cited article entitled "Hate Clubs of the Air." It was not only the alternative press that noticed the large number of superpatriot broadcasts. In 1967, *TV Guide* published a scathing article on the ten thousand right-wing broadcasts airing in America each week.[14] If both the alternative and the mainstream press were aware of the surge in right-wing activity, academics were not far behind in studying the movement, though not focusing specifically on its presence on the airwaves: a number of books by historians and sociologists appeared such as Seymour Martin Lipset and Earl Raab's *The Politics of Unreason: Right Wing Extremism in America, 1790–1970*, Bell's *The Radical Right*, and, of course, Hofstadter's famous essay.[15]

It's hard to say with certainty why the superpatriots have been so little studied since their heyday. By the 1970s, when the ultras were finally decimated by the Internal Revenue Service, the Federal Communications Commission (FCC), and, of course, by the rise of better organized, more "legitimate" and well-funded groups, all were eager to get the bitter taste of the fanatics out of their mouths. In the fall of 1961, attorney general Robert Kennedy had approached Joseph Rauh Jr., a civil rights lawyer, and Walter Reuther, the president of United Auto Workers, for advice on wrangling the radical Right. The result was a twenty-four-page document, widely known as "The Reuther Memo," which advised submitting Fairness Doctrine complaints against right-wing broadcasters to the FCC and pursuing IRS investigations to ferret out tax violators among the extremist organizations. The IRS initiative was dubbed the "Ideological Organizations Audit Project."[16] Both the FCC and IRS strategies were quite effective, and the very existence of the memo made for endless conspiratorial tirades from the extremists (in this case not without cause, for the brothers Kennedy really did have it in for them). By the end of the decade, liberals were glad to be done with the extremists, hardly imagining that a conservative triumph was still in the works, guided by the capable hands of people like Paul Weyrich and Richard Viguerie. At the same time, the new conservative groups wanted to distance themselves from the embarrassing antics of the extremists. Years later Viguerie would go so far as to contend that there simply were no real extremists—it was all a liberal smear campaign.[17] Regardless of how embarrassing the ultras may have been to later conservatives, the reality is that they did exist; they were not simply fantasized by liberal-communist intellectuals and a left-wing media bund embodied by Walter Cronkite and *TV Guide*. As Ingrid Bergman exclaims when she finally realizes that her husband has been pulling a fast one on her in *Gaslight*, "I'm not mad!" Cold war right-wing extremists were real, not the figment of an overheated liberal imagination.

There are multiple explanations for the ongoing amnesia surrounding the ultras. First, the contemporary right has mainstreamed itself, and it is unpleasant to pull extremist skeletons out of the closet, especially since the ultras so strongly opposed the civil rights movement. Another explanation for the amnesia is that it's hard to remember broadcasters who made a giant splash and then seemed to disappear without a trace. Of course, they didn't really disappear insofar as they finely crafted a conservative discourse that has lived on in different guises to this day. Fox News pundit Bill O'Reilly opens his book *Culture Warrior*, for example, by claiming to oppose both the "extreme right" and the "extreme left," and then he attacks "secular pluralists" using language that sounds very much like that used by cold war extremists.[18] Yet even if many of their rhetorical strategies do seem to have persevered, none of the cold war superpatriots persisted into the 1970s and 1980s or—notwithstanding some of Billy James Hargis's interesting efforts—played crucial, active roles in the formation of the New Right or the New Christian Right. The cold war broadcasters were washouts who forged something mighty, then quickly receded. This does make them seem forgettable. Yet what they forged was intricate and fascinating while it existed. Dan T. Carter concludes his masterful study of George Wallace by observing that Wallace "was the most influential loser in twentieth-century American politics." If ultimately not as *important* as Wallace, the cold war broadcasters were certainly among the most *interesting* losers of twentieth-century American politics. Finally, it has been convenient for liberals in particular to forget these broadcasters because they were driven off the air by the Fairness Doctrine and a cold war liberal conception of what it meant to serve "the public interest." Contemporary conservatives claim that liberals only want to restore the doctrine to drive conservative talk radio off the air, a claim that is not without some justification. So liberals gain nothing by remembering that this is, indeed, how the doctrine was used at one moment in the past.

*   *   *

*What's Fair on the Air?* presents an analysis not only of the cold war extremists rejected by what would become the mainstream conservative movement but also, specifically, of the FCC's battle against extremist broadcasters. According to the Communications Act of 1934, broadcasters were required "to serve the public interest, convenience, and necessity." This phrasing originated in the Transportation Act of 1920; the public interest was invoked as a rationale to decide issues such as "whether new or duplicating railroad construction should be authorized or an existing line abandoned."[19] Thus, the public interest was understood in strictly practical, technical terms; transferred to communications regulation, this conception of the public interest would be interpreted to mean that overlapping radio signals did not serve the public interest. Therefore, the government needed to license individual broadcasters so that such technical problems could be eliminated.

That the public interest might have a strong political valence (beyond the obviously politically charged implications of choosing who exactly gets a license) became clearer to policy makers later, particularly in the years leading up to World War II. In 1939, the National Association of Broadcasters had, Alan Brinkley notes, "adopted new codes sharply limiting the sale of radio time to 'spokesmen of controversial public issues.' "[20] This was in no small part a response to Father Coughlin's radio diatribes against Jews, FDR, and American engagement in the war, and by the end of 1940 Coughlin had "virtually no access to the air."[21] The FCC's 1941 *Mayflower* decision declared that "the public interest—not the private—is paramount. . . . A truly free radio cannot be used to advocate the causes of the licensee . . . In brief, the broadcaster cannot be an advocate."[22] *Mayflower* was a decision against editorialization, hot on the heels of the silencing of Coughlin. Coughlin had been both wildly popular and wildly controversial, and although the *Mayflower* case was not directly connected to him, there was, because of the use he had made of the US airwaves (not to mention Hitler's and Mussolini's harnessing of the power of radio overseas), wide concern that radio could be a very dangerous tool when left in the wrong, opinionated hands.

The 1941 decision would evolve to the next level with the FCC's crafting of the Fairness Doctrine as part of the commission's 1949 report on editorializing. With this report, the FCC removed the prohibition on editorializing, instead requiring broadcasters to cover controversial issues of public importance, and, when providing such coverage, to present multiple points of view. In light of the broadcasting industry's later hostility toward the doctrine it's hard to believe that, at the time, the president of the National Association of Broadcasters declared the 1949 decision "a victory in [sic] behalf of freedom of expression."[23] At that moment, broadcasters did not feel shackled by the notion of balanced coverage but rather relieved by the lifting of the ban on editorials.

The Fairness Doctrine itself remained a measure that would be only sporadically enforced before the proliferation of the broadcast ultras in the early 1960s, when it would be used quite successfully against right-wing speech. By the early 1970s, the last of the superpatriots were off the air. The ultras, in effect, pushed the FCC to deliberate the meaning of not only "the public interest" but also "the public." Were the superpatriots a legitimate part of the public? Did segregationists have a right to rebut integrationists on the news? Could the Fairness Doctrine possibly be enforced in a neutral manner? Ultimately, the FCC was more reactive than proactive in addressing such questions. The government agency did not go out of its way to hunt down right-wing (or left-wing) speech but instead waited for citizens to lodge complaints, with occasional input from the FBI and the Kennedy, Johnson, and Nixon administrations, to be sure.[24]

To the great distress of the commission, following the 1966 *United Church of Christ v. FCC* court of appeals decision citizens would attempt to redefine "the public interest" as social and political, not purely technical. The *United Church of Christ* decision forced the commission to allow citizens, as opposed to simply business competitors, to petition to deny license renewal. In other words, before 1966 a "petition to deny" could only be filed by one corporate entity that wanted the right to operate a station on which someone else had staked a claim.[25] Citizens had no "standing" in the process and were legally invisible when it came to license renewal. For citizens to usurp the language of "the public interest" (for the public, in effect, to attempt to define the public interest) was a radical shift, and one that did not delight the FCC.

When forced to define "the public," the FCC tends to refer to consumerism rather than citizenship, apparently seeing the former as more politically neutral than the latter. As Steven D. Classen has shown, for example, the FCC's ruling (linked to the *United Church of Christ* court case) against WLBT, a racist Mississippi TV and radio station, was not viewed by the commission as a triumph for *citizens* opposing racism but rather as a triumph for *consumers*, who deserved a high-quality product. Similarly, consumer interests are protected by regulations against plugola, payola, and deceptive advertising (here, the Federal Trade Commission is involved too), and by regulations regarding access for political candidates and regulations against indecency. Further, the FCC's 1960 policy statement created the concept of "ascertainment," stating that broadcasters were obliged to ascertain local community needs, but shying away from actually defining "community needs." Generally speaking, then, the FCC has tried to keep the public as depoliticized a concept as possible, but the growing number of Fairness Doctrine challenges against extremist broadcasters throughout the 1960s was a challenge to this neutral stance. The Fairness Doctrine itself was doomed, in part, because it was an attempt to serve an inchoate idea of the public.

As I've noted, the doctrine stated that broadcasters—station owners, as opposed to individual commentators—were obliged to cover controversial issues of public importance, and when broadcasters aired one point of view on a controversial issue they were also obliged to convey the other side of the issue. This did not necessarily have to be done within a single program, though it could be. Further, one did not have to give precisely equal time to the opposing side. Each side simply had to be given the opportunity—literally given, if it could not afford to purchase airtime—to express its perspective. Obviously, the most efficient way to fulfill the doctrine was simply not to make attacks on one point of view and therefore not to be obliged to allow representatives of the other point of view to come on air to make a rebuttal. Instead, journalists themselves would strive for balance so that no Fairness Doctrine complaints could be raised. Further, broadcasters were obliged to provide public-service programming, so this was one place where issues could be discussed from different angles. Such public-affairs programs were often ghettoized on Sundays, when the least amount of advertising revenue was at stake.

The deregulation of the broadcast industry by Reagan's FCC is typically cited as the moment when the concept of "public service" began to rapidly decline, finally all but disappearing. Reagan's administration flatly

declared the marketplace to be the best measure of public needs: quality could best be gauged by profitability. If children's TV, distance learning, and public-affairs programs could not garner high ratings, then they should be replaced by something more lucrative. From this perspective, programs with high ratings are, intrinsically, those that serve "the public interest." The demise of the Fairness Doctrine in 1987 enabled a renaissance of right-wing broadcasting—beginning with Rush Limbaugh and coming to a head with Fox News and, in particular, with the very highly rated *O'Reilly Factor*, and, later, *Glenn Beck*. Ascertainment has been eliminated, and the notion that broadcasters should specifically serve *local* needs has been seriously diluted. Clearly, deregulation brought the end to an older conception of the public interest.

This all sounds very bleak. And it also has a romantic undertone, as if broadcasters *used to* serve the public interest or community needs. It may be tempting to wax nostalgic about the days before deregulation, but broadcasting's public-service function never truly lived up to anyone's high expectations. Michael Curtain has shown how New Frontier documentaries served the Kennedy administration's global agenda, and Laurie Ouellette's research on the origins of American public television further complicates our notions of how TV serves the public and conceptualizes "good citizenship."[26] Further, Classen's work shows how the White Citizens' Council's TV and radio programs were understood as serving "the public interest," using a very narrow definition of who constituted "the public."[27] Reagan's FCC may have undermined the regulatory concept of serving the public interest, but there was no golden age when broadcasters indisputably properly served that interest.

If one takes an inclusive view of "the public," then, as the FCC claimed to in the cold war years, the problem with the ultras from a regulatory perspective was not that they used the airwaves to promote a right-wing agenda, but rather that the stations that gave or sold them time did not also attempt to serve the interests of moderates and progressives. These stations thought it was acceptable to define a particular segment of viewers and listeners as "the public" in its entirety. Citizen petitioners opposing license renewal of stations carrying such programs, conversely, did not see right-wing viewers and listeners as a legitimate part of the public at all. The positions on all sides were flawed: the superpatriots were broadcast on scarce, publicly owned airwaves, and stations airing them thus violated the terms of their licenses by providing only one political perspective; the FCC's claim of neutrality was impossible—they *were* perplexed, for

example, by the fundamentalist perspective conveyed on right-wing radio stations, and they could not possibly hope to define the public interest impartially; and many liberal petitioners against the superpatriots did
think that certain kinds of speech should be regulated away. Such extreme,
unbalanced speech was inappropriate on the scarce, publicly owned airwaves, but, still, "regulation" should be understood for what it was—a
euphemism for "censorship."

*   *   *

In the course of researching *What's Fair on the Air?* I've often been disturbed by what I've encountered. Research trips are always precious, with
not a minute wasted, but I simply had to leave an archive early one day
after hearing Dan Smoot describe the March on Selma as little more than
a "sex orgy" led by "filthy degenerates." On a good day, on the other
hand, I've had a chuckle—reading, for example, about how Carl McIntire
planned to parade a platoon of Peking ducks in front of the White House
gates to protest Nixon's rapprochement with China. Though there's plenty
of such fodder, my intention is not to poke fun at the ultras. Yet they were
mostly a humorless bunch, and it would be ridiculous to be equally severe
and avoid sharing some of the more unusual, occasionally comic details
of their stories. There has been a tendency among scholars of the Right
to treat their subjects quite respectfully, compensating to some extent for
Hofstadter's condescension, and "smoothing over the baroque strangeness of the American right," as Kim Phillips-Fein puts it.[28] In these pages,
this baroque strangeness will not be muted.

The argument that every president between Herbert Hoover and Ronald
Reagan was a communist dupe seems to me more than a little absurd, but
what is interesting is not so much disputing this kind of claim but rather
understanding its proponents' explanations of why their beliefs were rational and not right wing in the slightest. In part, then, *What's Fair on the
Air?* is a study in how the relationship between extremism, conservatism,
and moderation played out during the cold war, especially in the 1960s.
How did the superpatriots attempt to prove they were conservatives, not
extremists? How did the FCC attempt to define its own position as "moderate" or "neutral" in these years, even as the superpatriots insisted that
the commission was hopelessly liberal?

Chapter 1 centers on oil magnate H. L. Hunt's public-affairs radio and
TV programs, which he made throughout the 1950s and 1960s, first in col-

laboration with Dan Smoot, and later in collaboration with Wayne Poucher and Melvin Munn. Smoot and Hunt began working together in the early 1950s, creating half-hour programs such as *Facts Forum* and *Answers for Americans* that featured "balanced" debate on political issues. By the 1960s, Smoot and Hunt were producing unabashedly right-wing public-affairs programs, such as Hunt's 1960s radio and TV show, *Life Line*, which was conceptualized as an advertisement for free enterprise. In charting the development of Hunt's propaganda machine, we can clearly discern the shift from 1950s "consensus culture" to that culture's dissolution in the wake of the progressive social movements of the 1960s. Hunt was the super-patriot who was in the broadcasting game the longest, and, although he did endure some amount of government investigation because of the spurious nature of his not-for-profit (untaxed) educational and religious operation, he managed to escape punishment time and time again.

Chapter 2 examines Smoot's broadcast activities after leaving Hunt's operation in 1957. From then until the early 1970s, the *Dan Smoot Report* was a successful newsletter, radio show, and TV program. The radio version of the *Report* was aired almost exclusively on small independent stations owned by fundamentalists, while the TV show was aired mostly on stations in small markets, though sometimes with national network affiliations. The program featured an implicitly racist states' rights stance closely aligned with that of Smoot's ally, the JBS. Smoot talked a big game but never had sufficient political muscle to carry through on his ideas. This chapter considers Smoot as a political failure but, simultaneously, as an example of triumphant right-wing localism, situating him within the FCC's attempts to regulate the meanings of "the local," "the public," and "the public interest."

Chapter 3 turns to the Reverend Carl McIntire, a pivotal figure between separatist fundamentalists and the newly emerging neoevangelicals epitomized by Carl Henry, Billy Graham, and other proponents of the new worldly form of born-again Christianity that emerged in the cold war years and sought to pull fundamentalists out of their post–Scopes trial separatism into worldly engagement. It was this movement that would eventually morph into the New Christian Right in the 1970s.[29] Notably, in the 1930s, between the Scopes trial and the emergence of the postwar fundamentalist extremists, America had seen a surge of fascist anti-Semites—epitomized by figures such as Gerald B. Winrod, William Dudley Pelley, and Gerald L. K. Smith—generally grouped together under the banner of the Old Christian Right. In his landmark study, Leo P. Ribuffo argues that the careers of

Winrod, Pelley, and Smith "show that the 'extremism' of the far right often converged with the cultural and political mainstream. Theses three agitators attracted intermittent support from prominent officials and businessmen . . . [T]heir favorite countersubversive, racist, and anti-Semitic motifs had long circulated through American society."[30] McIntire and his fellow extremist broadcasters, too, both tapped into and fostered the already entrenched prejudices of their listeners, but in the years following the defeat of fascism in Italy and Nazism in Germany, overt anti-Semitism in public discourse was pushed farther to the "fringes" of society than it had been in the 1930s. McIntire and the other broadcast extremists were not above an occasional reference to the *Protocols of the Learned Elders of Zion*, but they were more inclined to tap into a different set of prejudices, fostering in particular a fear and hatred of communism, and a willingness to project communism onto virtually any manifestation of liberalism, especially the civil rights movement. At the peak of his success in the cold war years, Ribuffo notes, Billy Graham was proud to proclaim that he was opposed by both "extreme fundamentalists from the right and extreme liberals from the left."[31] For their part, McIntire and his cohort were proud to be exactly those "extreme fundamentalists" who rejected Graham.

McIntire represents the old-school fundamentalist camp, yet I argue, contrary to previous accounts, that he was not squarely a separatist insofar as he was very active not only as a broadcaster but also as a high-profile political protester. He was, ultimately, an embarrassing reminder of the extremist, uncompromising image that the new evangelicals hoped to cast aside. This chapter veers away from media issues to consider not McIntire the broadcaster but McIntire the religious and political figure, though the two roles are difficult to separate insofar as McIntire was a thorn in the side of the neoevangelicals—and even a problem for his own fundamentalist constituency—precisely because of his high-profile media presence.

Chapter 4 turns to McIntire's FCC hearing. At his height, McIntire was on over six hundred radio stations, more than any of the other ultras. He not only hosted his own show, he also owned his own station, and he was under constant FCC threat for violating the Fairness Doctrine. Whereas the typical story of this era, as told by the defeated right-wingers, is simply that their stations were taken away by a bigoted, unfair FCC, by examining the eight-thousand-page transcript of McIntire's nine-month-long hearing to retain his station we can decipher a more complicated story, in which a hearing commissioner and his witnesses spent almost a year debating what the difference was between religion and politics, what was fair and unfair, what it meant to be "controversial" or to make a "personal attack," and what it ultimately meant to serve the public interest and satisfy the Fairness Doctrine. McIntire emerges as a fascinating symbolic figure of fundamentalism in confrontation with secular modernity, as represented by the FCC.

Chapter 5 turns to the Reverend Billy James Hargis, the only figure of the four who truly understood how to play politics. Successfully allying himself with other groups and rallying grassroots activists, he was able to stall and finally shut down a major California public-school sex-education initiative, a huge triumph in an era when most of the ultras were incapable of effective political mobilization. Further, Hargis was a maverick in direct-mail fundraising and adept at on-air fundraising via his *Christian Crusade* radio and television show. He was both a prototypical televangelist and an important link between the cold war Christian right and the New Christian Right that emerged in the 1970s.

Perhaps the longest surviving link to the cold war extremist programs is William F. Buckley's *Firing Line* (1966–99), a show that can be understood, at least in part, as a spirited intellectual retort to the superpatriots. Buckley began his career in the company of these characters, appearing regularly on Hunt's *Answers for Americans* and even writing a guest column for Hunt's *Facts Forum* newsletter. If Buckley differed in many ways from the ultras, he did share their disdain of the Fairness Doctrine, all the while abiding to it, unlike the ultras, by offering multiple points of views on issues. This was not about "fairness," from his perspective. It was simply the intelligent way to talk politics. Buckley interviewed a few of the characters who appear in the following pages, including Barry Goldwater, Fred C. Schwarz, and Rush Limbaugh. Of these three *Firing Line* guests, Limbaugh is the one who currently has the most cultural resonance—and his rise is directly interconnected with the fall of the superpatriots. In the wake of Reagan's suspension of the Fairness Doctrine in 1987, right-wing broadcasting has experienced a renaissance, with Limbaugh being one of the players in the forefront. Although some of the concerns have shifted, right-wing TV and radio pundits today have also recycled much of the free market and libertarian rhetoric that the sixties broadcasters crafted, even targeting some of the same issues—most obviously, opposition to federal health care and federal taxation. Subject to ratings, supported by big advertising dollars, nationally broadcast, and not presenting themselves as fulfilling the FCC's public-service mandate, however, broadcasters like Limbaugh, O'Reilly, Glenn Beck, and Sean Hannity are in a new league.

Hunt, Smoot, McIntire, and Hargis were, conversely, abject failures. They were skilled at passionately attacking the political status quo yet had little practical sense of how change might actually be effected. Anticommunism and opposition to government spending were not enough to forge a coherent social movement. It took abortion, gay rights, the Equal Rights Amendment, and other hot-button, emotionally resonant *social* issues to finally make a New Christian Right coalesce. As Viguerie wrote in 1979, "The New Right is looking for issues that people care about, and social issues, at least for the present, fit the bill."[32] Taking a swing at the Business Roundtable, a conservative businessmen's group obsessed with economic issues, Weyrich noted that same year that "We talk about issues that people care about, like gun control, abortion, taxes, and crime. Yes, they're emotional issues, but that's better than talking about capital formation."[33] If one substitutes "communism" for "capital formation" this could be a retort to the ultras, who were similarly unable to drop their core issue—communism—and remained stuck in that groove like a needle on a scratchy old LP. A politically effective movement could not be built in the 1970s based only on opposition to communism, and, in the 1960s, secular and fundamentalist ultraconservative groups had not yet latched on to the emotional issues that would foment a movement. Moreover, they were simply too individualistic—and cranky—to forge productive tactical alliances.

Only Hargis was capable of long-term fundraising and coalition building, but, ultimately defeated by sexual and financial scandals, even he failed to fully transition to the new era of the Moral Majority, the Eagle Forum, and other successful organizations that emerged in the 1970s and 1980s. The cold war extremists simply were not power players in the "Reagan Revolution." They were the oddities who finally had to be left behind—by Buckley and the *National Review*, by Governor Ronald Reagan, and by the architects of the New Right, Viguerie and Weyrich—in order for the conservative movement to gain ground and, finally, legitimacy.

So, can the cold war extremist broadcasters shed any light on today's "legitimate" right-wing broadcasters, many of whom rail against attempts to reinstate the Fairness Doctrine yet also claim to be, à la Fox News, "fair and balanced"? It's tempting to assume that today's crew has simply picked up where the old Right left off. In fact, though, many of today's radio and TV commentators rant and rave in a way that actually exceeds anything heard during the cold war years. McIntire, the most abrasive of the four central figures examined in *What's Fair on the Air?*, seems almost mild mannered compared to Beck. Ultimately, we cannot draw straight lines from the cold war extremist broadcasters to contemporary TV and radio personalities like Hannity, Limbaugh, O'Reilly, and Robertson, but there are dotted lines connecting the old broadcasters to the new. Of course, certain beliefs have carried over—that there is a left-wing media conspiracy, that federal spending on social welfare is evil, and so on. But the strongest clear connection between old and new may well be the relationship of each to the Fairness Doctrine. The cold war broadcasters went off the air because of the doctrine, and the new broadcasters went on the air almost immediately after Reagan suspended the doctrine. While Hunt, Smoot, McIntire, and Hargis lost the battle against Big Government in general and the FCC in particular, there is no denying that they ultimately won the war.

# "A Strong Reek of the Not-Quite-Crackpot"

## H. L. Hunt, Right-Wing Radio's "Constructive" Conservative

Winston Churchill . . . is reported to have said about a tedious socialist of unconventional sexual disposition that he had managed to "give sodomy a bad name." Mr. Hunt has done his share among capitalists he has known to give capitalism a bad name, not, goodness knows, by frenzies of extravagance, but by his eccentric understanding of public affairs, his yahoo bigotry, and his appallingly bad manners. —William F. Buckley Jr., *Execution Eve*, 1975[1]

Haroldson Lafayette Hunt was a very strange man. Owing to incredible intuition, business acumen, and just plain good luck, he was able to capture billions of barrels of Texas oil. In fact, for some time he was considered the richest man in America. He loved making money, although he didn't particularly relish spending it. He did splurge by buying a home in Dallas, Texas, that was a duplicate of Mount Vernon, with one major difference: it was five times larger. As an octogenarian in the 1970s, he still went to work everyday, wearing a blue suit that had slowly changed color over the years, as he had only the bottom half dry cleaned. At lunchtime, the old man pulled out a sack lunch of fresh dates, pecans, apricots, celery, and perhaps a Thermos of thin broth, laying it all out on a makeshift tablecloth made of newspaper (figure 7). His office was spare, the only decoration a picture of his mentally unbalanced son, Hassie. For years, Hunt had sought various magic cures for the boy; one day the answer was valium, the next prostitutes. Finally, lobotomy took a bit of the edge off of Hassie's violent fits. But just a bit. Other than curing Hassie and sharing the bounty

FIGURE 7. Penurious billionaire H. L. Hunt drove himself to work everyday, parked in a free lot to save money, and carried a sack lunch of fruits and vegetables. Bettman/Corbis, 1972.

of his own gene pool—he had fifteen children (that he acknowledged, at least)—Hunt had one great passion: exposing the evils of communism and the goodness of the free market. A friend had once described his political philosophy as "to the right of [President William] McKinley," adding that Hunt thought that "communism began in this country when the government took over the distribution of mail."[2]

Now, many wealthy men have opposed taxation, government regulation, and social-welfare programs. What made Hunt unique was that he was extremely, even obscenely wealthy, and the one thing that he really enjoyed spending money on was anticommunist media. From 1951 to 1975, his anticommunist, pro-free-market broadcasts ran almost continuously, in every state, on hundreds of radio stations; for one year the show was even on a small number of television stations. The message was sent out via subscription newsletter as well. With "his eccentric understanding of public affairs, his yahoo bigotry, and his appallingly bad manners," as William F. Buckley Jr. put it, Hunt became the symbol of the so-called right-wing lunatic fringe—hardly "fringe," if you could tune it in on almost any radio in America!—that emerged in the postwar years and peaked in the 1960s.

By the 1970s, Hunt's sons had entered the limelight as well. Lamar Hunt founded the American Football League and was an innovator in the promotion of professional tennis and soccer. Herbert and Bunker Hunt had been caught attempting to corner the world silver market. (Could the crooks really have thought that no one would notice an ongoing attempt to purchase all the silver in the world?) They were also entangled in a wiretapping caper. Like his father, Bunker became notorious for not only his right-wing politics but also for his success in business. He became one of the biggest contributors to the John Birch Society in the US; he discovered massive deposits of oil in Libya; he raised prize stallions; he contributed a quarter of a million dollars (in cash, in a briefcase) to the 1968 George Wallace presidential campaign as a "rainy day" fund for emergency use; and he put up a million-dollar secret "trust fund" to persuade Curtis LeMay to be Wallace's running mate.[3] A flurry of books appeared in the late 1970s and early 1980s to cash in on public interest in the scandalous Hunt family of Dallas. One was even endorsed by Larry (J. R. Ewing) Hagman.[4] Indeed, it would have been hard to have viewed the 1978 premiere of *Dallas*, in which J. R. watches television in disgust as a lumpy man in unflattering plastic-rimmed glasses testifies before an investigatory committee, and not note the lumpy man's striking resemblance to Bunker.

In fact, Bunker made similar TV appearances in the 1970s and '80s, his hand caught in innumerable cookie jars.

H. L. Hunt had a few run-ins with the authorities himself, but he never *really* quite got caught at anything. A brilliant gambler, so good at memorizing cards that he simply didn't need to cheat, Hunt thought there was something special about himself that raised him above other men. He had learned to read before he was three years old and had been clever with numbers from an early age.[5] That he had nursed at his mother's breast until the age of seven was a point of pride, further evidence of his innate specialness.[6] Normal rules didn't apply to him, he reasoned. In point of fact, he did seem impervious to the slings and arrows of his own outrageous fortune. In 1934 his second wife, Frania Tye Lee, discovered that her husband of nine years was also married to another woman, and that he was H. L. Hunt, the richest man in America. She had not even known his real first name, though perhaps a seed of suspicion had been planted when he insisted upon naming their first child (inconveniently a girl) Haroldina. His secret exposed, H. L. tried to convince Frania to move to Utah and convert to Mormonism so that their bigamous relationship would be legal. When that didn't work, he bought her off. He learned a valuable lesson and did not actually marry the next woman, instead setting her up with their children in a house a few miles away from where his legitimate "first family" lived in Dallas. It's easy to see why Buckley and others felt that H. L. Hunt gave conservatism a bad name. He was an indisputable scoundrel, an eccentric, and, worse, a buffoon.

But he *did* keep a propaganda machine oiled and running on American radio for twenty-four years. There were many prominent anticommunists, like Fred C. Schwarz, who made successful sporadic forays into media production, but only Hunt spread an anticommunist message seven days a week, year in and year out. How did he pull it off? What did he accomplish? How did the endeavor change over time, as anticommunist diehards of the 1950s were forced to contend—grudgingly, painfully, angrily—with the countercultural ethos of the 1960s? And, if Hunt was the preeminent creator of extremist media in the 1950s and 1960s, what exactly did it mean to be "extreme" in those years?

Clearly, simply being anticommunist didn't make one an extremist. It was a question of *how* one was anticommunist. For cold war liberals and moderates, the strategy for dealing with communism, in theory if not in practice, was "containment" and "peaceful coexistence." By the 1960s, communism was still seen as a threat—indeed, the war in Southeast Asia was accelerating—but the credibility of obsessively focusing on internal subversion and conspiracy was waning. It was a liberal commonplace that communism was an *external* threat. To see it as an internal threat—to go so far as to accuse President Eisenhower of being a "dedicated, conscious agent of the Communist conspiracy," as John Birch Society founder Robert Welch had in his book *The Politician* in 1963—was to court the "extremist" label.

Still, even far from the extremist fringe, anticommunist alarmism was alive and well. In 1965, when the *CBS Evening News* infamously aired footage of Morley Safer showing Americans setting Vietnamese huts ablaze with Zippo lighters, "President Johnson immediately called CBS president Frank Stanton to excoriate Safer as a 'communist' who had 'just shat on the flag,' and had the reporter's background investigated for communist leanings."[7] Though not a communist, Safer was, the investigation revealed, *Canadian*, a fact that government officials would use thereafter to cast doubts on his loyalty and objectivity.[8] Notwithstanding their official understanding of the communist menace as an external one, Democrats of the 1960s clearly were not above making accusations of subversion.

At the same time, by the late 1960s, and certainly by the 1970s, the moderate-liberal view was that clinging to the anticommunism of the early HUAC years was a sign of being out of touch. Signaling an official sea change, Richard Nixon himself would even grandly claim in a 1970 speech that "the postwar period in international relations has ended."[9] Peace, he explained, required "trust among friends."[10] Whether or not we can take seriously such a proclamation from Nixon, he was at least striking a rhetorical claim for an end to cold war paranoia. CBS's controversial *Selling of the Pentagon* (1971) made its own call for an end to paranoia, with narrator Roger Mudd explaining, "It has been more than a decade since the national policy of peaceful coexistence replaced the harsher rhetoric of the early cold war years, but to the filmmakers at the Pentagon, with at least 12 million dollars a year to spend, 1946 seems to have lasted a whole generation." Here was the network news arguing that Pentagon filmmaking was a waste of taxpayers' money. A fracas ensued. It was not the first time that both extremists and run-of-the-mill conservatives would proclaim the mainstream media in general, and TV news in particular, to be hopelessly liberal at best, and communist at worst.

But what was to be done? Accuracy in Media emerged in 1969 to combat liberal media bias, filing complaints repeatedly with the FCC and pursuing lawsuits. Yet for most right-wing organizations of the time, the tactic to combat mainstream media bias—the kind of bias that dared to claim anticommunism passé—was to complain as loudly as possible. In other words, to complain on the radio. All four of the central figures examined in this book did exactly that, but Hunt's enterprise did it the longest and the loudest.

For Hunt, like McCarthy and his supporters, virtually all political events could be understood as part of a totalizing plot. History was made by conscious agents of the Communist Party, fellow travelers, and, on the other side, by the courageous opponents of such fiends. If China fell to the communists, and the US didn't stop it, it could only be because communist subversives in the US government had enabled China to go red. Or, as Buckley put it, the JBS fallacy was "the assumption that you can infer subjective intention from objective consequence."[11] Liberal intellectuals such as Daniel Bell, Richard Hofstadter, and Seymour Martin Lipset had already undercut such conspiratorial views of history in their research, but on the media front the figure that came to symbolize liberal anti-anticommunism most prominently was CBS newsman Edward R. Murrow.

Today it is widely acknowledged (even mythologized) that it was TV, particularly Murrow's famous 1954 *See It Now* broadcast and the televised Army-McCarthy hearings, that finally emboldened public opinion against Senator McCarthy. As media historian Thomas Doherty aptly puts it, "Milton Berle may have been the first superstar made by television, but Joseph McCarthy was the first superstar undone by television."[12] The case for television bringing down McCarthy is somewhat overstated, both underplaying the role that the print media played in critiquing the senator and overplaying the TV networks' heroism. After all, the Army-McCarthy hearings were not shown in their entirety on CBS and NBC; both networks decided against what would have been a loss of thirty-six days worth of daytime advertising revenue. CBS showed no hearings in their entirety, instead airing a daily forty-five-minute summary at 11:30 p.m., far from primetime, while NBC showed the hearings live for just two days, then shifted to running summaries as well.[13] ABC and DuMont did air the hearings, as the value of their daytime advertising was much less. In other words, only the underdog networks were willing to broadcast the hearings in full. But clips did recirculate on the news. Joseph Welch's famous rhetorical question, "Have you no sense of decency, sir, at long last?," was not only televised live by both ABC and DuMont on day thirty of the hearings but also repeated dozens of time on radio and TV that night.[14] Following McCarthy's attack on General George C. Marshall, former president

Harry S. Truman appeared on Murrow's *See It Now* and expressed his own feelings about McCarthy: "The man who made that attack isn't fit to shine General Marshall's shoes."[15]

The story of both Murrow and the Army-McCarthy hearings has already been well told by others.[16] It is worth adding, however, that as much as Murrow was a hero to liberals he was disliked by conservatives, and, more importantly for our story, loathed by the superpatriots. Today Murrow is widely described as courageous for his anti-McCarthy programs, but at the time there was hardly consensus on this point. His son Casey was hounded at school by classmates calling his father a red, and Murrow feared for Casey's safety.[17] Murrow himself received abusive letters, one suggesting that the Murrow version of the Statue of Liberty's inscription would be "Send me your Commies, pinkos and crackpots, and I will put them on television."[18] One hostile Hearst journalist habitually referred to him as "Egghead R. Murrow."[19] A *Daily Mirror* reporter called him a "Commy-tator," a "worm" polluting the airwaves.[20]

That Murrow was attacked by McCarthy supporters is well known. What is less commonly considered is how *See It Now* must have irked the Right with *all* of its coverage, not just its broadcasts directly relating to McCarthy. Murrow was fiercely patriotic; his America was an inclusive, democratic place in which citizens rationally discussed their problems. When Murrow took *See It Now*'s cameras to Korea for Christmas in 1952, he celebrated the sacrifices of the troops; Murrow also made a point of picturing an integrated platoon that included not only whites and blacks but also a Chinese American and a Korean American, a gesture that surely rubbed some viewers the wrong way. Only one week after *Brown v. Board of Education*, Murrow went to Louisiana to gauge attitudes of both blacks and whites; he included interviews with people who both supported and opposed integration, but he ended by showing Sunday services at black and white churches, with pastors at each giving sermons praising the Supreme Court decision. The program clearly sent the message that integration was not just a legal directive but also an ethical imperative. In 1955, a *See It Now* episode entitled "Two American Originals" featured Grandma Moses and Louis Armstrong. "Satchmo is one of our more valuable items for export," Murrow explains. "His recordings are hot on both sides of the Iron Curtain." Praising Armstrong in no uncertain terms for making music that would unite people of all political persuasions, Murrow seemed optimistic about peaceful coexistence. (He was also toeing the official government line; Armstrong was considered an official emissary of goodwill by the US State Department, which sponsored a number of his tours in the 1960s.) It was not a message that would endear him to the hawkish "better dead than red" crowd. Murrow was a televisual synecdoche of cold war liberalism.

Like many of the ultras, Hunt's operation used a newsletter to expose the liberal (socialist, communist, subversive) bias of mainstream newscasters like Murrow. Hunt's *Life Lines* newsletter, immune from Fairness Doctrine complaints and the FCC's personal-attack rules, and thus often harder hitting than the *Life Line* radio show, relished making bitter attacks on network newsmen such as "Chou En-cronkite" and "Ho Chi Rather."[21] The fact that Walter Cronkite was hardly a radical leftist, that he had even narrated a boilerplate anticommunist Pentagon film called *The Eagle's Talon* in 1962 in which he praised "the determination of free men everywhere to resist communist expansion by force of arms," did not in any way redeem him, for Cronkite had observed in a 1968 TV news editorial what must have been patently obvious to anyone paying any attention whatsoever: we were "mired in stalemate" in Vietnam. President Johnson famously responded, "If I've lost Cronkite, I've lost Middle America," but it was impossible for *Life Lines* editor Keith Kathan to consider the possibility that Cronkite spoke for Middle America. If Cronkite thought we were in a stalemate, he was a communist.

But on the airwaves, the need to be "balanced" was always in view. Hunt and his fellow extremist broadcasters deplored mainstream news as biased, but CBS, ABC, and NBC broadcasts were apparently "balanced" enough for most Americans, and for the FCC. Indeed, notwithstanding CBS's prestigious news operation, and commentators such as Chet Huntley and David Brinkley, much TV news in the 1950s consisted of little more than a handful of newsreel clips and newscasters reading aloud Associated Press wire stories. Neutrality was simply expected from news. Hunt would have liked to have produced a TV or radio show that obviously slanted right, but he had to come up with programs lacking obvious bias. It was quite a challenge. How could Murrow, Cronkite, and other incorrigibly liberal newsmen be countered if one were not allowed to simply articulate an overtly conservative point of view? Hunt would have to forge his tactics from scratch.

\* \* \*

In 1951, Hunt founded Facts Forum, an organization that was, theoretically, politically nonpartisan, educational, and, therefore, tax exempt. An early letter to potential constituents stated that, "Facts Forum is a kind of projection of the old New England town hall meeting idea. We have no ax to grind and no funds to raise."[22] Facts Forum advocated the setting up of small discussion groups (ranging from seven to forty-two members) to discuss important political issues. Every three weeks the organization would poll its members on current affairs and send out the results to be published in newspapers. A pamphlet explained that "What you believe and say is public opinion. Public opinion is a constant immutable force which can be altered or changed only by itself."[23]

Hunt wanted to challenge political apathy, but it would be going too far to say that his goal was "democratic." He favored an intelligent, wealthy ruling elite—government by oligopoly. In *Alpaca*, a futuristic novel he wrote in 1960, Hunt went so far as to advocate a society in which voting was based on wealth. Those with more money had more votes in Hunt's "graduated suffrage" system. Additional votes could be acquired by waiving government services such as retirement benefits. The book revealed how influential Hunt felt mass media was. In his perfect world, political discussion could only take place via the printed word; discussing politics on radio and TV, or speechmaking before an audience of more than two hundred people, was "outlawed as inflammatory."[24] It was widely reported that Hunt had hired someone to write the romantic parts of *Alpaca*, as he was only interested in the politics; when the book breaks from political exegesis, we find our right-wing lovers spouting inane dialogue such as "I am putty in your hands!"[25]

Self-published and self-distributed, and monumentally boring, the book could hardly be construed a success, and Hunt never got beyond conceiving a title for his next great work, *Yourtopia*. In any case, Facts Forum members were spared *Alpaca*, which was published two years after the demise of the organization, but they did have access to a mail-order library. Facts Forum also distributed small cash awards to members who wrote newspaper editorials and invented patriotic slogans, jingles, and songs. But there is no doubt that Facts Forum's most important and far-reaching activity was not its small group discussions or mail-order library but rather its delivery of messages to wide audiences via TV and radio. Indeed, the small group discussion idea never fully took off—though it no doubt bolstered Hunt's claims that his organization was educational and therefore should be exempt from paying taxes—and the production and distribution of the *Facts Forum* radio and TV show (and a number of other programs, such as *State of the Nation*, a live weekly interview program that aired as free public service on 315 Mutual radio stations)[26] soon came to dominate as the organization's driving mission. From 1951 to 1956, Hunt spent at least 3.4 million tax-free dollars on his broadcasts.[27]

While fundamentalist media pundits of the cold war era such as Billy James Hargis and Carl McIntire focused on politically inflected sermonizing, the format of choice for the more secular crew, embodied most powerfully by H. L. Hunt and his announcer Dan Smoot, was the public-affairs program designed to serve a speciously conceptualized "public interest." Beginning with his first set of TV and radio programs in 1951, under the aegis of Facts Forum, Hunt succeeded on the air—with Smoot as his spokesman, since Hunt himself was terrified of public speaking—because he was willing to temper his archconservatism by giving "two sides" to the political issues discussed. Hunt packaged his TV and radio programs as balanced and educational so that the networks would provide him free public-service airtime—five million dollars worth per year, Hunt would recall in a *Playboy* interview some years later.[28] In 1954, Hunt's free yearly airtime was estimated at five hundred million dollars.[29] Regardless of how one calculated the financial *value* of the time, the *amount* of time was fairly straightforward. Over twenty-five thousand hours of free radio and TV time went to *Facts Forum* each year.[30]

The radio version of *Facts Forum* aired on Mutual, the fourth, underdog network. Mutual had only radio outlets, no TV.[31] Strapped for cash, the network was willing to run programs that the big three networks would not. For example, Mutual had previously aired *paid* religious programming,[32] which was taboo on CBS, ABC, and NBC, where religious programming was generally run as free public service until 1960. Mutual had also broadcast the ultraconservative *Manion Forum* from 1954 to 1957. Manion let the Mutual contract expire after the network refused to air an interview with Herbert V. Kohler, who was trying to break a strike at his plumbing firm; Mutual rejected Kohler's speech out of fear that it might be defamatory.[33] Yet Mutual was at heart neither left wing nor right wing in orientation, just eager to stay afloat financially. If the network's newscasters were notably less neutral than those of NBC and CBS, this was more a tactic to boost ratings than a political choice. On the conservative side, Mutual aired Fulton Lewis, while on the liberal side they aired Raymond Gram Swing. Mutual may have initially made its name with less controversial fare—*The Lone Ranger*—but the network was clearly open to "biased" news content, making it a logical home for *Facts Forum*.

The *Facts Forum* television show as well as Hunt's *Answers for Americans* appeared most often on the other weakling network, ABC. Unlike Mutual, ABC had television outlets, and it was certainly more firmly established and widespread than Mutual, yet it was for many years the poor cousin of CBS and NBC, and it was particularly incapable of competing with CBS and NBC in the area of news production. If CBS was widely known as the "Tiffany network," ABC would be stuck in a Woolworth's rut for decades. Lacking high-end news production facilities, and eager for cheap programming that would satisfy the FCC's public-service requirements, Mutual and ABC were naturally more receptive to Hunt's programming than CBS and NBC were.[34]

Later, in the 1960s, right-wing broadcasting would appear mostly on small independent radio stations, but in the 1950s more mainstream stations happily welcomed anticommunist public-affairs programs such as Hunt's. In fact, there was initially no reason for Hunt's programs to stand out as particularly right wing. There were, after all, a number of overtly anticommunist entertainment shows, like *I Led 3 Lives* (syndicated, 1953–56) on TV and *I Was a Communist for the FBI* (syndicated, 1952–54) on radio, throughout the cold war years.[35] As one journalist noted in the *Nation*, "almost any time you flick on your television set during the fall and winter of 1962–63, you can be sure of getting a hefty dose of rabid anti-communism."[36] Further, in the early postwar years and beyond, the Federal Civil Defense Administration had produced single-episode television programs such as *Prepare to Survive*, *What You Should Know about Biological Warfare*, and *Survival under Atomic Attack*, this last title narrated by Murrow himself.[37] NBC's twenty-six part *Victory at Sea*, a patriotic celebration of the US Navy's performance in World War II, premiered in 1952; ten years later it had aired at least once in 206 US markets, and had been rerun in multiple markets, with thirteen complete runs in Los Angeles and New York City alone.[38] All of which is to say that Hunt's programs were in many ways a good fit with the broadcast scene of the 1950s. In fact, as late as 1962 *Broadcasting* magazine would declare that the "Red threat" was "the hottest new program subject in television."[39]

Former FBI agent Dan Smoot hosted the *Facts Forum* TV show, a half-hour or fifteen-minute program designed to serve the FCC's public service requirement by giving equal time to debating two sides of an issue. (Hunt hired so many former G-men that by 1957, "there was a saying around the FBI that former agents had two retirement plans—the bureau's and H. L. Hunt's."[40]) The program aired on 222 radio stations and fifty-eight TV stations.[41] On the surface, *Facts Forum* seemed like a textbook execution of the Fairness Doctrine; programs did not have to adhere to the doctrine, of course, only broadcast license holders did, but that's exactly what

FIGURES 8–9. H. L. Hunt's *Facts Forum* TV show pretended to be educational and nonpartisan. Low-tech graphics over a spinning globe framed the opening and closing, and citizens were encouraged to write letters in response to programs. MacDonald & Associates, c. 1954.

made a putatively "balanced" news program like *Facts Forum* appealing to stations. To fulfill their public service obligation, TV and radio stations might air religious programs, educational broadcasts, news editorials, or public-affairs programs. Many didn't have the resources to produce this kind of stuff themselves and were thus happy to run free anticommunist Pentagon films and other such offerings. To stations eager to satisfy the FCC and not court controversy, Hunt's programs at first appeared made to order. On the television version of *Facts Forum*, Smoot typically sat at a desk as he responded to a weekly political question by giving two points of view, one liberal and one conservative.[42] On the surface, Smoot's approach was in keeping with a conception of America as a democratic "consensus culture." We all agreed about the dangers of communism, it was widely presumed, and as long as we operated under this premise we could engage in spirited debate. *Facts Forum* seemed like the epitome of neutral public service (figures 8–9). Many individual episodes were actually reasonably balanced and asked questions that did not necessarily have an inherent bias: Should American foreign-aid programs be continued? Are US defense policies essentially sound? Should Congress amend the Taft-Hartley Law and make it more acceptable to organized labor?

Yet ultimately, the "two sides" that the programs offered were not so much liberal and conservative as conservative and ultraconservative.[43] For example, one episode of *Facts Forum* asked whether those advocating the violent overthrow of the US government should be subject to the death penalty. On the pro side, the answer was, yes, of course, such a conspiracy was worse than murder. On the con side, the argument was that such conspirators were only dupes or communist sympathizers. Dangerous, yes, but these were just misguided pawns whose civil rights should be respected. "Thus," as one critic described it, "a 'negative' argument against the death penalty for Communist conspirators turns into a positive affirmation that the nation is in imminent danger of collapse from subversion—a favorite *Facts Forum* thesis."[44] In a 1954 exposé, Ben Bagdikian observed that "when *Facts Forum* refers to 'pro-Soviet' and 'un-American,' it includes the Roosevelt and Truman Administrations and the people who supported them" and that "when it refers to 'American freedom,' it means, among other things, a total absence of governmental regulation in business and a withdrawal from the United Nations."[45]

Smoot was not always so blatantly biased, but in many *Facts Forum* programs he did flatten the nuances out of the liberal perspectives he expressed. In arguing as a "liberal" for the legitimacy of HUAC witnesses' taking the Fifth Amendment, for example, he noted that "Congressional investigators don't recognize that some communist association could be innocent,"[46] which was a far cry from the liberal contention that much of what HUAC claimed to be communist simply was not; liberals certainly did not perceive every liberal organization as a communist front. Smoot did at times manage to offer a passable version of the liberal perspective on a daily question, but his manner was generally more impassioned when he spoke in support of the right-wing side that he truly believed in. In feigning leftist sympathies, Smoot might complain about "isolationists crying crocodile tears," but foreign aid, when he wore his conservative hat, was a "Quixotic stupidity." In answering the question "Is Eisenhower cleaning up the corruption in Washington DC?" Smoot first explained yes, Eisenhower was balancing the budget, cutting taxes, and ridding the government of disloyal (communist) workers. On the no side, Smoot launched into an isolationist tirade that took him far from the original question:

> From president McKinley's exalted nonsense about America's responsibility for uplifting and civilizing backward Asiatics, Wilson's airy evangelism about making the world safe for democracy, Roosevelt's cynical rationalization of World War II as a means of guaranteeing freedom from want and freedom from fear, to Truman's unconstitutional police action without victory in Korea, America has been on a ghastly treadmill of wars and preparation for wars. In the name of collective security for the whole world, we have given up our own security . . . Every fight on earth is now ours . . . It was our high destiny to build in this hemisphere an indestructible citadel of freedom which would stand as a beacon of hope to all peoples. This we have given up for a crazy thing called internationalism.[47]

The question posed did not really call for a discussion of "internationalism," but at least the query's presumption that the audience agreed about the existence of government corruption wasn't much of a stretch.

More often, though, questions were of the "When did you stop beating your wife?" variety. One program, for example, asked, "Should there be a realignment of both political parties?" The assumption was that Republicans and Democrats were identical, and the question was simply what to do about it. On the liberal "no" side Smoot argued that most voters are "sensible middle-of-the-roaders" who would have no place to go after a realignment placed all the extreme right-wingers in one party and the extreme left-wingers in the other party. On the "yes" side, which Smoot agreed with, he argued that

> The leaders of both parties are essentially internationalists who scorn your point of view as reactionary and isolationist. If you happen to think that federal compulsory Social Security is a main prop of state socialism, identical in principle with the system that Bizmark set up in Germany years ago, and which paved the way for Hitler's Nazi state, what political party will you turn to? Leading Republicans and Democrats have identical views on Social Security . . . In 1952 as in 1948 as in 1944 the Democratic and Republican platforms were essentially two identical bags of wind.[48]

A Republican who liked Ike might have had some reservations about Social Security, but it is unlikely that he or she would just "happen to think" that Social Security was the inevitable precursor to fascism. This was a right-wing position, not simply a conservative one.

Shown on twenty-two TV stations and 360 radio stations, another Hunt-funded public-service program, *Answers for Americans*, was a live, half-hour weekly panel discussion program airing nationally on ABC and featuring the same liberals each week, former congressman George Hamilton Combs and New York University professor Charles Hodges.[49] On the other side of the platform sat William F. Buckley and a rotating guest conservative. The liberals had their say, but the mellifluous Buckley seemed to win every scuffle. Combs did not fare well under the harsh studio lights, and although most of the participants chainsmoked, it was only Combs to whom the smoke seemed to cling in a thick film. In his three-piece suit, with carnation boutonniere, he effused a stereotypical "East Coast liberal establishment" persona. Professor Hodges was articulate but often came across as a cartoonish liberal intellectual, or worse, an old windbag. Buckley spoke in easily digestible conservative sound bites

FIGURES 10–13. H. L. Hunt's *Answers for Americans* panel discussion program claimed to be politically balanced but pitted unappealing liberals against more eloquent conservatives. MacDonald & Associates, date unknown.

such as "we would rather die than be enslaved" by communism. Hodges, conversely, spoke of "tactical issues," the need for "differentiation in our thinking," and details that one should "watch closely as a barometric." When Buckley attacked FDR, Combs aridly responded, "I am always enthralled by this exhuming of the past."[50] The clever Buckley was clearly underwhelmed. On one episode the host Hardy Burt even jokingly introduces Professor Hodges as someone "who doesn't necessarily believe that brevity is the soul of wit"[51] (figures 10–13).

Though *Facts Forum* and *Answers for Americans* were flawed as "objective" public-affairs programs, they did in some ways make more than a token gesture of balance. Smoot did not visibly smirk and wince as he gave the liberal perspective; a liberal voice was often expressed, if sometimes caricatured. *Answers for Americans* also sought balance, though there was clearly bias in selecting articulate conservatives and unattractive liberals. And could Hunt have *really* been unaware that Professor Hodges bore a striking physical resemblance to Lenin?

Hunt may have stacked the deck, but he was not simply lying about the objectives of his various public-service TV and radio programs. He *did* vociferously promote the value of debate as a tactic to defeat political apathy. In at least six episodes, the *Facts Forum* format is even altered to include debate by phony audience members. Though tightly scripted, the artificial debate did, on the surface, convey different opinions. As audio-visual texts, though, the programs are perplexing, their aesthetics undoing their ostensibly balanced content. The episode on "Our Policy in Indo-china" pictures Smoot at a podium giving a pro and con position on said policy, interspersed with questions from two ersatz audience members.[52] The film does not even pretend that more than two people are in attendance, and the camera never cuts to the questioners, staying fixed instead on a head-and-shoulders shot of Smoot. Further, disconcertingly, the two audience members are recorded at the exact same audio level as Smoot. Now, it is rather likely that the audience voices were actually recorded later, and that there were no real audience members at all when Smoot was filmed, but by recording the two lone questioners at the same audio level as Smoot the producers make them sound like they are actually at the podium, which they patently are not. The most novice sound technician knows to use different levels to cue where people are in a room, even (or, rather, *especially*) when the veracity of either people or room is in doubt. The artificiality of Smoot's self-debate is thus amplified, the static camera and flubbed sound recording conveying to viewers that any real debate with Smoot is as phony as a three-dollar bill. Indeed, Smoot does not interact with his phantom audience so much as smile and patiently wait for them to pose their liberal and conservative questions before giving a definitive answer clearly not open to debate. Smoot gave two points of view, but the show conveyed one message: respect authority (figure 14).

If mainstream cold war news conveyed a neutral stance, it also projected an air of civility. Hunt's version of the news used a patina of balance to feign neutrality, and this worked particularly well on *Answers for Americans*. The conservatives always came out ahead, but the exchanges were relatively polite, notwithstanding Buckley's smirking contempt for the inferior debaters across the dais. Smoot took great pains to maintain the same civility on *Facts Forum*, yet his language and tone when speaking for the conservative position frequently teetered just on the edge of pathos.

For example, in answering the question, "Should we continue to handle Korea as a limited police action?" Smoot first dryly answered in the affirmative, quoting Adlai Stevenson: "Korea . . . is the most remarkable effort the world has ever seen to make collective security work. In choosing to

FIGURE 14. As *Facts Forum* host, Dan Smoot lectured on both the "pro" and "con" side of every issue, but was often more passionate when speaking for the conservative side that he truly believed in. MacDonald & Associates, date unknown.

repel the first armed aggression of the communists, we chose to make bitter sacrifices today to save civilization tomorrow." On the negative side, Smoot drew a portrait of a hypothetical soldier named Joe: "It's cold up here in the winter—sometimes thirty below zero. If a boy cries his tears turn to ice. And then there is the enemy, always the enemy . . . [and] the kind of fight that man fought centuries ago. Knives and fists, fingers groping for eyes, and teeth seeking a soft spot in the neck. Maybe Joe will die in the slit trench, and maybe he will live—his hands sour and gummy with half-digested rice gruel ripped out of the stomach of a bleeding bundle of rags and bones at his feet."[53] Needless to say, the more upright public-service programs did not refer to disembowelment. Not every program was so disturbing, but Smoot was certainly more likely to engage in name calling when he gave the conservative position. Smoot could somehow snarl "effeminate egghead" in such a way that it sounded infinitely worse than "son of a bitch." Even when he restrained himself, he wasn't fooling anybody.

Hunt's two-sided format conceived to engage in television's polite, civil discourse on the dangers of communism was clearly a failure, an irksome reminder of the tenuous nature of the whole notion of consensus culture. *Facts Forum* provided a world of caricatured, dueling binaries, with no possibility for common ground. In the epilogue of *The End of Ideology*, Daniel Bell argues that "ideologists are 'terrible simplifiers'" and that "ideology makes it unnecessary for people to confront individual issues on their individual merits. One simply turns to the ideological vending machine, and out comes the prepared formulae."[54] One would be hard pressed to find a better example of the vending-machine mentality than *Facts Forum*.

Even before Democratic congressmen began to complain about *Facts Forum*'s ideological persuasion and tax-free status, a red flag was raised when it was revealed that Hunt had links to Joe McCarthy. The senator only appeared once on the program, but his former researcher—and future wife—Jean Kerr was an early *Facts Forum* staffer, as was Robert E. Lee, a former FBI man who had assisted in compiling an early version of McCarthy's infamous list of 205 communists in the State Department.[55] Lee would only work for Hunt for a short period of time—developing *Facts Forum* for TV and briefly serving as moderator—before Eisenhower appointed him FCC commissioner in 1954. Senate confirmation was delayed by debate over Lee's connections with McCarthy and Hunt, not to mention his blatant lack of qualifications. Lee readily admitted both that McCarthy was a friend ("I like him. I think he's a great guy.")[56] and that his only experience in communications was his work on *Facts Forum*.[57]

Lee ended up serving a record-breaking twenty-eight years on the FCC. His presence there did seem initially to provoke the networks to give McCarthy more response time to attacks than they might have otherwise.[58] But over the long term Lee could hardly be characterized as a right-wing commissioner. Indeed, in 1978 he testified with other commissioners before Congress in *opposing* a proposed replacement of the public-interest standard of communications law with a marketplace standard, and his major contribution as commissioner was consistent cheerleading for the development of UHF, a development not universally supported by the communications industry.[59] So it would be farfetched to conclude that Hunt's programs were on the air for so long, even as other right-wingers were driven off by Fairness Doctrine complaints, simply because he had an inside man at the FCC. It would be more accurate to say that Lee's connection to both Hunt and McCarthy helped to raise Hunt's public profile and to reinforce the public perception of Hunt as a McCarthyite and an extremist.

Having a public profile was a relatively new thing for Hunt. Before forming the Facts Forum organization in 1951, Hunt had kept himself out of the public eye. In fact, few outside of Texas had even heard of him until 1948, when *Life* magazine surreptitiously snapped a photo of him to illustrate a story on "the richest man in America." Hunt suffered from stage fright—hence the front men on his radio and TV shows. As a youth he had once even swallowed a plug of tobacco to get out of giving a speech. But after the *Life* profile and the creation of Facts Forum, Hunt was suddenly a public figure, linked not only to McCarthy, the most famous anticommunist in America, but also to a controversial FCC commissioner who was a friend of McCarthy. Without really trying, Hunt became the public face, if not the actual on-camera or microphone presence, of Facts Forum.

Hunt eventually could not convince anyone that his broadcasts had no political agenda, and, with his organization's tax-exempt status becoming increasingly tenuous, he shut down the entire Facts Forum operation in 1956. Facts Forum had been a tax write-off for Hunt, but *Human Events* was apparently the only one truly to prosper from the seven-year-old organization. The conservative magazine inherited (or more likely purchased) Facts Forum's enormous mailing list.[60]

*       *       *

One journalist aptly noted in 1954 that "a strong reek of the not-quite-crackpot Right clings to Facts Forum."[61] Nonetheless, abstract notions of balance and fairness had been central to the organization and its TV and radio shows. Two years after the demise of Facts Forum, Hunt undertook his second broadcasting venture, *Life Line*. This time around, the thin veneer of balance was replaced by the broad brushstrokes of free-market pontification. The two-sided approach was kaput, and Hunt didn't even call people liberal and conservative anymore. There were only "the Mistaken" on the left and, on his side, those who were "constructive." "Conservative" he explained in his 1966 *Playboy* interview, was "an unfortunate word. It denotes mossback, reactionary, and old-fogyism."[62] (Would anyone but a mossback actually use a word like "mossback"?) The openly one-sided *Life Line* "constructively" promoted isolationism and fiscal conservatism for almost twenty years. Begun in 1958, on only twenty radio stations, the fifteen-minute *Life Line* program was on over three hundred radio stations by 1964;[63] for one year only, a much shorter version appeared on fifty-four TV outlets in over forty states.[64] There was also the thrice-weekly

*Life Lines* newsletter, which had forty thousand subscribers by 1962.[65] *Life Line* was particularly popular in Texas; in Abilene you could listen to *Life Line* five times a day, and by the early sixties the show was enjoying thirty thousand hours of tax-exempt airtime each year.[66] The advisory board of Hunt's new endeavor included former Facts Forum board members such as Robert Wood (CEO of Sears Roebuck) and John Wayne, but, importantly, the new board also included a number of Christian ministers, such as W. R. White, the president of Baylor University.[67] Hunt announced that his new endeavor was both educational and religious.

Smoot having struck out on his own, Hunt's new announcer was the Reverend Wayne Poucher, who had been a campaign manager for Strom Thurmond's successful senatorial write-in campaign in 1954. Poucher may have had the religious and political credentials that Hunt was looking for, but it would take more than that to fill Smoot's shoes and become the new voice of Hunt. Smoot was an aggressive ex-FBI agent, with chiseled chin and a handsome build; Poucher was a Church of Christ minister, soft-spoken, and a bit doughy. Smoot's bold style had brought negative attention to *Facts Forum*, and perhaps Hunt reasoned that Poucher's more low-key self-presentation would help to deflect criticism. In an obvious attempt to deter the troubles he had had with *Facts Forum*, in the early days of *Life Line* Hunt made sure that exactly half of each Poucher broadcast was a sermon. Differing from Hunt's earlier programs, the new radio show was not run by stations as free public service, though the whole operation remained a massive tax shelter for some years. Hunt must have reasoned that not getting free public-service airtime would help keep the Mistaken—Democrats, socialists, communists—at bay. Initially, Poucher ended the show's political commentary by advising, "Don't forget to think." His devotional concluded with "Don't forget to pray." The second part of the program was clearly there so that Hunt could claim he ran a religious organization meriting tax exemption.

Poucher's theology was thin, his rhetoric jejune. In a sermon on the evils of cursing, he noted with wonder that "the human tongue is physically small, but what tremendous effects it can boast of! A whole forest can be set ablaze by a tiny spark of fire, and the tongue is as dangerous as any fire, with vast potentialities for evil. It can poison the whole body; it can make the whole of life a blazing hell."[68] Occasionally, he would muse poetically: "The Bible, in a metaphor, picks open the petals of every heart and twines the tendrils about the throne of God: it picks the frozen locks of frosty streams and sends them singing to the sea; and it kisses bud and bloom into life and lifts the ocean of sorrow to the clouds. Yes, Mr. Businessman, the Bible has a place in your business."[69] Inexplicably, Poucher's favorite pejorative was "pottage," as in, "We have been gradually surrendering our American spirit, based on initiative and self-reliance, for a social and economic mess of pottage."[70]

Over and over again Poucher correctly noted that *Life Line* did not attack minority groups, disparage labor unions, or directly accuse people or organizations of being communist. Indeed, by replacing "communist" with "mistaken," Hunt seemed to think that he could avoid all accusations of political bias. Of course, everyone did make the accusation, but it is striking that until the youth movement came to a head later in the sixties, *Life Line* was the blandest right-wing program imaginable, a program supporting capitalism and attacking government spending without ever calling anyone a bad name or, in fact, even identifying specific people by name. *Life Line* claimed to be positive, "constructive," offering helpful tips to improve society without resorting to government programs: "Community centers, picnics, and parties can get children off the streets and away from some temptations if they are run right. (And it is difficult to run them right. The fight against sin is a battle, not a picnic.)"[71] If churchgoers only loved their neighbors as they loved themselves, "there would be no possibility of America ever becoming a welfare state."[72]

On Sundays, the entire broadcast was given over to a Christian sermon. Nothing could have been more hypocritical on Hunt's part, for even if he did share views about the evils of communism and the virtues of the free market with broadcasters like McIntire, Smoot, and Hargis, he was not personally religious. His third wife (or second, taking into account that the first two were coterminous) was quite religious, and after marrying her he did join a Baptist church—a move calculated not only to please his wife but also to lend just a bit more credibility to the notion that *Life Line* had religious aspirations. Hunt was already familiar with his new pastor, Rev. W. A. Criswell; he had secretly had two hundred thousand copies of an anti-Catholic Criswell sermon printed for distribution at the 1960 Democratic National Convention. (As if it weren't bad enough that Kennedy was Catholic, he was making noise about revoking the oil-depletion allowance!)[73] Since Hunt had always deemed himself special and therefore above the laws of both God and man, it was hard to take his religious conversion seriously. Confronted by his young daughter June—who would later become a Christian singer and radio personality—about his constant womanizing, he curtly told her, "I'm not a Christian. I do not have to go

by Christian ethics." He then punished her by sending her away to board-
ing school.[74] He took the opposite approach when similarly confronted by
daughter Swanee: "King Solomon had seven hundred wives. And that's in
the *Bible*."[75]

Reading transcripts of early Poucher scripts, one cannot help but conclude that Hunt was so anxious to escape the controversy that had befallen
*Facts Forum* that he overcompensated. Smoot, by contrast, was now on his
own and free to give only his own point of view. He quickly made up for
lost time. During Castro's revolution, when American military were kid-
napped, "we should have sent a detachment of United States Marines into
the Cuban hills to drag those beatnik Castro punks out by their beards
and turn them over to the lawful government of Cuba."[76] Finally at liberty to give only the constructive perspective, *Life Line*, conversely, was
more circumspect. Asserting the importance of writing patriotic letters
to the editor and the value of patriotic advertising, Poucher blandly advised, "we can use our faith in America as a constructive basis on which
to resist and throw back the mistaken drive against freedom."[77] Letters to
the editor were a strong strategy because they would be widely read, since
"people have a natural curiosity about what other ordinary people have
to say."[78]

In a way, *Life Line* had painted itself into a corner. Having pledged
not to attack minority groups, only rarely to attack specific individuals by
name, and to offer positive advice to listeners, the only material it had to
work with was government spending. So while superpatriots like Smoot
fulminated against Martin Luther King and his "marauding bands of negroes,"[79] Poucher decried the wastefulness of foreign aid, asserting bathet-
ically that "the world must learn to help itself."[80] Poucher lamented that
the government was spending American tax dollars on teaching monkeys
arithmetic, storing duck and goose feathers, and buying the wrong cloth
for uniform pants pockets.[81] Further, the Agriculture Department had
recently consulted with the Supreme Court to determine which part of the
hog could legitimately be labeled ham.[82] Channeling Hunt's free-market
economic perspective, Poucher mocked virtually every governmental ex-
penditure. In one program he lamented that

> the foreign aiders . . . have come up with a scheme to spend 1,600,000 dollars
> to put American television sets in out-of-the-way villages of Asia, Africa, and
> Latin America. Since there's no electrical power in these places, the sets will
> be run on batteries recharged by merry-go-rounds propelled by children, or

by riders on stationary bicycles. No estimate has been given of the cost of the merry-go-rounds or the bicycles.[83]

Poucher became even more passionate when responding to claims that anticommunists were psychopathic, mentally ill extremists: "When we are told that patriotism is controversial, and that we must be guided to an unquestioning acceptance of a one world government, we had better be suspicious, or wind up either dead or slaves. One of the highest survival values is suspicion . . . Of course, *the Mistaken* do not want us to be suspicious of them or their motives."[84] The fact that obsessive anxiety about "one world government," not to mention insistence upon referring to all political opponents as "the Mistaken," was the shortest path to being branded "extremist" was beyond Poucher's ken.

Visually, the short-lived *Life Line* TV show was even flatter than Hunt's earlier programs. Poucher was framed in a head-and-shoulders shot in a barren studio space (figure 15). Although the television program only ran about three and a half minutes (with spaces for sponsors to fill it out to a full five-minute spot), it lost money and was discontinued after sixty-five weeks. The *Life Line* radio program, conversely, was long-lived, thanks to one thing only: canned goods. In 1959, Hunt had started a food business, HLH Products, which immediately became virtually the sole *Life Line* sponsor. HLH bled money over the years, while *Life Line* remained in the black thanks to income from HLH advertising. In a classic instance of the tail wagging the dog, one of the most repeated *Life Line* topics in its first few years was an urgent call for patriotic advertising. "In adding patriotism to advertising, business can strike a terrific blow on behalf of freedom."[85] Patriotic advertising would save America! Poucher never overtly said that the venue for all those patriotic ads should be *Life Line*, but it was obvious that Hunt was frustrated that no one seemed to want to support his show besides himself. It often seemed that the central purpose of *Life Line* was to procure advertising for *Life Line*, a futile endeavor, especially in the early years when the show truly stank.

Poucher was fired in 1963 when he refused to deliver a diatribe in favor of the oil-depletion tax allowance that Hunt supported.[86] Hunt also offended Reverend Poucher by making him plug overpriced Bibles on the show—Bibles that came complete with a plug for *Life Line* on the cover. Poucher was evicted from the home he rented from Hunt and proceeded to sue his former boss for back pay. Hunt was already in his seventies and apparently did not participate in the day-to-day business of *Life Line* after

FIGURE 15. Wayne Poucher was the first announcer on the *Life Line* radio show. He also appeared on the short-lived television show. MacDonald & Associates, 1963.

Poucher's abrupt departure. Certainly, though, the program continued to represent Hunt's views, or he would not have poured over one million dollars a year into advertising HLH Products on it. The show ran through a number of announcers after Poucher, before Melvin Munn finally settled in for the long term in 1965, staying on until the whole operation shut down in 1975.

\* \* \*

*Life Line* would never have survived from 1958 to 1965, when Munn came on board as writer and announcer, if it had been truly left to fend for itself in the free market. Munn had a keener sense of narrative and pacing than Poucher. He had a deeper voice and a rhythmic delivery method. And he resorted to purple prose less often. At heart, though, he shared Poucher's cornpone sensibility. (He was an "expert," he explained, "x" signifying an "unknown quantity," and "spurt" referring to "a drip under pressure.") Even in Munn's more capable hands, *Life Line* remained a bad show that couldn't get advertiser support but kept going because Hunt wouldn't give up on it. The country's most prominent free market propaganda machine was subsidized. Of course, Hunt's line was that it was all a conspiracy and that the only reason he couldn't get advertisers was that the Mistaken had convinced Constructives that patriotic advertising was controversial and should therefore be avoided. In other words, the fact that his program had no apparent value in the free market was merely the result of communist subversion: "The Mistaken learned long ago, my friends, that one lower-level advertising man is worth a dozen corporation presidents," Poucher had intoned in a 1959 broadcast. "We have seen it happen time and again, where a patriotic businessman has been persuaded to forego his patriotic advertising for the sake of money. He is told to be agreeable, to avoid controversy in the programs that he sponsors."[87]

Needless to say, *Life Line* was just as controversial in Munn's hands as it had been in Poucher's, repeatedly coming under attack for spewing Hunt's ideology. Astoundingly, Munn consistently denied that Hunt controlled the content. Granted, almost everything Munn said of his own inclination happened to match Hunt's own feelings. Yet Munn insistently identified Hunt as just one of numerous sponsors, although there were actually few others outside of a few banks and oil companies that Hunt did business with. Further, Munn maintained the Hunt had not even been the brains behind the whole enterprise in the first place. It had been started in 1958, he vaguely claimed, by "a woman in Miami, Florida."[88]

With his background in public relations, Munn knew how to stick to a story: Hunt just happened to be a major *Life Line* advertiser. Of course, the circumstances of Poucher's dismissal were public, and no one would have taken on the *Life Line* announcer job knowing he'd have to accept copy from Hunt every day, so it was credible that Munn had the editorial autonomy he claimed. But not even Hunt had the chutzpah to deny that he was the originator of *Life Line*. In fact, he celebrated it by erecting a pink-and-blue, six-feet-high, and twelve-feet-wide *Life Line* sign on his front yard.

Notwithstanding Munn's claims to the contrary, *Life Line* was Hunt's progeny, and, determined to make money off of it, he created a symbiotic (yet ultimately parasitic) relationship between the program and HLH Products. Here's how it worked. *Life Line* charged stations between $1.50 and $10.00 a day (depending on station size) to run the fifteen-minute program. Then, the station would sell ad time to sponsors. In addition to the flat fee of $1.50 to $10.00 per day, *Life Line* was given 10 percent of the revenue that the local station was able to procure from advertisers. The other 90 percent of the ad revenue went into the station's pocket. Stations did not pay for the Sunday programs, which were strictly religious, and no ad time was sold during those programs. (In the early Poucher years the program had been split between politics and religion, but under Munn only Sunday shows were religious.) The tricky thing was that local stations were quite often unable to find sponsors. So, HLH would step in and buy the ad time. In fact, HLH products were advertised in many areas where they were not even available for sale. It was a great system for the local stations, who paid a fair price for a show and then got most of the money HLH paid to advertise. It was a great system for *Life Line*, which pocketed a flat fee plus a smaller percentage of money paid by HLH to advertise. And it was a lousy system for HLH, which paid a ton of money to advertise but actually sold very few canned goods.

Like other right-wing broadcasts, *Life Line* had something of a piece-meal distribution strategy. As Munn later told the story, Mutual made a pitch to run the show on their broadcasting system, but *Life Line* would have had to sell local ad time itself, and it didn't have the resources to take this on. Given the situation with HLH Products, the story is a bit iffy, but the upshot was that unlike *Facts Forum*, *Life Line* was not networked, and it was a daily show, so the *Life Line* office had to send out hundreds of reel-to-reel tapes (at only two shows per tape) each week to individual stations.[89] They included a stamped envelope so that the tapes could be returned and reused; in theory, such tapes could be used an average of seven times each. But three-quarters of the stations did not return the tapes. Munn proposed an innovation: they switched from tapes to long-playing records. More broadcasts could go on each record, and *Life Line* did not ask for them to be returned, instead encouraging stations to donate the LPs to a local library.[90] In sum, the new system saved *Life Line* $72,000 in postage the first year, and, since the records could not be recorded over like the tapes (which may well be why the radio stations did not return the tapes in the first place), *Life Line* was potentially reaching an even larger audience through secondary circulation of the LPs.

*Facts Forum* had sunk under the weight of controversy, amidst accusations of fanaticism and cronyism, particularly in light of Hunt's connections with Commissioner Lee and Senator McCarthy. *Life Line* strove to be more "positive" than *Facts Forum* but still could not escape controversy. Critics wondered if the show should really be tax exempt, opining that if Hunt was saving millions in taxes, this ultimately meant that the American people were actually footing the bill for America's most ambitious right-wing propaganda mill. In 1964 a Democratic senator from Oregon lamented that "there is probably no one who gets more radical rightwing propaganda value for his tax-exempt dollar than Haroldson Lafayette Hunt."[91] In 1965, the IRS did finally rule that Life Line did not qualify for exemption as an "educational organization." With his enormous team of lawyers, Hunt could afford to appeal the decision endlessly, and it is not clear when or if the Life Line organization was finally subject to taxation. Hunt's bottomless legal fund made it difficult for any action against him to pan out.

Although the FCC apparently did receive many citizens' complaints about *Life Line*, nothing ever came of them. It would be jumping the gun to conclude that Hunt's man on the commission, Lee, had stepped up to bat for his former boss, since the FCC actually acted on relatively few complaints it received from citizens about any kind of broadcasting, from the left or the right—notwithstanding the ultras' complaints of relentless FCC harassment. And, of course, to be considered by the FCC a citizen complaint would have to be specifically against a *radio station* for being "unbalanced" in its political coverage. *Life Line* itself could not be held liable for Fairness Doctrine violations, and the wealthy Hunt could always jump ship and simply find another outlet if a specific station came under fire from the FCC. In any case, *Life Line* broadcasts were assiduously crafted to avoid making personal attacks, which meant that stations would not have to notify those who had been attacked and offer them free airtime to respond. While the broadcasts were not balanced, they were certainly less incendiary than the other right-wing shows of the time, which probably made them more appealing to vulnerable independent stations sympathetic to Hunt's doctrinal line but hoping to avoid the kind of controversy that Smoot, Hargis, or McIntire inspired.

When critics attacked the broadcast ultras, they always referred to Hunt as the leader of the pack. His programs were the most long-lived, of course, and the most widespread over the course of that period—though McIntire's station penetration did surpass Hunt's at one point. (Hunt's operation peaked at five hundred stations, while McIntire peaked at six hundred.) Hunt's wealth guaranteed his longevity on the airwaves—*Life Line* never hurt for a sponsor until HLH Products collapsed—and it was thus natural to point to *Life Line* as the epitome of right-wing broadcasting. It was seemingly everywhere, and for so many years. At the same time, it was a bit off base to hold up the show as emblematic of right-wing broadcasting, because in many ways it was unique. Most obviously, the other shows were more often and more blatantly racist. The *Dan Smoot*

*Report* attacked international aid as not only an unfair tax burden (and on this point *Life Line* agreed) but also because our money was being used to educate, feed, and industrialize the "colored have-not nations": "nothing could be more suicidal for us than to burden our own people with taxes in an effort to put African primitives on the same education and economic level with us."[92] Further, the United Nations was not only part of a "one world government" conspiracy (again, *Life Line* agreed) but also dangerous, according to the *Smoot Report*, because it gave power to primitive people: "With the admission of fourteen new colored nations to the UN in 1960, the balance of voting power in that organization would swing to the Communist and colored have-not nations of the world. A little nation of savage African tribes under a leftist dictator now has as much voting power in all UN agencies . . . as America has, although we pay most of the bills."[93]

*Life Line* was perhaps the least overtly racist of all the right-wing broadcasts of this era, although Hunt himself was not privately progressive about racial issues, and, according to his daughter Swanee, was ferociously anti-Semitic. In 1964, a journalist profiling Hunt did manage to dig up a few interoffice memos in which Hunt acknowledged that Gerald L. K. Smith was "a notorious racist and anti-Semite" but that he might be "doing more good than any other person in the present fight against communism." Hunt had also observed that the "Life Line [organization] is not anti-Semitic, but inasmuch as there will be practically no Jews who fail to fight Life Line, Life Line is not due to carry the torch for them."[94] (The Facts Forum mail-order lending library had originally offered Joseph Kamp's *We Must Abolish the United States*, in which Kamp announced, "I pull no punches in exposing the Jewish Gestapo or any Jew who happens to be a Jew.")[95] If *Life Line* was anti-Semitic or anti–civil rights, these sentiments remained submerged, though its general opposition to federal government "interference" had to be read, in part, as a reference to *Brown v. the Board of Education*. It was tame stuff compared to the pontifications of the other broadcast extremists.

Hunt thought overtly racist broadcasting was simply poor strategy: "Many of the two-hundred genuine anticommunist organizations . . . accomplish little and are of little effect . . . because they handicap themselves by making unwise attacks on minority groups."[96] The policy not to attack minority groups made *Life Line* truly unique—and did not make Hunt any friends among the other ultras. He usually refused even to make overt attacks on labor unions! The other anticommunist broadcasters saw the labor unions and civil rights activists as the absolute heart of the communist movement in America, so Hunt's tactics were downright bizarre to them.

Hunt was personally odd of course, and more or less incapable of making friends; this ostensible leader of the right-wing broadcasting pack operated in relative isolation. His few forays into playing the politics game had been limited. He had been an adamant supporter of nominating Gen. Douglas MacArthur for president, and, as an FDR hater, a fervent supporter of the Twenty-second Amendment, which limited a president to two complete terms. Hunt seems to have sunk some money into both campaigns, and he took full credit for the passing of the Constitutional Amendment, claiming it as his own single-handed accomplishment.[97] Perhaps some credit was indeed due to him, but bear in mind that Hunt also took credit for inventing the concept of hand lotion. His inflated sense of self often made it difficult to parse out his true accomplishments. He had also supported Americans for America, an organization chaired by Robert E. Wood of Sears Roebuck and designed to channel money to ultraconservative Republican candidates, and Wood, in turn, was an ardent *Facts Forum* supporter, advertising the show in his stores and in Sears advertising leaflets.[98]

But Hunt was unable to elicit support from others on the right. A 1953 FBI memo concluded that *Facts Forum* was a bona fide anticommunist show, but that it was "controversial" among other anticommunists and that Hunt had no luck securing sponsors because he was "personally disliked" by so many potential supporters.[99] Hunt periodically contacted the FBI asking them to investigate various anticommunist groups because they all "seemed to be against him,"[100] which, in his mind, threw their anticommunist credentials into doubt. In fact, Poucher made a number of sad, veiled radio appeals to the ultras who had rejected Hunt. With typical ineloquence, he explained, "When men eat each other, it is cannibalism. A political parallel of this revolting vice is being enacted today by Americans . . . [M]en who should be friends assail each other needlessly and futilely, engaging in hopeless internal strife . . . We must end the cannibalism and name-calling among freedom-lovers."[101] Needless to say, such flatfooted exhortations did not help Hunt to win friends and influence people.

The pacing and writing of the show did eventually improve. When *Life Line* became crankier in the early 1970s—attacking pornography, longhairs, libbers, and peaceniks—it became both more disturbing and more entertaining. *Life Line* had for years sidestepped the common superpatriot contention that the civil rights movement was a communist conspiracy, while expressing dismay about communism and generally maintaining a polite tone. But as the counterculture emerged in the late 1960s, and groups like the Black Panthers, Students for a Democratic Society, and the Weathermen became higher profile, *Life Line* switched gears dramatically. Still setting aside explicit discussion of racial issues, *Life Line* began an adamant counterattack against the young revolutionaries calling for the overthrow of the US government.

In the course of attacking the counterculture, *Life Line* also suddenly became vocal about Vietnam. *Life Line* had always been isolationist in orientation, pointing to Korea and Vietnam as mistakes and a waste of taxpayers' money. But once we were committed to fight, we had to fight to win, and only a coward would call for America to pull out of Vietnam. "PEACE," the *Life Lines* newsletter explained in 1971, stood for "People Existing After Communist Enslavement."[102] Though the newsletter did not partake in profits from sales, it did happily publicize a wildly popular mail-order bumper sticker distributed by a Texas-based group known as Faithful Americans and picturing a peace symbol with the tagline "Footprint of the American Chicken." Munn conceded that *Life Lines* editor Keith Kathan was "a good deal more hard hitting" than he was. Kathan was "at times a little coarse . . . a little raw." He was "a small man and quite excitable, and he'd get all worked up about something and get to that typewriter, and he'd just smoke."[103] And Munn wasn't talking about cigarettes.

What is particularly disturbing about both the radio and newsletter perspective on Vietnam was the complete disavowal of the possibility that atrocities had been committed by American soldiers. The John Birch Society had similarly denied that police brutality existed, and in a film in the late 1960s it had even referred to the revolt of "the supposedly poor and oppressed negroes" against "the supposed lynching, segregation, social ostracism, and exploitation of the white man."[104] The police did not beat people up, and blacks were not oppressed, they retorted. Case closed. An argument for the legitimacy of police violence or for the oppression of blacks would have been less disturbing than the contention that such things simply did not exist. Similarly, *Life Line* noted that every Vietnam vet opposing the war was a phony who had never actually fought in the war. Crying Vietnamese women pictured on TV were "supposedly" responding to the destruction of their homes. Buddhists who set themselves on fire were obviously communists, so there was no reason to be alarmed about self-immolation, just about such cheap communist bids for media attention. It didn't matter how many vets described the murder of babies, the rape of women, the throwing of prisoners out of helicopters, or the trading of "ears for beers" at the end of a long day of fighting.[105]

A defense of such atrocities—that's just the way war is, we have to do horrible things to defeat communism, etc.—would have been bearable compared to *Life Line*'s flat refusal to listen. The *National Review*, for example, had responded to reports of Vietnam atrocities by comparing them to the horrors of Sherman's march to Atlanta: Hadn't such rampant destruction been preferable to the dissolution of the union? Or consider the most impassive and uncritical soldier pictured in the Oscar-winning short film *Interviews with My Lai Veterans* (Joseph Strick, 1970): he's surprised that the massacre got so much attention, because it was just standard operating procedure, My Lai was an enemy stronghold, and, besides, the Vietnamese are a strange people who don't care if they live or die. Asked why women at My Lai were raped before being killed, he misses one beat, then responds simply, "I don't know."[106] He doesn't deny the events, just contests their interpretation. But no kind of testimonial would move the writers of *Life Line* scripts or the *Life Lines* newsletter. All reports of atrocities were simply part of a left-wing media plot.

Of course, Munn and his cohort were not alone. All the superpatriots (and many lesser patriots) thought that Lieutenant Calley was a hero.[107] And General Westmoreland himself had explained that "The Oriental doesn't put the same high price on life as does the westerner. Life is plentiful, life is cheap in the orient. As the philosophy of the orient expresses it, life is not important."[108] *Life Line*'s response to My Lai and other reports of atrocities, in other words, was not particularly unique, except that *Life Line* had worked so hard for so many years not to attack anyone and to package anticommunist radio messages that were alternately alarmist *and* hopeful. By 1968, *Life Line* was just alarmist. The *Life Lines* newsletter, immune from FCC consideration altogether, was even worse.

If *Life Line* was not atypical in its insistence that there were no war crimes in Vietnam—if conservatives all over America were placing "Free Calley" bumper stickers on their cars[109]—*Life Line* did stand out as a specifically anti-anti-Vietnam *media outlet*. All the radio ultras attacked the peace activists, but *Life Line* spread the antipeace message the longest, to the widest audience. It was a largely reactive move: they saw the networks as all-powerful and hopelessly biased against the conservative cause. Of course, the mainstream media was hardly the socialist-communist enclave that *Life Line* claimed it was. All the media outlets refused to believe that the ex-soldiers testifying at the 1971 "Winter Soldier" hearings in Detroit were actually veterans, for example.[110] More generally, as Daniel Hallin has argued, the media dutifully reported official government policy regarding Vietnam for years, only breaking with the official line after the Tet Offensive in 1968.[111] By the time *The Selling of the Pentagon* appeared on CBS in 1971, a huge number of conservatives—not just the extremists—were up in arms over mainstream media bias. If *Life Line* was showing its true extremist colors in attacking war protestors, those colors didn't look terribly different from those of the "silent majority" that had reelected Nixon as a law-and-order candidate.

In any case, *Life Line*'s final years attacking the counterculture were the last hurrah for Hunt's propaganda mill. It was a terrific struggle to keep going after HLH Products, riddled with internal corruption and debt—having sucked some eighty million dollars from Hunt's coffers,[112] a fraction of that having gone to *Life Line*, with the rest stolen by corrupt employees, sunk into defunct real estate, or simply lost—finally withdrew sponsorship in 1970. Hunt would have hung on forever, but he had become too old to fight back, and his family would no longer tolerate HLH's tremendous losses. The *Life Line* operation hobbled along until 1975, when it finally shut down. Munn started up Munco, Inc., a map vending-machine venture, pursued public appearances in which he recited the Sermon on the Mount from memory, and became executive secretary of the ultraconservative, JBS-dominated Association of American Dentists. Right-wing broadcasting's most long-lived program had disappeared with a whimper, not a bang.

\* \* \*

In so many ways Hunt operated alone—incapable of working with other superpatriots, unwilling to sink money into political campaigns, surrounded by mistresses yet utterly lacking friends. Yet we can place Hunt, the loner, within (or at least adjacent to) the cold war movement of conservative businessmen opposed to labor unions, the welfare state, and, in general, the legacy of the New Deal. As historian Kim Phillips-Fein explains, by the 1960s there was a growing "sense in a part of the business community that ideological and political engagement was an appropriate, legitimate and absolutely essential part of being a businessman. Businessmen needed to fight on behalf of the free market, against the monopolistic threat of unions and the welfare state that threatened to exercise illegitimate power over the state."[113] Hunt may have been incapable of collaborating with other free-market businessmen, but he certainly shared their antipathy for government spending.

In the 1950s, Hunt had been the biggest funder of right-wing propaganda in the US, but by the time *Life Line* appeared, many other wealthy businessmen had joined the fray. Patrick Frawley, a maverick in ballpoint-pen promotion in the postwar years (indeed, the man behind PaperMate), would later become the head of Schick Safety Razor and chairman of Technicolor in 1961. He was a cochairman (with Walter Knott) of TV for Goldwater-Miller, the organization that produced the famous televised half-hour speech in which Ronald Reagan pledged support for Goldwater. Frawley supported Fred C. Schwarz's Christian Anti-Communist Crusade, and his companies provided "public-service" advertising (i.e., write-off-able expenses) for Schwarz's three-hour 1961 telecast from the Hollywood Bowl, *Hollywood's Answer to Communism*. Frawley also had Technicolor shoot an address by J. Edgar Hoover to be distributed to anticommunist groups. Frawley was a fervently anticommunist, conservative Catholic; he even sent out a mass mailing of Phyllis Schlafly's *A Choice Not an Echo* to priests, with a note on Schick letterhead. Frawley never had a regular radio or TV program like Hunt, but he did sink a lot of money into conservative media. In fact, according to the executive producer of *Choice*, the ill-fated half-hour Goldwater promotional film that never aired (Goldwater rightly recognized the film's racism and ordered it nixed, but too late—the DNC already had its hands on a print), Frawley actually financed *Choice*.[114]

Walter Knott of Knotts Berry Farm fame similarly pursued anticommunist objectives via his California Free Enterprise Association, a clearinghouse for a wide range of right-wing films, publications, and tapes produced by the John Birch Society, by Fred Schwarz, and by the National Education Program, a patriotic film operation based at Harding College. Knott's organization also sold books by Dan Smoot, Cleon Skousen, and John T. Flynn. D. B. Lewis, dog food manufacturer, as well as owner of a sulfur company and president of the Nuclear Fuels and Rare Metals Corporation, purchased advertising time to sustain not only the *Dan Smoot Report* but also television presentations by Major Edgar Bundy's *Church League of America* and the widespread *Manion Forum* radio program.[115] Hunt would only sponsor his own show; Lewis, by contrast, was a right-wing hero for advertising widely.

Of course, it's a bit simplistic to lump all of these fellows together. Hunt and Lewis brought a sharply conspiratorial edge to all that they did; these were not names that most politicians wanted to be publicly connected with, unless they were of the Strom Thurmond or Lester Maddox ilk. Knott and Frawley were ultraconservatives but were, to put it bluntly, able to play with others—to collaborate with the Goldwater campaign, for example. Regardless of such differences among the extremist businessmen, the point is that by the 1960s big money was flowing from the right, much of it not into the hands of the Republican Party but instead into the freelance production and distribution of conservative media.

A great many right-wing businessmen supported the John Birch Society by advertising in its publications and via direct cash donations. In 2008, Buckley audaciously claimed that the society "had been run out of town by *National Review* in 1962," when the magazine had first repudiated the leadership of the organization, while still holding out hopes for its members.[116] But Buckley's 1962 critique had not even come close to slowing down the expansion of the society. The JBS grew dramatically after Goldwater's defeat, recruiting members with a distinctively dull and direct new slogan: "*Now* Will You Join the John Birch Society?" The Anti-Defamation League of B'nai B'rith reported in 1966 that "by the end of 1965 the Society was spending well over $5 million a year. Add items for capital outlay and for local Society activity, such as full-page newspaper advertisements, and it is clear that Robert Welch achieved his goal of a total Society cash flow of $6 million for 1965. The Society grossed $1.6 million in 1963 and $3.3 million in 1964. Robert Welch's financial goal for 1966 is $12 million."[117] The JBS only briefly experimented with radio, preferring more low-tech media projects such as bumper-sticker and billboard campaigns. The most well-known billboard campaign was the one with the slogan "Support Your Local Police." Others included "Get us out of the United Nations!" and a pro-police billboard picturing an officer giving a boy mouth-to-mouth resuscitation, with the tagline "Some call him pig." The JBS had its own publishing imprint, American Opinion Books, and a few other front-organization publishers. (You can be pretty sure that any conservative book published in Belmont, Massachusetts, in the 1960s or 1970s is a product of the Birchers.) The JBS also sold books, filmstrips, and LPs at their American Opinion bookstores, and they arranged for local set-ups by which one could phone a special number to hear a recorded patriotic message. This was known as the "Let Freedom Ring" campaign. In 1962, Buckley had criticized Welch but spared JBS members, but in 1965 he rejected the organization completely. Its "psychosis of conspiracy" had become a threat to the legitimate conservative movement.[118] It was one thing to support the defeat of communism in Southeast Asia and to oppose the United Nations, quite another to believe, as Hunt, the Birchers, and their cohort did, that the government was planning to intern all American right-wingers in camps in Alaska, and that fluoridation was a "mass medication" communist-socialist conspiracy. Buckley finally had to concede that, like Hunt, Welch and his followers were nuts.

In the 1950s, Hunt had been a big fish in the small pond of right-wing media, but ten years later, with the rise of Smoot, Hargis, and McIntire, and the financial backing of Frawley, Knott, Welch, and others, the swimming hole had expanded tremendously. A 1962 *Nation* exposé on oil money and the radical Right noted that Hunt and a few other oil billionaires had been the main funders of the radical Right in the fifties but that a new crew of "Respectables" was now on board. In fact, "business millions were being channeled, not into the coffers of the Republican Party, but into the causes of Radical Right extremism."[119] How "respectable" the business tycoons redirecting their contributions from moderate Republican candidates to the growing hard-line fringe really were is open to debate. But the *Nation* hit the nail on the head in pegging Hunt as *less* respectable than men like Schick and Frawley. Respectable businessmen gave money to the causes in which they believed. Hunt wouldn't even give to local Dallas charities, much less political campaigns. Asked to contribute to diabetes research, Hunt responded, as summarized in an FBI memo, that "society would be better off if persons who were permanently disabled or physically incapacitated and unable financially to care for themselves were let to die rather than to be a burden on society."[120] One politician was lured to his office expecting a contribution but left with only an ample supply of Hunt's Gastro-Majic indigestion pills. Another, George Herbert Walker Bush, met with Hunt in 1962 hoping for a contribution to his congressional campaign; his heart must have skipped a beat at the end of the meeting, when Hunt discreetly gave him a bulging envelope. It was filled with Life Line pamphlets.[121] But the leaders of PaperMate Pen, Tidewater Oil, Richfield Oil, Knott's Berry Farm, Carnation Milk, Coast Federal Savings and Loan, and Southern California Edison Co. were another matter. These people were willing to open their wallets to a wide range of conservative political activities. Indeed, Coast was so gung-ho about anticommunism that it scheduled over one hundred screenings of patriotic films each month for employees in 1962, focusing on HUAC's *Operation Abolition* and Pepperdine College's *Communist Accent on Youth*.[122] By channeling funds toward superpatriot causes, "The Respectables," the *Nation* concluded, "have turned the Radicals from freaks into a force."[123]

Such right-wing businessmen did not spend their days writing "constructive" letters to the editor of every newspaper in America, like Hunt did. They might have shared Hunt's ideas about the dangers of communism, but they had the good sense to keep a lower profile. One might go so far as to say that the very thing that critics of Hunt attacked throughout the 1950s and '60s, his propaganda machine, was exactly what made him completely ineffective. He could spread his anticommunist "educational" information ad nauseam, but no political candidate would ever want to be officially endorsed by him; candidates could only be harmed by support from Hunt's TV and radio shows. In fact, in the course of his run for reelection, President Nixon advised his campaign manager to publicize the fact that Angela Davis, Abbie Hoffman, and Jerry Rubin supported McGovern. The idea was to defeat McGovern with a reversal of a tactic used against Goldwater: "One of the factors that brought Goldwater down to such a shattering defeat in 1964 was the success of the media in tying him to ultra-right-wing supporters like H. L. Hunt, the John Birch Society, etc."[124]

Even the rumor of an association with Hunt could be damning for a candidate, especially after Hunt was investigated in connection with the Kennedy assassination. Hunt senior was not actually involved: his son Bunker had financed a virulent JBS newspaper ad attacking Kennedy; an associate of Jack Ruby had approached Lamar Hunt looking for a job in his bowling alley shortly before the assassination; *Life Line* had broadcast a tough attack on JFK on the day of the assassination; and Jack Ruby had had *Life Line* pamphlets in his pockets at the time he murdered Lee Harvey Oswald (Ruby was disgusted by the pamphlets and no fan of Hunt's).[125] This was all very bad luck for Hunt, not to mention very gripping for conspiracy theorists for many years thereafter. Death threats against Hunt and his family ensued after the assassination.

The upshot was, Hunt was political poison, and his radio enterprise would be dismissed as extremist rubbish regardless of what kind of information it actually put out. It didn't matter than the newsletter, with a smaller circulation, was much tougher than the radio show, or that the radio show quite often came across as conservative, but not really extremist, per se. Expressing concerns about the Weathermen and other youth groups calling for violent revolution, for example, was hardly the exclusive domain of the Far Right in the late sixties. Hunt had created an organization that put out a right-wing newsletter and a blandly conservative but occasionally nutty radio show, but given Hunt's *Facts Forum* history and circumstantial link to the Kennedy assassination, *Life Line* was destined to be branded extremist no matter what. It didn't help that Hunt operated from Dallas, widely seen as the extremist center of America. JFK himself had referred to the city as "nut country."[126]

Nonetheless, Hunt kept plugging on for years after the assassination, convinced that spreading the correct information about communism, news bias, and the free market would inevitably help the country shift right. But the Right didn't *need* anticommunist information on radio and TV in the 1960s and 1970s. It needed, in brief, four things. First, organizational skills and a behind-the-scenes cash flow to the appropriate causes. A wealthy, eccentric tightwad like Hunt was no help whatsoever on this front. The need for organization and cash flow was intertwined with a second need: think tanks and organizations such as the Moral Majority, the John M. Olin Foundation, and the Heritage Foundation. As Alice O'Connor explains, in the 1970s, conservative business elites, "catalyzed by the 'social revolution' of the 1960s . . . cultivated a critique of the foundation-funded liberal establishment that—minus the overt anti-intellectualism of earlier right-wing critics—brought intellectual respectability and sophistication to largely familiar charges of creeping collectivism, cultural relativism, internationalism, and liberal elitism."[127] Hunt embodied the "minus," the anti-intellectualism and yahoo bigotry that Buckley rejected.

Third, the Right needed an issue besides communism: emotional issues like the family, abortion, culture wars, opposition to the Equal Rights Amendment, and so on would soon emerge as the cornerstone of the New Right. The Republican Party did begin to veer right in the post-Goldwater years, which made it more appealing to people like the so-called Respectables, but these wealthy businessmen would need to change, too: they needed to shift their agenda from communism to culture. By the 1980s, Coors and Domino's, among others, would emerge as the corporate face of the new Respectables. In a 1979 *Conservative Digest* essay, "Building the Moral Majority," Paul Weyrich spelled it out this way: "The family will be to the decade of the 1980s what environmentalism and consumerism have been to the 1970s and what the Vietnam war was to the 1960s."[128] Communism was the Right's big issue in the 1960s, and this is implied by Weyrich's reference to Vietnam, which inspired not only an antiwar movement on the Left but also a prowar movement on the Right. But Weyrich specifically references liberal social movements as the model for the New

Right. These were the movements that had traction. Frawley and Knott were smart to keep a lower profile than Hunt and to spread their money more widely, but they were still stuck on communism.[129] If those same businessmen, and new players in the growing conservative surge, could shift gears, a new movement could be created around issues like opposing abortion and gay rights. It worked, of course.

Fourth, as far as media was concerned, *Life Line*'s hokey style simply would not do. The Right needed slick media if it was to mainstream and modernize itself, pulling away from its extremist image. *The Silent Scream* (Bernard Nathansan, 1984) perfectly embodied all of these goals. It was about abortion, the new big issue that could bring together conservative Protestants, Catholics, and Jews. It was slickly produced, including sono-gram imagery. And it could be used to inspire activists and to fundraise.[130] This was practical propaganda. What *use*, conversely, did *Life Line* have, beyond serving as an easy target for irate *Nation* writers and indignant senators pontificating against Hunt's abuse of the tax code?

We can't be sure if anyone ever listened to *Life Line* and then decided to organize against the youth movement and in support of the war in Viet-nam. But did *Life Line* ever directly suggest such activities? Hunt virtu-ally never promoted direct political activity, instead sinking vast sums of money not into movement building or political organizing but in simply revealing facts that he thought would necessarily spur people to action. There was an implicit theory here as to how politics worked, a theory shared by most of the ultras: there were vast conspiracies in place, but ex-posing them to the light would inevitably weaken and destroy them. Thus, the richest man in America, who could have easily endowed right-wing political action committees or think tanks, instead spent untold millions on radio messages, newsletters, and pamphlets. To make these materi-als more effective, readers and listeners were encouraged to share Hunt's ideas with others. To this end, every *Life Line* mail-order radio transcript encouraged readers to share the transcript with friends. The program also devoted time to celebrating patriotic advertising, encouraging listeners to buy products from sponsors, and encouraging new sponsors to come on board. And Munn and Poucher often reminded listeners to enter *Life Line* essay contests. To fight dirty movies, *Life Line* suggested that listen-ers encourage theaters to show more wholesome fare. Offering an inspira-tional example, they told how a group of small-town high school students had successfully pressured a local theater to replace the undeniably smutty *Kiss Me, Stupid* (Billy Wilder, 1964) with something more virtuous, and the school principal had made sure that teachers didn't give homework so that the kids could go to the morally upright replacement film. *Life Line* had not been behind the attack on the film and did not follow up with tips on cultural activism. They certainly offered no model upon which to build a movement. Ultimately, the thing that *Life Line* did best, it seemed, was promote *Life Line*, not the tactics of conservative social change.

## CHAPTER TWO

# Right-Wing Broadcasting's Supreme Individualist

*Dan Smoot and the Tactics of Constitutional Conservatism*

For ultraconservative Dan Smoot, talking was doing. Skilled at making verbal assaults on the politicians and policies he disagreed with, his single attempt to enter politics himself as a candidate for public office was an unmitigated failure. Yet Smoot did succeed as a radio and TV pundit. How did he become the only long-term, regularly scheduled, and widely televised ultra? What were his tactics? What legacy, if any, would Smoot leave behind? And who exactly was this self-declared constitutional conservative?

To say that Smoot was a self-made man would be an understatement. Born in Missouri in 1913, Smoot was orphaned at age eleven. Thereafter, he and his brother Jewell worked long hours sharecropping with their Uncle Hez. Their days filled with mending fences and tending hogs, there was virtually no time for schooling, and the roads to school were impassible most of the time anyway. On the rare occasion that the boys did attend school, they were the poorest children there. While others had lunch pails and real victuals, Dan and Jewell each arrived with an old sorghum molasses can containing a piece of cornbread and a bit of hog fat. "We were ashamed," Dan recalled, "to eat it in the presence of others who had such store-bought dainties as peanut butter and crackers, and baloney on lightbread."[1] Dan's father had taught him to read, and he had run through *David Copperfield*, *Tom Sawyer*, and *Moby-Dick* by the age of seven, but Uncle Hez had no books to share, to Smoot's great regret. (Some years later, Smoot's wife would give him money she had painstakingly saved for him to buy a smart topcoat, but on the way to the store he would spot a fine ten volume set of Shakespeare that he could not resist buying instead.) If there was no money for soap, there certainly was none to spare for literature. Smoot and his neighbors were so hungry that rabbits, raccoons, squirrels, and possums were practically extinct in the area. At age fifteen, Dan was taken to the dentist for the first time, by a kindly aunt. Never having owned a toothbrush, he was only narrowly saved from dentures.

It was a hardscrabble existence, but not one that Smoot resented. In a 1961 speech he seemed positively relieved that the Big Hand of government had never offered him food or shelter:

> As a boy, I had spent a great deal of time making a living in an occupation which would, today, have me classified both as a Child Laborer and Migrant Farm Worker. I didn't find out until years later . . . that great, rich people like Mrs. Roosevelt and Edward R. Murrow, felt sorry for folks like me, and considered us a shameful blight on the American scene, and wanted to improve us . . . It is true that . . . I didn't enjoy enough leisure to become a juvenile delinquent; and I was so ignorant that I didn't even know I was oppressed.[2]

The grinding poverty his family had experienced in the 1920s had been caused by the federal government's spending on World War I, he explained in his autobiography, and the New Deal only made things worse. He had watched his mother die in excruciating pain of an untreated ruptured appendix, and his grandfather had wandered homeless after a stroke before finally being committed to "some sort of prison" as "a public menace," where he was apparently murdered.[3] Yet the notion that the government should provide assistance for the poor never entered Smoot's mind. These personal events pained him, but what could be done? People got sick and died. That's just how things worked.

Smoot ran away from Uncle Hez's place when he was fifteen, picked up what work he could, and made his way to hobo jungles when he needed tips on riding the rails. He finally landed in Dallas, Texas, and in 1931 enrolled in high school, while also working forty-four hours a week as a clerical worker for a fruit and vegetable distributor. Incredibly, given his distaste for handouts of any kind, Smoot accepted a scholarship to Southern Methodist University in 1934, earned his BA and MA, and then proceeded to Harvard in 1941 where he pursued (but ultimately did not complete) a PhD in American civilization. He was fond of the students but disgusted by the unpatriotic attitudes he encountered among the faculty; he enjoyed the company only of his dean and Robert Frost. Following Pearl Harbor, Smoot hoped to enlist but was rejected by all branches of the military because of color blindness and flatfeet. In 1942, he left Harvard for the FBI, where he initially pursued draft dodgers and later was put to work on communist cases before being transferred to more general criminal investigations. Already a talented orator, Smoot also regularly gave speeches for the FBI, basically doing public-relations work. Frustrated for years by the bureau's "fetid corruption" and failure to root communists out of the federal government, Smoot finally resigned in 1951.[4]

Smoot quickly made a new career for himself as the voice (and face) of H. L. Hunt. But he soon grew tired of giving two points of view on every issue. The liberal perspective left an unbearably bitter taste in his mouth. So in 1955 he resigned from his ventriloquist act at *Facts Forum* to begin his weekly *Dan Smoot Report*, a newsletter that in 1957 would become a fifteen-minute weekly TV and radio program aired throughout the South, Midwest, and West Coast.[5] Upon starting his new solo broadcasting venture he announced that he would no longer give the "totalitarian liberal" perspective as he had been forced to do by Hunt. Now he would speak only for "constitutional conservatives"—a constituency that he named, then claimed as his own.[6] In his publication and broadcasts, Smoot voiced his opposition to civil rights, communism, foreign aid, the United Nations, Earl Warren, and so on.[7] Although major media markets like New York City and Chicago did not air the *Report*, Smoot was a small-time celebrity, already a known face from his years with Hunt. In fact, appalled liberals had labeled him the "hired voice of the Texas Oilionaires," and he was sufficiently famous that in the late 1950s, when he bumped into senator Lyndon Baines Johnson exiting a TV station in Austin, Johnson immediately shook his hand and exclaimed, "You're Dan Smoot! Oh, if only I had your voice!"[8]

The Facts Forum office had handled the hundred thousand letters sent to Smoot in the four years he worked for Hunt, forwarding around thirty thousand letters to Smoot himself. Smoot's secretary had made an informational index card for each letter, and Smoot took the cards with him when he left Hunt's operation.[9] Smoot sent out the first copy of his newsletter for free to the thirty thousand addresses from these cards. Within a week he had received nine hundred requests for subscriptions, as well as enthusiastic letters from Barry Goldwater (addressed to "Dan" and signed "Barry"), William F. Buckley Jr., South Dakota senator Karl E. Mundt, South Carolina senator Strom Thurmond, and a number of businessmen.

A recurrent motif of the letters was relief that Smoot had finally thrown off the two-sided mantle and disappointment that Hunt had not made this move himself. (He would, of course, a few years later.) One correspondent noted indelicately, "It must be a relief not to be working for H. L. Hunt and family. I've never met anyone who could get on with that S.O.B."[10]

Smoot presented himself more as pedant than S.O.B. Although occasionally sarcastic and bitter, his style was just as often humorless and dry as he hammered home his arguments. He hoped to ignite indignation more through logic than emotional exploitation. In this way, he differed starkly from fundamentalist broadcasters like McIntire and Hargis who hoped to seduce listeners with their passionate discourse. It seemed like the more tears they could provoke, the more contributions would pour in. This would have been quite distasteful to the ever-angry but rarely fully emotive Smoot. His power as a broadcaster came from his authoritative, masculine address, yet his masculine reserve also meant that he would not pull at heartstrings to bring in donations, and this ultimately held him back. That is, it held back the growth of his enterprise. Since he never solicited funds on-air, his endeavors could not develop into an organization of the magnitude of Hargis's Christian Crusade. This inevitably limited the power and scope of Smoot's undertaking. Thus, although Smoot had a small support staff, he did not have a political organization the way that Hargis did. The *Dan Smoot Report* had twenty-two employees at its peak, yet always remained more or less what it sounded like, a one-man operation.

Smoot's 1961 radio/TV audience has been estimated at six million, though this may well have indicated his *potential* audience rather than the number that actually tuned in. With no ratings of Smoot's programs available, audience data is virtually nonexistent, but we do know with certainty on exactly which stations Smoot aired. In 1961, the *Report* had thirty-one TV outlets and fifty-two radio outlets, with a particular concentration in California, Washington, Idaho, and Arizona. By 1966, Smoot aired on ninety-one radio stations and forty-four TV outlets in thirty-eight states, with an estimated audience of seventeen million and a newsletter subscription pool of forty thousand.[11]

Smoot devoted much of his TV program, radio show, and newsletter to attacking presidents Kennedy, Johnson, and Nixon. All three were "totalitarian liberals," and none got credit for escalating a war against communism in Southeast Asia or deferring federal action to further school integration. That evidence seemed so clearly to indicate that Kennedy was a centrist, LBJ a north-by-northwest liberal, and Nixon a conservative meant nothing to Smoot. He was no mere conservative. He was a "constitutional conservative."

Smoot could not stomach the application of labels like "ultra" and "extremist" to himself and other superpatriots. In a 1961 issue of his *Dan Smoot Report* newsletter, he responded to liberal attacks by painting a positive picture of the expanding conservative movement: "A most hopeful and wholesome development in 1961 was the tremendous growth of the patriotic movement in America—a movement composed of well-informed men and women of all age groups, from all occupations, in all parts of the country. The movement is wider, deeper, more intelligent, more orderly, and more determined than it has ever been before." This movement would succeed once the federal income tax was abolished and the US disengaged from the United Nations, he further explained. Next, Smoot attacked Robert Kennedy for referring to the JBS and the aptly named National Indignation Convention as "vigilante" groups and explained that "the 'liberals' are scared: that's why they use lies, distortion, mis-quotations, guilt-by-association, nasty labels, and ugly innuendoes, in their all out campaign to discredit the 'super-patriots' and 'extremists.' " Finally, Smoot quoted Thomas Jefferson to boost morale among his superpatriot following: "The patriot, like the Christian, must learn that to bear revilings and persecution is part of his duty."[12]

Though a fierce individualist, Smoot was not alone on one count: all the superpatriots harumphed that they were not extremists. No one from the Ku Klux Klan to the White Citizens' Council to the Christian Crusade was eager to self-identify as a radical organization outside of "the mainstream." The John Birch Society in particular was keen to portray itself as upscale, sensible, and normal; recruitment films pictured Birchers in banquet halls in tuxedos eating New York strip steaks and listening to inspirational speeches, as Miss Indiana circulated and made small talk. Goldwater boosters had been widely caricatured in the press as "little old ladies in tennis shoes,"[13] but the gentlemen pictured in the 16mm John Birch Society recruitment films projected in suburban living rooms all over America sported wives with lovely bouffant hairdos and elegant beaded gowns. The JBS bent over backward to convey an image of upscale normality. These were patriotic businessmen with a taste for dry martinis, not Molotov cocktails.

What, then, constituted "extremism," from the Birchers' perspective? A 1969 JBS film argues that there are two kinds of extremists. On one end there are anarchists who advocate no government at all. On the other end are those who advocate total government control—communists and Nazis. (This was an argument precisely reiterated by both Smoot and Billy James Hargis.) Since Birchers were opposed to both the extreme of anarchy and the extreme of totalitarianism, the film argues, they are actually America's "real middle of the roaders."[14] Similarly staking a claim for non-extremism, in the script of a radio broadcast intended for an ABC series that never materialized, Smoot again quoted Thomas Jefferson on the importance of state sovereignty and concluded that "Jefferson and Daniel Webster sound exactly like the Americans whom Gus Hall [leader of the American Communist Party] and other 'leftists' call 'right-wing extremists' today."[15]

Looking back today, labels like "liberal," "conservative," "ultraconservative," "extremist," and "right-wing" quickly become confusing. American politics have moved rightward since the postwar years, and what was deemed liberal or conservative fifty years ago would not necessarily sound liberal or conservative today. However, many if not most Americans in the late 1960s and early 1970s were capable of perceiving Nixon as conservative, even if they fundamentally disagreed about whether he was too conservative or not conservative enough. Herein lies Smoot's "extremism," in part, for he was incapable of understanding that Nixon remained a conservative, even as he played the game of politics. A more flexible thinker might have realized that conservative politicians could not support every single tax cut; the fact that they made compromises did not simply transform them into socialists. But taxation for federal spending on anything but national defense was unconstitutional, Smoot believed, and proved that one was a totalitarian liberal, the polar opposite of the constitutional conservative. Thus, from Smoot's perspective, he was no extremist. It was the presidents who illegally enforced civil rights and spent money on public housing, education, and welfare who were left-wing extremists. For their part, Kennedy, Johnson, and Nixon intuited that the ultras were not only true enemies (and largely symbolic enemies, with more bark than bite) but also good straw men. The high-profile right-wing broadcasters represented a radicalism that cold war presidents could point to as proof of their own sensible moderation. It was Political Strategy 101.

The broadcast ultras would ultimately be shut down by a combination of actions taken by the FCC, the Democratic National Committee, citizen activism, and the IRS. It was Kennedy's administration that began to use the Fairness Doctrine to attack right-wing broadcasting, although the grand poobah of them all, Carl McIntire, would only finally be ousted from the airwaves during Nixon's administration, as we will see in chapter 4.

Intuitively, it might seem odd that the ultras made Nixon's Enemies List. After all, Nixon's call for "law and order" and his stand against student radicals and other longhairs were, at points, closely in line with the extremists' own attitudes, and Nixon also nominated Supreme Court justices with records of supporting "states' rights" and opposing integration. As late as 1970 he would go so far as to claim that integration was simply moving too fast. But Nixon had opened relations with China and did not intend to discontinue social (or rather, Smoot and others insisted, *socialist*) welfare programs. He simply wasn't anticommunist enough to pass the ultras' severe ideological litmus test.[16] Indeed, more reputable, intellectually inclined conservatives like Russell Kirk and William F. Buckley Jr. were also disenchanted with Nixon.

Nixon's opposition to integration—and busing in particular—was no consolation to Smoot, for Nixon was part of the establishment and, like virtually all politicians, was a pawn of what Smoot called "the Invisible Government," a cabal composed of the Council on Foreign Relations, the Trilateral Commission, the United Nations, the World Bank, and other dastardly villains. Few politicians escaped the tentacular grasp of the Invisible Government, according to Smoot. Smoot's book, *The Invisible Government*, became a centerpiece of the John Birch Society's media distribution network, going out via mail order and widely available in JBS bookstores, commonly called "American Opinion Libraries." Smoot claimed *The Invisible Government* sold almost two million copies, a figure that does not seem unlikely given its status as a conspiracy-theory classic.[17] In fact, in 1967 Smoot's book was included in the society's "One Dozen Candles," their list of books considered indispensable Americanist classics and crucial reading for new recruits.[18]

If H. L. Hunt was willing to make certain compromises (like avoiding attacks on labor unions and minorities) in an attempt to retain his tax-exempt status and avoid getting stations in trouble for Fairness Doctrine violations, Smoot was more like Carl McIntire: unwilling to bend or compromise in any way. And like both McIntire and Hunt, Smoot had difficulty forming pragmatic political alliances, notwithstanding a long-standing friendly relationship with the Birch Society. Smoot himself was a living model for what he imagined the Constitution to be, a self-enclosed document that provided clear-cut guidelines with no room for multiple interpretations. If the fundamentalist ultras of the 1960s took John 3:16 as their inspiration—"For God so loved the world that he gave his only begotten son that whosoever should believe in him would not perish but have everlasting life"—Smoot's Rock of Gibraltar was the Tenth Amendment:

"The powers not delegated to the United States by the Constitution, nor prohibited by it to the States, are reserved to the States respectively, or to the people." States' rights were the key to America's political salvation.

*   *   *

When the ultras' numbers swelled in the wake of McCarthy and Goldwater, they were roundly attacked by the liberal intelligentsia. A slew of both academic and more popular publications attacking the superpatriots appeared. Books like *Danger on the Right, Report on the John Birch Society, 1966,* and *The Politics of Doomsday* provided elaborate (and often repetitive) summaries of the ultras' political beliefs. Plowing through these books, it becomes hard to keep all the different players straight. They begin to melt together into a single giant hate group spewing propaganda. And this was not Leni Reifenstahl–style propaganda, driven by an aesthetic imperative; the ultras' broadcasts were perceived by critics at the time merely as vehicles for right-wing content. It is a mistake, however, to paint the extremists' radio and TV shows with broad strokes as "just propaganda," as if the programs were only vessels for manipulative information. The *Report* was an audiovisual text, albeit often an exceedingly dull one, with a zero-degree style.

The black-and-white weekly program opens with a gentle orchestral arrangement of "America the Beautiful," with titles offering a literal interpretation. America, as represented by the flag, is superimposed flying over "amber waves of grain" and then over "purple mountains majesty." The title of the program appears onscreen, and then Smoot himself appears, sitting behind his desk, always dressed neatly in a suit and tie. Behind him is a bookcase with matching volumes, a globe, and a small houseplant. Visually, Smoot offered viewers the very picture of good taste and middle-class respectability. One imagines the books behind him must be the Harvard Classics series, which were promoted with the notion "that every American should engage in perpetual education through self-guided reading . . . and that anyone could acquire learning through no more than fifteen minutes of reading a day."[19] Smoot, too, would offer self-improvement in fifteen-minute doses.

Fifteen minutes was a standard programming length with roots in radio; the format would finally die out in the early 1970s, shortly after the demise of Smoot's program. When the *Report* premiered in the late fifties, produced on a shoestring budget and running fifteen minutes, it wouldn't have looked very different from most public-affairs programs. While a number of early TV soap operas that had carried over from radio ran fifteen minutes long, thirty minutes was already the standard for TV soaps by the late 1950s, with only *Guiding Light* (CBS, 1952–2009) and *Search for Tomorrow* (CBS, 1951–82; NBC, 1982–86) holding at fifteen minutes until 1968.[20] Further, both CBS and NBC had extended their nightly news programs from fifteen to thirty minutes in 1963.[21] Yet as late as 1968, local news still held at fifteen minutes in many markets, and, though produced at a higher cost than the *Dan Smoot Report*, local news still kept costs down by centering on studio-based talking heads. All of which is to say that Smoot's program might have stood apart for its right-wing ideas, but in terms of format it was quite unremarkable as a news program, and its similarity to locally produced news was quite appropriate, since this was a program striking a claim to debunk the "totalitarian liberal" national news.

After the *Report*'s opening titles, Smoot would introduce the day's topic, the film would cut to allow insertion of a sponsor's plug, and then Smoot would deliver his message, which appeared perfectly memorized, though he did actually use a teleprompter. This was a model performance of seriousness and rigor. Of all the broadcast ultras, Smoot was the most careful and refined in his use of language. Hargis and McIntire were drawn to a fire-and-brimstone style, and Hunt, who had crafted a two-sided approach thickly packaged as "fair" in the fifties had embraced more eccentric discourse in the sixties. But Smoot was a precise rhetorician, a man who clearly loved his thesaurus. Once his careful monologue was completed, another brief sponsor break would follow, and then Smoot would give a quick conclusion and close by telling viewers that they could learn more by subscribing to his report. The script of the *Report* television program was virtually identical to Smoot's paper version, with editing for length. Aside from the cutaways for sponsors, the entire program was composed of a single long shot. This appeared to be a show utterly drained of aesthetic ambition (figure 16).

In effect, Smoot gave lectures that deliberately avoided taking advantage of what gave TV an edge over print and radio: the ability to reveal things visually and dynamically. One might chalk this restraint up to financial limitations. Smoot had no budget for stock footage of the foreign lands he discussed and no crew to gather footage of the communists he attacked. Although it is true that Smoot did not have the resources for a more visually dynamic presentation, I also believe that the "non-aesthetic" that

FIGURE 16. The same tasteful mise-en-scène is on display in every episode of the *Dan Smoot Report*. MacDonald & Associates, 1965.

he chose to use suited him quite nicely. After all, Robert Welch made a number of JBS recruitment films without ever stepping out from behind a podium (figure 17). That Welch was a notoriously dry speaker was acknowledged by even the most devoted Birchers. If the man who symbolized the American patriotic movement didn't have to liven things up with a backdrop more ambitious than a curtain, why should Smoot waste time on elaborate mise-en-scène?

The whole point of Smoot's presentation was that he had facts to deliver. To illustrate the facts with fancy pictures would have demeaned them by implying that *showmanship* could improve the message. Network news of the 1950s and '60s used illustrations freely, and did that make the coverage any better? Indeed, liberal media historian Eric Barnouw clearly holds radio news in higher esteem than TV news, noting that, beginning in the early 1950s, "the camera, as arbiter of news value, had introduced a drastic curtailment of the scope of news. The notion that a picture was worth a thousand words meant, in practice, that footage of Atlantic City beauty winners, shot at some expense, was considered more valuable than a thousand words from Eric Sevareid on the mounting tensions of Southeast Asia. Analysis, a staple of radio news in its finest days . . . was being pushed aside as non-visual."[22] Smoot would not fall into this trap. When he holds up the paper version of the *Report*, a viewer might gather that he is using a visual aid, but this would be a mistake. The newsletter pictures Smoot in the upper-right-hand corner and a title that duplicates the program title. Since Smoot's programs were rarely if ever repeated, and there were no consumer VCRs, the newsletter represents not so much a visual aid as simply a chance to consume the program again. And if you missed the TV show and weren't a subscriber, you could hear the exact same fifteen minutes of audio on the radio.

The single-shot format was not merely a means of saving money on editing. The uncut shot helped to further remove the program from the realm of interpretation and manipulation; only tricksters needed to use crafty editing to cobble together their arguments. The liberal Edward R. Murrow, who shamelessly promoted *democratic* values, depended on the smoke and mirrors of manipulative montage sequences, as in the infamous 1954 episode of *See It Now* composed of extracts from McCarthy speeches. As a *constitutional conservative*, by contrast, Smoot needed only himself and a loaded 16mm camera to deliver his story to an audience that valued

FIGURE 17. John Birch Society founder Robert Welch gives a ninety-minute lecture without the benefit of visual aids in the 16mm recruitment film *Tower of Sanity*. His single attempt at rhetorical panache: "The whole official line as to what we are doing in Vietnam is as nutty as a pecan pie." MacDonald & Associates, c. 1965.

not democratic debate but rather the simple facts that would restore America to its lawful status as a *republic*. And one can only assume that the perfectionist (and budget-conscious) Smoot shot all of his programs in just one take. If he messed up at any point, he would have had to scrap the whole thing and start over. The perfect delivery within the single-shot format conveyed polish, professionalism, and imperviousness to error.

Smoot's anti-aesthetic was connected to his dislike of flashy protest. To march in the street with a picket sign, for either a conservative or a liberal cause, was deeply distasteful to him. The problem was not merely that civil disobedience was a tool of communist civil rights activists but also that civil disobedience functioned by *disobeying*. Constitutional conservatives should not stoop to rowdy activism, Smoot maintained. Rather, they should protest with "facts and ideas . . . until enough people are enlightened by the truth to take legal, political action to restore the crumbling foundation of our Republic."[23] Smart tacticians on both left and right have long realized the power of using protest to draw media attention, but for Smoot, stage-managed protest demeaned one's cause. In a script he wrote for ABC (which was never aired), Smoot discussed a conservative demonstration against Adlai Stevenson staged at the United Nations building. A picketer had "accidentally bumped Stevenson on the head" in Smoot's version of the story, and the liberal mainstream media had run with the story. Smoot empathized with the demonstrators, but he did not approve of their tactics: "Picketing and demonstrating are poor means of expression, which I have never approved." Smoot added that "the way to answer Stevenson is not to wave signs at *him*, but to reach *others* with facts to expose the fallacy of his views."[24]

Some years later, as the anti-abortion movement gathered steam, conservative activist groups like Operation Rescue would perfect the art of making "the whole world" watch. They understood that movements need visibility, symbols, and media coverage. But for Smoot, to adopt the headline-grabbing techniques of lawless hippies was unthinkable. Smoot would not give anyone the satisfaction of a vulgar dog-and-pony show when straightforward facts delivered from behind a desk were the only authentic means of staging protest.

Smoot could spread his ideas, but with an aversion to showy protest and virtually no fundraising he couldn't run a political campaign, lobby against a law, or fight an FCC policy. Smoot was a committed individualist who didn't get involved in activism on the ground, perhaps because it would have meant collaborating with others. He had many loyal subscribers and viewers, but he never rallied his constituency into taking specific political actions. However, he did almost become a political candidate himself. In 1969 Smoot was approached by the American Independent Party of Texas and asked to run for the Senate. Most often remembered as the organization that supported Wallace in his 1968 run for the White House, the American Party was clearly making an ill-fated attempt in Texas to broaden its purview. Smoot agreed to take his place on the ticket, provided he could first raise sufficient funds for the campaign, but he ultimately returned the money he raised and decided not to run. His financial supporters were many, but diffuse, without a clear concentration in Texas that would translate into votes: only 21 percent of his contributions and 19 percent of his pledges came from Texans. Further, the American Party itself ultimately faltered in its support for Smoot, as the continuance of Social Security was part of the party's platform, and Smoot, naturally, opposed Social Security.

Notwithstanding his brief alliance with the American Party, Smoot preferred to maintain his independence. Along with Clarence Manion, he had been a national chairman of For America in the 1950s, and he had also been a director-at-large of We, The People!, an organization in which Hargis would later be active, but he devoted most of his energies to running his own outfit. Smoot was in great demand as a speaker at engagements of numerous right-wing organizations. He not only fit the bill ideologically but also had a deep, appealing voice and was rather handsome. Indeed, one Elaine Kregeloh, who wrote to Smoot often—mentioning her husband Hubert not infrequently, presumably to mask her simmering crush—commented, "You look a bit like Murrow—thank God you don't have his 'objective' ideas!"[25] The problem was, all he had were ideas—strategies, without the muscle to carry them out. Even at For America there was not much practical activity. A central objective of the group in 1956, for example, was to get a so-called spare tire presidential candidate on the ballot so that true conservatives would have an alternative to Eisenhower in order to make "an impressive protest vote."[26] A large protest vote would demonstrate that many *dis*liked Ike, but it was a symbolic act, and the very notion of the spare tire did not convey any great ambitions. Buckley's *National Review*, by contrast, took the pragmatic high road in officially declaring, wryly, "we prefer Ike."

\* \* \*

By the time the *Dan Smoot Report* premiered in 1957, the civil rights movement was already a frequent topic of discussion on the networks' national news programs. The public interest would be served, many local station owners apparently assumed, by balancing out the "biased" national news with the putatively more objective *Report*, which opposed civil rights and exposed the movement as a communist conspiracy. Smoot would have been shocked by the suggestion that his programs were racist. Was it his fault that communists were behind civil rights? Why couldn't his totalitarian liberal opponents understand that American blacks had a higher standard of living in the US than their savage counterparts in deepest Africa? Although the *Report* covered a wide range of topics and timely issues (developments in the United Nations, changes in foreign-aid packages, new Supreme Court appointments), states' rights were always implicitly at stake. Every kind of federal government action could be blamed on the unlawful violation of the Tenth Amendment, and on the unlawful existence of the Fourteenth Amendment, which Smoot repeatedly claimed had never been properly ratified. As the ultimate expression of communist influence and symbol of encroaching federalism, the civil rights movement was always implicitly at issue in Smoot's broadcasts. For his loyal listeners, every evocation of the disempowerment of the states—even if the explicit topic were Social Security or Medicare—would have brought civil rights to mind.

Smoot's belief in white—specifically American white—superiority was undoubted. A three-week tour of South America in 1963 confirmed all that he had believed before he left the US. Of Panama he wrote in a letter home: "It has pleased me to see my previous opinions of this land confirmed by observation. It is a jungle which was the pest-hole of the world until American money and brains converted it into the most wholesomely healthful and comfortable nation of all Latin America. The natives themselves have done nothing. The fascinating and colorful old ruins are the remnants of what Spaniards built. The present beauty and development are American-made."[27] Peru fared no better: "In Peru . . . the big population of indolent and stupid Indians hangs like an albatross on the nation's neck, inviting political demagoguery which results in social unrest, political instability, and economic uncertainty—the very conditions which discourage the inflow of foreign capital and the proper use of domestic capital."[28] Smoot spoke highly of a Peruvian guide who shocked others in his tour group by declaring that "most of the 'low' breeds who people the smelly slums are there because they are too indolent, or stupid, to work. She says there is plenty of work for all to do, but most of the slum-dwellers prefer to live like pigs and beg."[29] These private letters matched the tone of Smoot's public discourse almost exactly, although he also would have contended that, practically speaking, it ultimately did not matter whether or not blacks, poor people, or the uneducated were inferior to white, prosperous, educated people: federal mandates about who could vote or where you had to send your child to school were a violation of both individual rights and state sovereignty, as per the Tenth Amendment. Race and class were, theoretically, tangential to the most important thing of all: states' rights.

It was typical for conservatives in the 1960s to oppose civil rights on the grounds that it was a communist or communist-inspired movement and on the grounds that the federal government had no right to force school integration. One thing that made Smoot more unique, however, was that he opposed universal voting rights not only based on the idea that states themselves should determine voter eligibility requirements but also because universal voting rights were not constitutionally guaranteed. And if it wasn't explicitly in the Constitution, it wasn't legal. Laws should reinforce, not interpret, the Constitution; that the law and the constitution or laws might change over time based on changing social or political conditions was lunacy, as far as Smoot was concerned. Case law was a foreign concept to him, and he had little use for amendments beyond the Bill of Rights.

In line with the JBS, Smoot argued that the US was not a democracy. In fact, one of the society's slogans was "This is a republic, not a democracy — Let's keep it that way!" The motto was a bit ungainly for bumper stickers, but a JBS textile-mill owner did successfully requisition a printing plate with the slogan so that all of his metered mail would proclaim these words of wisdom. The Pitney-Bowes meter-machine makers routinely produced specialized plates, as long as the statements were not "controversial," and a fracas later ensued when Pitney-Bowes learned that the slogan was inflammatory. Officials from the company, who had approved the plate without any clue about its JBS roots, demanded return of the plate and pleaded ignorance: "some dictionaries define a republic as a democracy. It seemed rather meaningless."[30] Indeed, to the masses outside of the extremist worldview, the distinction between a republic and a democracy was not widely understood, or seen as a particularly compelling issue. Although H. L. Hunt had called for some decidedly undemocratic measures in his utopian novel, it appears that the JBS and Smoot were the ultras most actively driven to opposing democracy on principle.

It was certainly true, as Smoot claimed, that America had been devised as a republic and that the founders had not envisioned universal suffrage.

Two hundred years later, Smoot did not see any reason to alter course. He did not baldly state that only white male property owners should be enfranchised, but he had no problem with poll taxes, literacy tests, and other means of determining voter eligibility. That a literacy test in Alabama might involve asking an African American to read a Chinese newspaper was not the kind of patently unfair (and bizarre) scenario that Smoot was likely to expose on his program. There simply was no racial injustice in America, as far as he was concerned. In holding this attitude, Smoot was not atypical. "An illusory ideal rallied many in the white South" during the years of the civil rights movement.[31] There had been no "race problem" before outside agitators stirred things up, and local blacks had been perfectly content under Jim Crow. It seemed like everyone who made this claim had a happy black housekeeper or gardener to offer up as proof of black tranquility and passivity. John Hope Franklin elaborates: the white South's "obsession was to maintain a government, an economy, an arrangement of the sexes, a relationship of the races, and a social system that had never existed . . . except in the fertile imagination of those who would not confront either the reality that existed or the change that would bring them closer to reality."[32]

Many who opposed African American access to the polls in the 1950s and 1960s believed in their fertile imaginations that blacks didn't really want to vote anyway; communists had taken advantage of their simple minds and manipulated them to demand suffrage. Some approved of any means to keep blacks away from the polls (including violence, which Smoot never sanctioned), but Smoot emphasized the constitutional validity of preventing democracy. Some years later, having agreed to serve on the board of an organization called Western Goals, Smoot was shocked to come across a positive reference to democracy in the organization's legal paperwork. He immediately decided to step down, exclaiming, "How could I explain [my presence on the board] to people whom I taught to despise democracy as an evil kind of government—people who learned from me the rule of thumb that America is (or at least was and should be still) a Republic, not a democracy?"[33] The founder of Western Goals—congressman, John Birch Society chair, and former urologist Larry McDonald—satisfied Smoot and kept him on the board by promising to "delete the egalitarian phraseology."[34]

In the republic envisioned by the Constitution, Smoot believed, only those fully *qualified* would vote. At a speech in Boston in 1970 he spoke of a constitutional amendment that had been approved by the House and was being considered by the Senate that would have provided for popular election of the president. This, he predicted, "would be the death blow to the American constitutional Republic," which would be replaced by a "mobocracy."[35] The real danger was that "with direct, popular elections, a million adult reliefers in a few large cities—people who never worked or paid direct taxes—could outvote all income-taxpaying citizens in any one of forty of our fifty states. Two or three precincts in a big northern city, densely populated with welfare families, could outvote all income-taxpaying citizens in Alaska, Delaware, Nevada, Vermont, or Wyoming."[36] Democracy, in other words, was a dangerous thing.

Given Smoot's strong connections with the JBS, it's not surprising that the Birchers agreed with him about the perils of democracy. The society went so far as to contend that a lynch mob was the ultimate expression of democracy, since it was an expression of majority rule, with only one dissenting vote. A nondemocratic republic, by contrast, would offer limited majority rule that protected the minority.[37] To meld Smoot's rationale with the Birchers', one might summarize that big-city reliefers voting en masse were a lynch mob oppressing the elite, more rational crowd to whom voting rights properly belonged. Thus, the JBS and Smoot could implicitly explain how black voters oppressed whites, and justify only allowing whites to vote, without directly discussing race. "Minority," in this lopsided equation, referred not to African Americans or other ethnic groups but rather to the minority of white Americans truly qualified to vote.

One would be hard put to deny that racism and extremism were in play as the conservative movement began to swell in the 1960s. Naturally, this notion is distasteful to the "legitimate" Right that came into its own in the Reagan years. Richard Viguerie even argues that, contrary to reports fabricated by the "liberal media" of the 1960s, which smeared conservatives as racist crackpots, there were few real extremists in the 1960s. Even George Wallace and his staff privately acknowledged that the Birch Society and the White Citizens' Council (both groups ardent Wallace boosters) were all a bunch of "nuts,"[38] but JBS founder Welch, Viguerie contends, was "against segregation," and "he purged the Society of both anti-Semites and racists."[39] In a tell-all exposé, former JBS employee Gerald Schomp tells a different story: "While the Society has denounced anti-Semitism for public consumption, it endures anti-Semitic and racist members as long as they don't 'spread such views,' or publicly embarrass the organization. But by tolerating anti-Semitic and racist views within the membership, Welch practically insures that such views will ultimately be disseminated to more members."[40] That Welch urged bigots to bite their tongues did not absolve his organization of racism.

Of course, everything hinged on how one defined "racism." In the 16mm recruitment film *This Is the John Birch Society* (1969), narrator G. Edward Griffin explains that people like to associate with those who are like themselves; this is normal discrimination that has nothing to do with hatred. The society, he elaborates (and exactly in line with Goldwater on this point), was equally opposed to a state government forcing segregation as it was to a federal government forcing integration. Instead, both federal and state government should leave integration and segregation up to individual choice. This libertarian language didn't use racist slurs, but it certainly made it clear that individuals should be "free" to act as racist or nonracist as they desired. Whether this might have a negative impact on black Americans was not a question the film was interested in raising, though the narrator does cheerily note that "there are all-negro John Birch Society groups and all-white ones." The objective of the film was clearly to convey an image of the society as hyperrational, not extremist.

*Civil Rights or Black Power?*, a late 1960s filmstrip distributed by the JBS and produced by a Los Angeles group called The Voice of Watts (probably one of the Birch Society's many front organizations),[41] aptly illustrates the stance of conservative groups conceiving themselves as middle-of-the-roaders at this time. A white couple observes that "We know a lot of good colored people, but lately they've been acting kind of funny." Husband Ron exclaims, "I'm an oppressor? I work the same job and make the same money!" A helpful African American—"Charlie"—explains that "You and your wife Vicki are supposedly oppressing the mailman." Charlie adds that "These so-called black leaders have been created by the media . . . what they're really doing is preaching racial hatred." All three agree that segregation is bad, but just because integration would make the world better was no reason for Negroes to transfer their "primary loyalty" to race. Charlie explains that Martin Luther King made a list of demands and told the world that if they were not met immediately the result would be militancy and the burning of ghettos, and that's why rioters torched Watts. Thanks to militants, the police have been perceived as symbols of oppression, when "there is no real police brutality." Ron and Vicki remain befuddled: Do Negroes want integration, as per the civil rights movement, or separation, as per black power? Why are "shaggy degenerate liberals" teaching revolution in "black studies" classes? Charlie explains that "no matter what whites do, Negro leaders claim it's a conspiracy against Negroes." King now wants a separate black state, and groups like the Committee on Racial Equality, the Southern Christian Leadership Conference, and the National Association for the Advancement of Colored People "are all agents of a communist plan." Soon, the government will take on dictatorial powers, like Hitler, to stop the rioting. But it's not too late! You can make a difference by taking a stand against the racial hatred embodied by the black power movement.[42]

It's interesting that the filmstrip actually comes out against segregation (not totally out of keeping with the JBS, but a move that Smoot would never make), but what is even more provocative is the filmstrip's earnest and balanced tone. Charlie, Vicki, and Ron are all upset about militancy, but it hasn't turned them into hateful mean-spirited racists. They are perplexed by rioting because the only true oppression against blacks is segregation; everything else is a fantasy created by black radicals and furthered by the liberal media. Before black power activism, apparently, racism was not a crisis (even though segregation was wrong), and Ron and Vicki supposedly had lots of colored friends. It's a powerful, earnest fantasy of a world lacking systematic oppression of African Americans. And, indeed, there may have been no reason for the fictional Ron and Vicki to have noticed such oppression in the 1950s. Ron even thinks that he earns the same salary as blacks do, which, though not impossible, is hardly likely. *Civil Rights or Black Power?* diverges from the Smoot approach in that it does not advocate Constitutionalism as the cure for all ills and it lacks Smoot's fancy prosody. There are no "venal" politicians violating the Constitution in this story. At the same time, in its insistence that blacks' problems were created not by whites but by other blacks, and ultimately by communists, and in its implicit insistence that this argument is rational, sensible, and not in any way racist or extremist, this filmstrip strongly echoes the Smoot approach.

It is worth noting that national polls of whites in the 1960s revealed consistently that, as historian Dan Carter recounts, "half of all Americans believed that the Communist Party in the United States played a significant role in both the demonstrations and the riots. Another quarter of those polled believed that communists had played 'some' role in racial disturbances."[43] This makes labeling the belief that communists were behind civil rights as "extremist" a bit precarious. Could one actually brand half of America in the mid-1960s as "extremist"? Of course not. It is a tricky label, to be sure. Notably, Carter observes that whites were "often contradictory in their assessment of the causes of racial unrest, careening back and forth from a recognition of the role of prejudice and poverty to a denunciation of lax law enforcement and the inherent lawlessness of minorities."[44] It is this uncertainty and confusion that is lacking in the hardcore extremists. More "mainstream" Americans, both liberal and conservative, were alternately certain and uncertain of the links between civil rights and communism. Superpatriots like Smoot never vacillated. Further, the superpatriots took the link between black activism and communism as an unfalsifiable fact. Like a creationist who cannot believe that fossils are millions of years old, regardless of any proof to the contrary, there was simply no evidence that could convince ultraconservatives like Smoot that their beliefs about the communist roots of civil rights were flawed.

Indeed, any challenge to such beliefs would be answered not with counterarguments but with more "facts." Cold war extremists were information packrats. No detail was too minor to find a place in a filing cabinet. As Richard Hofstadter noted in "The Paranoid Style in American Politics," "The entire right-wing movement of our time is a parade of experts, study groups, monographs, footnotes, and bibliographies."[45] The liberal media's version of the civil rights movement could thus be systematically rebutted with counterfacts from less sympathetic sources. Was the Selma to Montgomery march a response to political disenfranchisement? Did Alabama police beat and murder marchers? No. And, in any case, the "facts" proved that the marches were a threat to "public safety" and therefore "dangerous." Smoot describes the march in one of his broadcasts:

> Many of the marchers were human scum. Beatniks, prostitutes, degenerates, drunks, bums, and communists, some of whom were paid to join the march. US representative William L. Dickson, Alabama Republican, has made a careful investigation of the Selma to Montgomery march. Here is a sample of his findings [picks up *Report* to read from it]: "Drunkenness and sex orgies were the order of the day in Selma, on the road to Montgomery, and in Montgomery. Negro and white freedom marchers invaded a Negro church in Montgomery and engaged in an all-night session of debauchery within the church itself." This is a bunch of Godless riffraff that have left every campsite between Selma and Montgomery littered with whisky bottles, beer cans, filth. The Communist Party is the undergirding structure for all of the racial troubles in Alabama in 1965. And what about the King? King Martin Luther. Martin Luther King himself has amassed a staggering total of more than sixty communist front affiliations since 1965.[46]

There was no room for refutation, and this was certainly not the kind of balanced political exchange that the FCC's Fairness Doctrine required from broadcast license holders. Indeed, reading this kind of rhetoric now, one has to wonder how Smoot got away with it as long as he did. A subscription newsletter was one thing, but these one-sided diatribes were airing on television and radio. How on earth did he pull it off?

*     *     *

The key to Smoot's success lay in his program's *local* rather than *national* distribution. The FCC was specifically encouraging of local programming in the 1960s, and there is no doubt that cold war right-wing broadcasting was the ultimate in local (and regional) programming. Hunt and Smoot's TV and radio shows came from *Texas*, after all. Indeed, they are certainly the most widely viewed TV shows to ever come out of Texas.[47] Nashville, Tennessee, can lay claim to *Hee Haw*, to the *Grand Ol' Opry* TV and radio programs, and to much programming that appears on the Great American Country cable channel, but there has otherwise been little Southern-produced programming that has found a national viewership.[48] Smoot's program was a source of local and regional pride to those who supported it. At the same time, the show functioned as a symbol of marginalization and resistance to a supposed left-wing media monopoly. After all, Smoot certainly didn't choose to be distributed on a state-by-state basis, on local stations, rather than being fed out via a national network feed. Looking back on his glory days in a speech at a banquet celebrating the John Birch Society's twenty-fifth anniversary in 1983, Smoot explained: "My broadcasts were commercially sponsored, and I had outlets from coast to coast and in a majority of states; but my audience was small in comparison with what each network newsman has every day. The networks would not sell time for my broadcasts. Hence, I had fewer station outlets, and none of the promotion and regular prime-time scheduling that the TV networks give their commentators. Limited as it was, mine was the only Americanist (or, as I called it, constitutionalist) television program in existence."[49]

There is both pride and bitterness here. If right-wing television was a symbol of localism and states' rights for its producers and viewers, it was also a symbol of the oppression of the states by the national networks. From this perspective, NBC, CBS, and ABC operated with all the imperiousness of the federal government and, more specifically, the Supreme

Court, by making decisions that should have been made purely at the local level. Smoot did not always explicitly discuss civil rights and states' rights, but by virtue of being non-network, self-distributed, grassroots, Texas television, the *Report* in and of itself consistently symbolized states' rights and opposition to federalism. To fully understand Smoot, then, requires discussion of a number of issues: the FCC's invention of "ascertainment" and its definition of "the public interest" and "public service," the importance of localism to US broadcast history, and the history and wider context of racially sensitive material on the air.

By the 1960s, to the dismay of many intellectuals, the New York City–produced live anthology dramas were dead, and production moved to Hollywood, a sausage factory efficiently pumping out formulaic "telefilm" series.[50] Yet TV was never simply the innocuous vast wasteland that FCC commissioners and high-culture snobs of the 1960s presumed it to be. As TV scholar Aniko Bodroghkozy argues, programs such as *The Smothers Brothers Comedy Hour* (CBS, 1967–70), *The Mod Squad* (ABC, 1968–73), and the revived *Dragnet* (NBC, 1967–70) all engaged with political and social issues.[51] The networks hoped to strike a balance, providing relevant programming to draw viewers (especially young, socially conscious ones) while avoiding offense and controversy that might alienate older, more conservative viewers. It could be a precarious balancing act. *The Smothers Brothers* was appealing to the suits in charge because it drew desirable demographics; when the savvy program became too controversial, though, it was axed. TV with edge could be profitable, but as a general policy in the 1960s the networks hoped to secure the widest audiences, offending as few viewers as possible by offering what is sometimes referred to as "LOP," least objectionable programming. How is it possible, then, that Dan Smoot appeared on TV delivering his anti–civil rights—his anti-almost-everything—diatribes? The short answer is that the networks had nothing to do with the *Report*. The longer answer is a bit more complicated, requiring consideration of the differences between national and local programming, as well as the bigger picture of the history of controversy surrounding televisual representations of African Americans.

In the postwar years, black viewers had high hopes that they would get a fair shake from America's new mass medium, television. They were immediately disappointed when *Amos 'n' Andy*, one of radio's all-time most popular programs (indeed, American radio's very first hit serial),[52] was transferred to television in 1951 with its racist stereotypes intact. The only concession to sensitivity was casting the series with actual blacks instead of using whites in blackface; the radio series had only used white actors. Within two years *Amos 'n' Andy* had lost its sponsorship and ceased production. Faced with the possibility of further black protests, the Big Three decided that the only way not to irk activists with "negative representations" was to remove blacks almost entirely from entertainment programs. Positive images of blacks were almost beyond their imagination, and, further, the national networks claimed that they did not want to risk alienating Southern affiliates. Throughout the fifties, of course, and into the sixties African Americans did appear on TV, but most often on the news in the context of civil rights coverage. Only by the late sixties were the networks finally ready to attempt to produce "positive" entertainment programs featuring African Americans, starting with *I-Spy* (NBC, 1965–68) and *Julia* (NBC, 1968–71).

But *Amos 'n' Andy* had not actually disappeared in the interim between its cancellation and the later appearance of the new "positive" TV shows. *Amos 'n' Andy* continued airing in syndication well into the 1960s. According to the received histories, it was rerun in the Deep South, but Doug Battema reveals that the program was syndicated nationally, receiving its highest ratings (in 1955–56, at least) in Atlanta, Detroit, Baltimore, Boston, and Cleveland.[53] Most discussions of the rise and fall of *Amos 'n' Andy* end with a note that the show continued in syndication, as if this were the epilogue to the story.[54] But syndication is not the postscript to the *Amos 'n' Andy* story. It's the heart of the story. Or at least it should be.

In the wake of Derek Kompare's research on syndication and reruns, it is now clear that nationally aired first-run programs are really only the tip of the iceberg of American TV history. In terms of sheer numbers of episodes, many more programs are run in local syndication than in first run; recycling programs is the norm, not an afterthought. Where *Amos 'n' Andy* was concerned, innumerably more people watched the locally syndicated *Amos 'n' Andy* between 1953 and 1966 than had watched the program when it was first aired nationally in 1951–53. Kompare explains that, "though popular, particularly in the south, *Amos 'n' Andy*'s profile began to wane during the early 1960s amidst the civil rights movement. Chicago station WCIU's plans to return the series to that city's airwaves in 1964 were cancelled after viewers protested, and sales to Kenya in 1963 were similarly cut off. CBS quietly removed the series from the air in 1966 in the light of increasing complaints about the program's representations of African Americans."[55] Altogether, *Amos 'n' Andy* had a fifteen-year run that coincided with the years of the civil rights movement. As far as the national networks were concerned, though, the show had been canceled in 1953, and the "problem" of representing African Americans had been solved until it reemerged in the late 1960s. *Amos 'n' Andy*—not unlike *Life Line* and the *Dan Smoot Report*—flew beneath the radar of the Big Three precisely because it was programmed locally. Such potentially controversial local programming was of no concern to the networks.

The *Amos 'n' Andy* story provides helpful background for understanding Smoot on several counts. The *Report* was not an isolated controversial program in a sea of seemingly innocuous fare like *Green Acres* (CBS, 1965–71) and *The Beverly Hillbillies* (CBS, 1962–71).[56] The national networks had made every effort not to offend minorities in the fifties and sixties, not out of any progressive instinct but simply because it was good business. Local stations, conversely, while certainly not hoping for controversy (they too wanted to sell advertising time, which seemed to work best when programming did not stir up trouble) made every effort to satisfy their white local constituency, and *Amos 'n' Andy*, like the *Report*, fit the bill perfectly. In some areas, whites were a majority of the audience, while in other areas whites were the minority, but, regardless, particularly throughout the South and Midwest, they were understood as "the public." For WLBT in Mississippi, serving the public meant flashing a phony "Sorry, cable trouble" sign on the screen when Thurgood Marshall was pictured on screen and substituting an episode of *The Loretta Young Show* for an episode of *The Rifleman* in which Sammy Davis Jr. was to make a guest appearance.[57]

Television news must have appeared schizophrenic in many American towns, as the national network news attempted an evenhanded, sometimes sympathetic presentation of the civil rights movement, while local news programs and public-affairs programs like the *Report* and *Citizens' Council Forum* (produced by white supremacists) took a quite different approach. These programs were quite rightly attacked by activists for their racism. At the same time, their local and regional status could have worked to their advantage at license renewal time, in theory, because the FCC had long claimed to value localism. As right-wing broadcasting grew in the 1960s, and the FCC invoked the Fairness Doctrine in response to citizen complaints, local TV and radio stations must have been both angry and confused. The doctrine, as we will see in chapter 4, was designed to ensure the expression of a diversity of opinions on the airwaves: broadcasters had a sacred responsibility to the public to balance their political coverage. From the perspective of local stations airing anti–civil rights public-affairs programs, what they were doing was completely fair. The national news, segregationists felt, portrayed a liberal perspective on civil rights, and the local news and programs like the *Report* balanced this out with the opposite perspective.

But what exactly did the FCC mean by "local," and how could stations prove to the commission that they served their local constituencies? The mandate of the Communications Act of 1934 was that broadcasters serve "the public interest, convenience, and necessity," but it was left to individual license holders (that is, stations) to determine what "the public interest" was. The FCC's 1960 policy statement noted fourteen types of programs that would serve the public interest, and "entertainment programs" (which dominated the programming of most TV stations) were not given top billing. However, the independent radio broadcasters who aired nothing but right-wing programming day in and day out theoretically satisfied no less than six of the areas cited in the policy statement. The radio ultras offered little in the way of traditional entertainment programs (outside of religious music), instead offering religious programs, educational programs, public-affairs programs, editorials, and news programs. The FCC's 1946 Blue Book had voiced concern that broadcasters were ignoring local programming in favor of more profitable network entertainment programs, but radio stations owned by McIntire, John H. Norris, and other fundamentalists aired only right-wing programs like the *Dan Smoot Report*, *Manion Forum*, *Life Line*, *Christian Crusade*, and *Twentieth Century Reformation Hour* and ignored mainstream scripted entertainment altogether. They sacrificed the greater profit that came from entertainment programs in the name of serving the needs of their white, conservative constituents. When some locals who did not appreciate the right-wing message complained, the FCC came to their defense, ultimately agreeing that one-sided, right-wing programming did not serve the public. The FCC declined to address the uncomfortable fact that stations airing such programs did serve *a* public and thereby, arguably, represented a flawed attempt to fulfill the mandate of localism. The rationale for the Fairness Doctrine was, in part, that the broadcast medium was a scarce resource; thus, since only a few broadcasters could service a single area, all of the audience had to be served, the FCC reasoned.

Ostensibly, there was little room within this paradigm for specialized, narrowcast programming. In practice, though, as Victoria E. Johnson has revealed, the FCC's policy on niche programming varied by region, according to market size. In discussing the FCC's 1960 policy statement,

Johnson observes that " 'Rural' and, specifically, Midwestern stations, historically, were urged to guarantee a breadth of program types within one
station's schedule, while the FCC held 'northeastern' urban broadcasters
to a significantly different standard—allowed, as those stations were, to
'narrowcast' based on the broad field of competition in which they were
operating and the diversity of voices that composed their audiences."[58] In
other words, individual small-town stations were expected to do a little of
everything to serve the public interest, but big-city stations could niche
broadcast because so many different stations were available in these markets. This is directly relevant to the story of right-wing broadcasting in the
1960s, because the ultras were mostly concentrated in smaller markets. On
television, Smoot and Hunt were virtually the only right-wing presence;
they would have been mixed in with a variety of mainstream programming
(the network feed, the local news, etc.), more or less satisfying the FCC's
expectation of a wide range of programming. But on radio, right-wingers
were concentrated in particular on stations owned by fundamentalists
who played nothing but sermons, church music, and shows like the *Report*. Narrowcast programming was exactly what the FCC was wary of in
rural markets, so such programs raised a red flag even before the issues of
fairness and political balance came into the picture.

A number of these radio stations (and some TV stations as well) aired
the *Report* specifically as a service to the public, noting as much in filling
out their FCC license renewal forms. But how did they know who the
public was? We have no hard data about who was watching and listening
to right-wing public-affairs programs, but there was, technically, a system
in place for stations to define the public they were striving to serve. The
FCC's 1960 policy statement reiterated (as per the Communications Act
of 1934) that broadcasters had to serve the public interest but added a
new component by stating that broadcasters themselves were required
to determine community needs. Citing the First Amendment, the policy
statement emphasized that the FCC would not explicitly define the public interest; instead, the commission simply listed numerous categories
of programs that might serve local needs. The newly required process of
discerning community needs—officially known as "ascertainment"—was
left to local broadcasters, most of whom saw it as something of a joke; they
usually sent out short surveys in the mail to people they identified as representative community leaders. The completed surveys from this era that
I've seen do not reveal a local audience strongly asserting its demands.
Respondents seemed to take little time to complete the surveys, and spe-

cific demands for programs might boil down to little more than a request for programs in a language other than English (e.g., Polish Americans requesting Polish-language programming). It's not that local listeners and viewers didn't care about TV and radio programming, but rather that individual local broadcasters (whether right-wing or mainstream middle-of-the-roaders) rarely worked very hard to systematically ascertain audience needs.

Broadcasters are not sociologists skilled in polling techniques, and it's not surprising that their ascertainment methods tended to be less than scientific. Thomas Streeter is quite right to argue that ascertainment was, on the FCC's part, an attempt to give sociological method a "practical" application: "social scientific survey methods, the reasoning went, would . . . ensure that broadcasters serve the public without the FCC having to act as a censor. Sociological technique would let the FCC off the hook and square the circle of rights and regulation."[59] Streeter notes the naïveté of the FCC's attempt to make policy as rational and objective as possible, but the problem with ascertainment was not simply the commission's misplaced faith in the power of social science: in an effort to avoid the taint of censorship, the 1960 policy statement declared that stations should "canvas" the general public and undertake "consultations" with community leaders but offered no other practical guidance about how ascertainment should work.[60] Stations did not really want to ascertain community needs and were unlikely to pay high fees to polling agencies or other experts to do the dirty work of ascertainment for them. As far as license holders were concerned, if ratings were high, needs were being met, and advertising time could be sold. (This was, of course, the attitude that the commission itself would take twenty years later under the leadership of Reagan's FCC chair, Mark Fowler.) Thanks to the vague 1960 policy statement, station owners could take as lackadaisical an approach to ascertainment as they desired, although if their license renewal were ever in doubt a poor ascertainment record might come back to haunt them.

Kim A. Smith explains that "for the next two decades [after the 1960 statement], the FCC struggled to define and implement the ascertainment process with little success."[61] In 1971, the commission finally released a *Primer on Ascertainment of Community Problems*, but by that time most of the ultras had been thrown off the air. Several studies in the late 1960s and early 1970s showed that ascertainment was rife with methodological holes, and Smith concludes that "the ascertainment process appeared to have little impact on public interest programming by stations."[62] Finally, "in 1981, the FCC dropped the formal ascertainment requirement for radio licensees and in 1984 followed suit for television licensees."[63]

Obviously, in the Deep South and across the Sunbelt the stations willing to air Smoot's TV and radio show would be likely to survey exactly those citizens, politicians, preachers, and other community leaders most likely to confirm that Smoot did indeed serve the public. Ascertainment thus offered a clear opportunity for stations to produce a very one-sided idea of what the "local community" was. The "public interest," then, was not an empirical reality but rather a product of an ascertainment process whereby station owners reified their own version of the public through idiosyncratic survey techniques.

"The public" was a construct different from—though running parallel to—"the audience." The audience is an entity created by viewing logs, People Meters, and other corporate information-gathering strategies.[64] The audience never includes a measurement of everybody or fully captures the viewing patterns of those it does measure, but it is a necessary fiction for the TV and radio industries; the industrial players all have to agree on the validity of the concept in order for advertisements to be sold. As Eileen Meehan explains, "the ratings and commodity audience are themselves manufactured in the strictest sense of the word . . . In social scientific terms, the metered group is not a scientific sample of the viewing public since it is not randomly selected from and not representative of that public."[65] If *audiences* are created, measured, and counted to sell ads, the *public* has a different valence and, in theory, has an inherent integrity that the commodity audience lacks. Or at least this was the exalted ideal that the Kennedy administration promoted, with FCC chairman Newton Minow at the helm.[66] For these few years, then, before Reagan's deregulatory FCC—when the audience and the public collapsed into one another under the banner of the free market—serving audiences and serving the public were two conceptually different kettles of fish.

As far as right-wing broadcasting went in the sixties, the stakes in ascertaining what the public actually was were high, for if one opposed the right-wingers the public was a collection of rational, liberal (in the classic sense) citizens who opposed prejudice and supported democracy. Right-wing speech from this perspective could not respond to a community need but, rather, could only *create* undesirable communities. In other words, Smoot could only be understood as a propagandist fostering bigotry, not as a rational man responding to legitimate and complicated preexisting interests and concerns held by a certain segment of the population. If one was on Smoot's side, conversely, one could only conclude that there were numerous warring publics, some duped by communism and taken in by liberal media propaganda and others more rational and well informed, opposing democracy in favor of republicanism and championing individual freedoms (for whites in particular) above all else.

Once a station had, for better or for worse, ascertained what its public needed, programs had to be selected to satisfy those needs. Some TV stations were independent—independent radio was more affordable and hence more common—but most were affiliated with ABC, CBS, or NBC, and it was network programming that would fill much of their primetime and daytime schedules. Yet there was local time to fill too. Since few stations could afford to produce their own programs besides the news and cheap children's shows (typically a clown or cowboy adult host, with some puppets, screening scratchy old cartoons), satisfying local needs most frequently boiled down to airing syndicated rerun packages offered by the networks or, occasionally, by independent producers. Kompare argues that such local choices "facilitated an alternative model of broadcasting that placed national culture under local control. Syndicated programs thus 'belonged' to their local stations, advertisers, and communities in a somewhat dialectical manner in which network programs did not."[67]

Media historians have often valorized the local over the national. In the 1920s, activists and amateur broadcasters fought the Federal Radio Commission for use of the airwaves, Robert McChesney explains, but the feds won, and the big networks arrogantly took it upon themselves to monopolize programming and determine community needs.[68] Today, many would argue, control of national broadcasting comes from behemoths like Clear Channel or Rupert Murdock's News Corporation, while local programming such as public access and pirate radio represents an authentic grassroots.[69] The celebration of the local over the national is not a formulation without merit, and researchers like Deirdre Boyle certainly have proven how powerful local TV can be.[70] However, in practice, for better or for worse, local broadcasting seems to almost always be inflected with the national in some way. Most "local" programming selected by network affiliates during the times of day when they are not required to take the national feed has ended up being syndicated reruns of network programs. That grassroots right-wing TV also succeeded in finding local distribution forces us to tweak the conceptions of local versus national that prevail in media studies. Genuinely local and grassroots programming may well pose a challenge to the corporate media monopoly, but the content of such

programming can come from every political direction. There is no reason
to presume that "local" is synonymous with "progressive."

Local and syndicated programming—regardless of its political or, for
that matter, apolitical orientation—has long suffered from a low-rent image. Kompare explains that

> syndicated programs are sold directly to stations on an ad hoc basis, rather than
> transmitted simultaneously across a national network. While network series
> are ostensibly vetted at the highest levels of television, syndicated programs are
> "peddled" on a station-to-station basis. This difference has fostered a sense of
> syndication as second-class national programming: either not "up" to network
> standards, or, in the case of off-network syndication, regarded as an aftermarket
> of hand-me-downs. [Thus,] while prime-time network programming is regarded
> as "mainstream" . . . syndicated programming is seen as somehow exterior to
> this mainstream. Its audiences are typically historically regarded as too femi-
> nine, too young, too old, too poor, too ethnic, too provincial, or too crude for
> a mainstream, network sensibility. [Such] programming . . . is relegated, to the
> "fringes" of television: too early or too late for prime-time, or, on independent
> stations, located "off the grid" of the networks.[71]

Right-wing shows like the *Report* were not distributed in large syndicated
packages and were generally available not for lease but for sale (Smoot
charged $5.00 per film to each station in 1967). But, peddled on a station-
to-station basis, scheduled at undesirable times, and targeting an audience that was "provincial" from the national networks' perspective, they
were certainly outside of the "mainstream" (although they might not have
been perceived that way by those white Southern viewers who thought it
was the *CBS Evening News* that was out of touch with average patriotic
Americans) and had much in common with syndicated programming.
When the right-wing broadcasting movement was profiled by national
publications like the *Nation*, *TV Guide*, and *Time*, outraged readers responded with hostility in large part because the programs' politics rubbed
them the wrong way. Although it is difficult to prove this definitively, I
would wager that the negative response also came because the shows were
low budget, not up to network standards, and downright weird by virtue
of being independently produced. What were *individuals* doing making
TV and buying their own time on small local stations to spread their own
*personal* political ideas? In an era dominated by three major networks,
before cable, PBS or public access, not to mention YouTube, this seemed
strange, disreputable, dishonest by its very nature.

Right-wing shows differed from syndicated programs in several ways. Syndicated TV series were usually stripped (shown five days a week, in regular time slots) and shown over and over again; local stations basically leased popular programs like *Hopalong Casidy* with the intent to recycle them until their audiences tired of them.[72] But programs like Smoot's were often timely, responding to specific news events; they aired only once a week and would not repeat well. More importantly, most superpatriot TV and radio producers were strapped for cash and could not commit to long-term financial arrangements and deliver large packages of product to stations. *Hopalong Cassidy* was already in the can, and a local station could contract for a huge number of episodes, whereas right-wing public-affairs shows arrived in the mail piecemeal, once a week. The right-wingers thus functioned in a financially unique manner; if syndication in general was the poor stepchild of first-run TV, the ultras' programs were simply bastard embarrassments, enduring hand-to-mouth financial arrangements.

Right-wing programs were distributed on TV and radio according to a number of basic economic configurations, which sometimes overlapped. Often, it was the right-wing *producers* of the programs who purchased airtime from stations rather than the typical situation of *stations* buying syndicated "regular" entertainment programs from producers and then making their profits by selling ads. The right-wing producers would themselves sell advertising time in order to make back what they had paid for slots to air their programs. For fundamentalist program producers, there was a second option: they would pay for airtime but forgo spot ads and simply do on-air fundraising. As for Smoot, the stations would pay him a fee to run his show. The problem was that they might have trouble finding a sponsor to make back their investment, so Smoot generally had to dig up the sponsors himself rather than counting on the station to do so. Smoot, in other words, would be paid by the station and would provide a sponsor, who would in turn pay the station to advertise on the *Report*. A fourth option was for a station to pay the producer for his program, then to run it without ads (or sometimes with) specifically to satisfy the FCC's public-service requirement.[73] Finally, public-service programs might be run without any fee being paid to producers, but this was less feasible for financially strained or mismanaged smalltime right-wing outfits than for larger member organizations like the AFL-CIO or the National Association of Manufacturers.[74]

Smoot continually sought out conservative businessmen to be local sponsors for his programs. He griped that he received fan mail from successful businessmen but that few were willing to put their money where their mouth was and buy advertising time. "God deliver me from timid patriots!" he exclaimed.[75] Seeking to avoid controversy but wanting to support Smoot, some would buy time without actually running their ads. Ultimately, Smoot's principle sponsor was based in California—D. B. Lewis, the successful manufacturer of Dr. Ross dog food. Lewis's singularly uncatchy slogan was "Dr. Ross Dog Food for Dogs of Discrimination," and his company's stationery pictured an upright dog in checkered suit and tie, with a carnation in his lapel. In *The Fearless American*, a tribute album to Lewis produced in 1963 or 1964, Smoot recounts how one old lady wrote a fan letter to him saying that she had switched her cats over to Dr. Ross. They were finicky, but she "told those communist cats to eat Dr. Ross or starve!"[76] Lewis initially imagined that he might not make any profit from sponsoring Smoot and conceived the *Report* as a public-service venture, but, according to Smoot, he "soon made a surprising discovery: this once-a-week, fifteen-minute program, sold more dog food than Hopalong Cassidy used to."[77]

When he met Lewis, Smoot was not yet on television. He had been able to procure only three sponsors and was on four radio stations. As Smoot later recounted: "I cannot describe the struggle this man made to pioneer patriotic advertising on television. D. B., who at that time was the biggest TV advertiser on the West Coast, had to fight to buy time for my broadcasts on stations where he had been buying advertising since the beginning of television."[78] Smoot was introduced to Lewis by Rev. L. Wendell Fifield. Fifield invited Smoot to air his views about union bosses on his Claremont, California, radio show; Smoot warned him that if he did, Fifield would probably lose his sponsor, but Fifield assured him that the sponsor would not run. It turned out that Lewis was the fearless sponsor, and he and Smoot hit it off immediately. Lewis would enable Smoot's broadcasting venture to expand rapidly. "As soon as D. B. got us into television, we could offer our TV programs for one-station sponsors anywhere. By the mid-1960s, our broadcasts were on about one hundred and fifty stations in some thirty states, under about fifty different sponsorships. According to professional surveys which D. B. ordered, I had an audience averaging about sixteen million people a week."[79] Though some sponsors offered to support the program nationally, the three national television networks and four radio networks declined to air the *Report*; it would air widely, but never via national network feed.

Clearly, given such difficulties, right-wing broadcasting was not an inherently profitable venture. Hunt didn't need to earn money from his broadcasts, and Carl McIntire and Billy James Hargis kept afloat by claiming tax-exempt status (shamelessly asserting that their outfits were strictly religious) and soliciting funds on air. In never seeking tax-exempt status and keeping on-air fundraising to an absolutely Spartan minimum, the dignified Smoot took the moral high ground. Smoot was lucky to earn a living and only survived because he had a benefactor who bought most of his ad time. Other producers were able to continue for years (primarily on radio, a medium substantially cheaper than TV) because they were tax-exempt organizations or were otherwise subsidized. The anti–civil rights *Citizens' Council Forum*, for example, was a fifteen-minute talk-format series distributed throughout the US on both radio and TV, reportedly on over three hundred (probably more radio than TV) stations.[80] Beginning in 1955, the show "had direct ties to Mississippi state government and was allocated tens of thousands of taxpayer dollars during its first years of existence."[81] Ample access to state tax dollars constituted quite a subsidy.

Following the Reagan FCC's deregulation in the 1980s, a twist on the financial arrangements pioneered by—or, to put it more aptly, cobbled together by—the right-wing program producers would appear in the form of infomercials. The company hawking a product via infomercial would buy airtime, but then (like Hargis) would not need to sell ad time, since the show itself was an ad, and money would come in via purchases of the product. Also, in the 1980s the cash-plus-barter system was developed and used in particular for syndicated packages of children's programs such as *He-Man and the Masters of the Universe*. *He-Man*'s creator, Mattel, would sell a sixty-five-episode syndicated block to cash-poor independent stations at a very reduced rate. Then the station would allow Mattel to sell some (but not all) of the advertising time during the show. If Hargis, with his blatant self-promotion, was a progenitor of the infomercial, Smoot, forced to procure his own advertisers, was an early configuration of the cash-plus-barter syndication system. Not so ironically, then, it was cold war right-wing broadcasters, who so often touted a free-market philosophy, who were the first to engage in financial arrangements that would only become "legit" (and highly profitable) in the deregulated broadcast marketplace created by Reagan.

*   *   *

Aside from such interesting financial interconnections, Smoot did not leave much of a legacy on the economic front. He created no think tanks,

institutes, or endowments. Smoot thrived because he found a benefactor
in D. B. Lewis, and also because he was successful at selling subscriptions
to his newsletter. When Lewis died in 1965, he left Smoot and the John
Birch Society each a million dollars; Lewis also bequeathed one million dollars to Pepperdine College of Los Angeles, contingent upon the
school's awarding Smoot an honorary PhD. Pepperdine declined to grant
the degree and thereby forfeited the bequeathal. Lewis dedicated another
million dollars to funding a new organization to be called The Defenders
of American Liberty, which was to be a right-wing version of the ACLU
defending the Constitution as it stood in 1950. (One suspects that Lewis
really meant for his organization to ignore not so much the post-1950 Constitution as all Supreme Court decisions made after 1950.) Lewis willed his
wife a paltry $1,000 per month allowance, but she contested the will and
finally won most of the estate. According to Smoot, "D. B. (individualist
to the end) had written his own will, having his signature witnessed by
a man on the night clean-up crew" at the dog food factory.[82] The anti-
ACLU organization did not materialize, and the JBS apparently lost out
completely. A few relatives received part of the estate, including three
"children of Lewis but not by Mrs. Lewis," each with a different surname.[83]
(Hunt was clearly not the only millionaire skirt-chaser supporting right-
wing broadcasting.) In 1986 Smoot finally received $75,000 from the es-
tate, $25,000 of which went to his lawyer.

Smoot simply could not stay afloat without D. B. He met with a lawyer
for financial advice in 1968, as his finances "had been declining danger-
ously for some time," but the real estate investments the lawyer suggested
were "complicated procedures" that Smoot confessed he did not understand.[84] An astonishing admission from a man of confidence who imagined
himself impervious to error! Not particularly clever with money, Smoot
felt doomed from the start because the federal income tax sucked away
half of his income. Without Lewis's help, he could keep up his newsletter until health problems slowed him down, but he didn't have a chance
of staying on the air. Financial troubles forced him off TV completely by
1967, and his radio coverage fell by more than half, although his newsletter
continued until 1971.

In 1960 Smoot admitted that his "prolonged, intense mental exertion"
had upset his body chemistry and caused occasional ulcers, even though
there was "no anxiety or worry involved" in his work.[85] By 1971 Smoot admitted more candidly in a private letter that "during the past fifteen years,
I have had countless stomach ulcers. They have caused so much scar tissue

to build up in my stomach that vital passages are now in danger of being blocked. My doctor says I must eventually have most of my stomach taken out."[86] Reluctantly, he realized that he had to release himself from his "choking weekly deadline," and he issued his last printed *Report*, supporting himself thereafter on speeches to organizations such as the JBS, the Association of American Dentists, and The Daughters of the American Revolution. He also wrote articles for the JBS's monthly *American Opinion* and weekly *Review of the News*.

Smoot lived to see Reagan elected, but the eighties were no better than the sixties as far as he was concerned. In 1984—when the New Right was crowing that the conservative takeover had finally been achieved—Smoot remained angry and disaffected: "At the present low point in the degradation of our Constitutional Republic, strict constitutionalism is the most hated position that a person in public life can take."[87] What good was Reaganomics if the Fourteenth Amendment was still in place and federal courts still exercised power over the states? The Bush and Clinton years could not have been any better for Smoot's ulcers, and he finally passed away in 2003, literally done in by his own bilious nature.

Clearly, Smoot was an individualist, not a strategist or a movement builder. Shortly after he went off the air, one-sided conservative broadcasting largely disappeared until new right-wing figures such as Limbaugh and, later, O'Reilly appeared in the wake of Reagan's suspension of the Fairness Doctrine. Like Smoot, the pundits of Fox News oppose federal government regulations and spending on social-welfare programs. Yet the contemporary crowd is varied and nuanced, their hard extremist edges often—though not always—blunted. And, more importantly, they are entertainers. Smoot wanted to inform; people would tune in because they wanted the truth, not because the delivery of the truth was flashy or fun. Rush Limbaugh's listeners ("dittoheads") love him not only for his conservative ideas but also for his style. Limbaugh—or, as he calls himself, "El Rushbo"—is, first and foremost, an entertainer and, for those who enjoy his style of humor, a comedian. Bill O'Reilly, too, offers a good show, hollering at guests and cutting off their mics if they dare to disagree. Smoot was above such shenanigans.

Between Smoot and Limbaugh, conservative broadcasting was scarce, but not gone completely. Milton Friedman's ten-part 1980 PBS series *Free to Choose*, a tribute to the glories of the free market, echoed some Smoot ideas, but in a cheery, can-do manner. The first half hour was shot on expensive locations, with the second half hour devoted to a Q&A session in which Friedman interacted with both liberals and conservatives. Though the Reagan Revolution had only just begun, the program today seems like a crystal ball revealing the eventual triumph of deregulation. William F. Buckley's *Firing Line* ran from 1966 to 1999, and, upon Buckley's passing in 2008, was widely trumpeted as the first conservative TV show, "an obvious precursor to shrill modern-era programming like *Hardball, Tucker, Hannity and Colmes,* and *Scarborough Country,*" according to the *New York Times.*[88] Buckley's highbrow program encouraged lively, intelligent debate from all sides, and was very different from Smoot's. Although it is extremely unlikely that Sean Hannity has ever heard of Dan Smoot, his dogmatism and inability to engage with those he disagrees with make him more stylistically akin to Smoot than Buckley. In any case, the idea that Buckley was the first conservative with a TV show seems particularly silly in light of the fact that Buckley himself was a permanent guest on H. L. Hunt's *Answers for Americans* more than ten years before *Firing Line* premiered!

The eulogizers got it right on two counts, though. First, William Kristol noted correctly that "it's hard today to appreciate that before Buckley, there was no American conservative movement. There were interesting (if mostly little-known) conservative thinkers . . . Buckley created conservatism as a political and intellectual movement."[89] Smoot was no movement builder, just an incredibly persistent man who talked loudly and did not carry a big stick. Second, Hugh Kenner observed that "Bill [Buckley] was responsible for rejecting the John Birch Society and the other kooks . . . [W]ithout him, there probably would be no respectable conservative movement in this country."[90] What is left unsaid here is that Buckley began as a JBS supporter; his insight was that kooks like Welch and Smoot had to be cut loose for the movement to move forward.

However, it is mistaken to conclude that extremists such as Smoot and the John Birch Society were simply inconsequential to the conservative movement that would follow. For one thing, the extremist broadcasters had many listeners and viewers, which translated to a lot of voting power down the road. Smoot and his compatriots got conservatives riled up to make big changes. But for whom could they vote? Smoot often advised his followers not to vote in presidential elections, feeling that candidates were basically the same—all totalitarian liberals. However, he did encourage people to vote in state and federal congressional elections and local elections, where he saw more room for true conservative candidates. It was a tactic that would work particularly well for the Christian Right throughout the 1990s, when it dramatically consolidated its power not in the White House but on schoolboards and in state legislatures.

How fitting, finally, that Buckley's penultimate posthumous publication would be a tribute to Barry Goldwater, the man who emboldened Smoot and his right-wing compatriots at last to go to the polls and vote for a real conservative presidential candidate who was not a "spare tire." Was Goldwater an "extremist," an "ultra," a "superpatriot"? The labels didn't matter in the end. He lost the election, but a conservative movement blossomed in his wake. That people like Smoot had to be left behind was par for the course. Less than a spare tire, Dan Smoot was a third wheel. Such third wheels were the awkward, embarrassing, and strange roots of the conservative movement to come.

# God's Angriest Man

## Carl McIntire, Neoevangelicalism, and the Long-Lingering Fundamentalist Fires

500 years ago Moses said, "Pack your camel, pick up your shovel, mount your ass, and I shall lead you to the Promised Land." 500 years later, F. D. Roosevelt said, "Lay down your shovel, sit on your ass, light up a Camel, this is the promised land." Today, Nixon will tax your shovel, sell your camel, kick your ass, and tell you there is no promised land.

> P.S. I am glad that I am an American
> I am glad that I am free
> But I wish I were a little doggy
> And Nixon were a tree—Anonymous, memo to "The American People"[1]

There was no shortage of Nixon haters in the 1970s, but this angry would-be poet was hardly typical. This is not the voice of a Vietnam War protestor, a woman's libber, or a civil rights activist. Anonymous is not a liberal at all but, rather, a devout fan of fundamentalist radio broadcaster Carl McIntire. An outspoken anticommunist who saw Nixon's rapprochement with China as nothing short of high treason, McIntire used his radio station, WXUR, his weekly newspaper, the *Christian Beacon*, and his nationally broadcast radio program, the *Twentieth Century Reformation Hour*, throughout the 1950s, 1960s, and early 1970s to attack his enemies: the NAACP, the Anti-Defamation League, the AFL-CIO, the National Council of Churches (NCC), the World Council of Churches (WCC), the Pope, Billy Graham, the National Association of Evangelicals (NAE), and the Federal Communications Commission (FCC). McIntire reserved a special wrath for the FCC because it had, by 1973, succeeded in using the Fairness Doctrine to force him to cease using the radio for his one-sided diatribes. Anonymous was a lot like McIntire: angry, a bit crude, and vociferously resistant to change.

FIGURE 18. Carl McIntire, pictured here at a Victory in Vietnam rally he staged in Trenton, New Jersey, was a highly charged symbol of the conflict in the 1960s and 1970s between old-time religion and the forces of modernity. Photo courtesy of Gary K. Clabaugh, 1970.

Historians and religious studies scholars have portrayed McIntire primarily as a distasteful icon of old-fashioned fundamentalism, while media studies scholars have ignored him altogether. (Indeed, while there is a body of sociologically grounded research on Americans, religion, and media—embodied by the work of scholars such as Stewart M. Hoover and Lynn Schofield Clark[2]—the more humanities-oriented side of American media studies has displayed scant interest in religion.) But McIntire was much more than just a splenetic fundamentalist. He was an activist, a preacher, and, most importantly, a highly charged *symbol* of the conflict in the 1960s and 1970s between old-time religion and the forces of modernity (figure 18).

This chapter and the next examine McIntire's two greatest battles, one with the FCC and the other with both the forces of neoevangelical change and with McIntire's own fundamentalist constituency. Without McIntire, Billy Graham and the New Evangelicalism still would have risen, the New Christian Right would have followed, and the FCC's Fairness Doctrine would have fallen, but McIntire played his own role in the early history of these dramas, while also playing a role in helping fundamentalists define themselves. For if the neoevangelicals defined themselves, in part, as "not like the fundamentalist McIntire," it did not necessarily follow that fundamentalists wanted to define themselves as "like McIntire."

As the only radio broadcaster to lose his license because of the Fairness Doctrine, McIntire was a central player, both literally and symbolically, in the history of governmental regulation of speech. McIntire's story—and the bigger story of the rise and fall of the doctrine—deepens our understanding of the legal system's historically shifting definitions of what constitutes censorship, free speech, and the "public interest." Such issues will be the focus of the next chapter, which will examine McIntire's battle for his radio station in some detail.

Here, though, our focus is on McIntire's relevance as a religious and political figure: McIntire's career complicates previous conceptions of both the history of American fundamentalism and the emergence of the New Christian Right in the late 1970s and early 1980s. McIntire is important, then, not only as a figure in the history of media regulation and as a symbol of fundamentalism in conflict with liberalism and modernity, but also as a symbol of the cold war Old Christian Right in conflict with the New Christian Right, and of fundamentalism in conflict with itself.[3]

Unlike today's conservative Christian activists, McIntire was largely incapable of achieving his political objectives. McIntire was what one might call a "successful failure." In fact, his failed attempts at politics made him a negative model for the neoevangelicals and later for the Christian Right. McIntire lost to both his secular foe, the FCC, and his Christian foes, the neoevangelicals. (Of course, since neoevangelicals had tainted themselves by compromising with modernity, they were barely "Christian" in McIntire's mind.) Both defeats had interesting long-term implications. McIntire's FCC case was used as evidence by right-wing senators like Strom Thurmond for years as they persistently fought the Fairness Doctrine in Congress. This erstwhile "extremist" position against government regulation would, under President Reagan, become normalized as merely "conservative." Making a similar shift from right-wing "extremism" to mainstream "conservatism," many fundamentalists became neoevangelicals in the post–World War II years, and, among these new Christians dedicated to being "in the world but not of the world," those who were politically inclined shifted toward the New Christian Right in the 1980s. This group was given the friendlier "conservative evangelical" label in the nineties, achieving a realignment with a more moderate conservative image. Rather than speaking Bible-thumping language in the political arena, many of today's conservative evangelical political leaders use a secular-sounding rights-based discourse that they have carefully shaped to meet their needs. One might say that the extremist rough edges have been rubbed off of both deregulatory discourse and, more generally, Christian right-wing discourse. And McIntire embodied those rough edges.

Born in Ypsilanti, Michigan, in 1906, McIntire grew up in Oklahoma, retaining a subtle Southern twang even though he lived in Collingswood, New Jersey, for over sixty years. McIntire was ordained as a minister of the Presbyterian Church in 1931, but five years later he was stripped of his ordination for his strident criticism of the church's "liberal" missionary activities. He had joined with J. Gresham Machen in making these attacks, and the two had left Princeton Seminary together in 1929 to found a "true church."[4] But McIntire thought Machen, who did not find premillenialism to be justified by the Bible, had compromised with "modernism" (secular humanism), and McIntire was also offended by Machen's belief that moderate alcohol consumption was acceptable. Shortly after Machen died in 1937, McIntire broke away to establish his own church, the Bible Presbyterian Synod.[5] McIntire founded the American Council of Christian Churches (ACCC) in 1941 and the International Council of Christian Churches (ICCC) in 1948 as alternatives to the NCC and the WCC, ecumenical Protestant organizations he condemned as "apostate" and hopelessly liberal. In 1955, McIntire was ejected from his own Bible Presbyterian Church because of his dictatorial leadership style, but his faithful followed him and insisted that they remained the true Bible Presbyterian Church.[6] McIntire remained with this reconstituted church until it finally forced him out in 1999. So at the age of ninety-two he created a new church, which met in his living room. McIntire was the überfundamentalist, largely incapable of even agreeing with other fundamentalists about anything. Never willing to give up, always looking for conspiracies when things did not go his way, and a model of fundamentalist hostility toward modernity, McIntire might well be described as God's angriest man.[7]

*   *   *

Even if much of the fundamentalist rank and file remained separatist in the cold war years, the common perception that twentieth-century right-wing Christian political engagement *began* with the Moral Majority is, in light of McIntire's activities and his large following of radio listeners, clearly inaccurate. Today's politically active evangelicals—and I'm speaking particularly of those at the top who play the media spin game, the talking

heads, leaders, and news personalities—often refer to America's historically "Christian roots" and reference the 1950s specifically as an era of
strong religious sentiment and high moral standards. The fact that the loudest politically engaged fundamentalist voices of the 1950s spoke out against
the civil rights movement is now seen as something of an embarrassment.
Thus, most figures of the cold war Old Christian Right tend to be conveniently left out of the nostalgic stories spun by the New Christian Right.

It should probably not be surprising that conservative Christian political leaders have not given their followers a nuanced understanding of the
history of American evangelicalism and fundamentalism. American political discourse—religiously inflected or not—is not known for its subtle
sense of historical context. It is more surprising, though, that the large
body of scholarly research on fundamentalism and evangelicalism has
largely accepted the teleological narrative of socially engaged evangelicals
overtaking fundamentalist separatists in the 1950s and 1960s. The narrative is not wholly incorrect, for it was indeed during the cold war years that
the neoevangelical seeds planted by Carl Henry, Harold John Ockenga,
and Billy Graham took root in America, and separatist Christian fundamentalists have been a dying breed ever since. Martin E. Marty said that in
the 1940s McIntire "was tending the lingering fundamentalist fires."[8] This
was true, but McIntire still had a following thirty years later, at the height
of the controversy around his right-wing radio station. One might say that
rumors of the death of fundamentalism had been greatly exaggerated.

After the 1925 Scopes trial, fundamentalists retreated from the wider
culture and built up their own separatist networks of schools, churches,
Bible colleges, and, of course, radio stations. They thus laid the foundation for the emergence of neoevangelicalism in the 1950s, a movement of
intellectually and culturally engaged Christians who would march under
the banner of Henry, Graham, and Ockenga. These born-again Christians
were culturally and politically conservative, but they were rhetorically
moderate compared to McIntire. Notwithstanding the nuanced narratives
of fundamentalist history and culture spun by researchers such as Joel
Carpenter and George Marsden,[9] historians of evangelicalism have tended
to paint the movement from fundamentalism to neoevangelicalism as a
teleological narrative of progress: fundamentalists were anti-intellectual and
rigid, but neoevangelicals were sophisticated and able to nimbly interact
with the wider world. Within this narrative, McIntire, who firmly rejected
neoevangelicalism, can only exist as a symbol of the past, a relic of the
fundamentalism-modernism debates of the early twentieth century.

Neoevangelicalism, the new worldly form of evangelicalism, did not come about overnight. In 1948, Ockenga, who was the first president of the NAE, coined the term, but the idea did not immediately catch on. Almost a decade later, in 1957, Ockenga delivered a sermon called "New Evangelicalism." This sermon was picked up by the Associated Press, and suddenly neoevangelicalism became controversial among fundamentalists. At this point, the labels become a bit confusing: the "fundamentalists" under discussion here were conservative, separatist, "Bible-believers"— people whom we might refer to as "born-agains" today. (Nancy Totem Ammerman observes that in the 1930s and 1940s, believers were comfortable using "fundamentalist" and "evangelical" interchangeably.) In the late 1940s, Ockenga and Henry indicted this group for not being socially engaged, hence their call for a New Evangelicalism. Ammerman explains that "For Ockenga there was a growing sense that fundamentalism had to learn to speak in terms the larger culture would understand and respect. Learning was highly valued (Ockenga boasted a PhD), and conspiracy theories were not. What separated him from McIntire was not so much the content of their beliefs about the Bible or evangelism or eschatology as the style of their relationship to the culture."[10]

The separatists and the neoevangelicals would do battle throughout the 1950s and 1960s, and Graham became the highest-profile popular-culture representative of the new approach. He collaborated with mainline Protestant churches during his crusades, which infuriated hardline separatists. Volie E. Pyles, a Baptist preacher who lived through these days, recalls that "at the grass roots level the question soon became simply, 'are you for or against Graham?'"[11] Graham was a major figure in Youth for Christ, which became a symbol of the new approach: fervent, committed, and also "normal," middle class, modern, and far from the old fire-and-brimstone stereotype. A Youth for Christ participant in the late 1950s, Mel White— later a ghostwriter for Pat Robertson and Jerry Falwell, and later still a gay activist fighting the Christian Right—recalls, "we would sing and we would pray. It was very much the in thing to do then. It didn't have any kind of sense of fanaticism or craziness to it."[12]

The move away from separatism in the 1960s was provoked by a number of factors. For many, it was a response to John F. Kennedy's election, since a Catholic president seemed very dangerous to many evangelicals.[13] The shift was also a reaction against the civil rights movement, the introduction of sex education into public school curricula, and the Supreme Court decisions against prayer and Bible reading in schools. Conservative Christian worldly engagement would receive a boost from Jimmy Carter's election to office (an evangelical, if a liberal one), and it would officially win out over separatism with the formation of the Moral Majority in 1979.[14] Opposition to abortion and gay rights would solidify conservative evangelical involvement in politics throughout the 1980s and into the twenty-first century. By the late 1970s, the "neoevangelical" label was already passé. To outsiders, at least, politically engaged evangelicals were now commonly called the "New Christian Right."

McIntire, then, was left behind, a symbol of the cold war Old Christian Right. His role in the narrative of the separatist-versus-neoevangelical controversy is usually summed up this way: he was the mold for the old-school separatist approach; he fought neoevangelicalism tooth and nail; he finally lost out to the inevitable forces of modernity; theologically, he wasn't much different from the neoevangelicals—it was their "worldliness," their modern style, that he resisted. There are a few problems with this way of telling the story. Ammerman is right when she argues that McIntire differed from Ockenga in terms of *style*. Ockenga knew how to interact with the mainstream; McIntire reveled in conspiracy theories that would forever mark him as an "extremist." But McIntire would have been appalled to have heard Ammerman characterize his beliefs about the Bible as the same as Ockenga's, for he saw the evangelicals' interaction with other religious groups as a biblical transgression. As he explained it, neoevangelicals "affirm their adherence to the fundamentals of faith but insist that they can accept and live within the inclusive church and be part of the World Council of Churches and the ecumenical apostasy. They . . . rationalize their action in disobeying the commands of God which call for separation from unbelief and which forbid the unequal yoke."[15] McIntire wasn't simply being stubborn and old fashioned when he resisted the neoevangelicals. He was certain that he had the Bible right and they had it wrong.

Another problem with the standard fundamentalist-versus-neoevangelical narrative is that, although McIntire was "old fashioned" in his interpretation of the Bible, he was, at the same time, aggressively modern in his approach to spreading his ideas. Religious studies scholar Randall Balmer has aptly called him the P. T. Barnum of fundamentalism.[16] McIntire was a relentless showman who knew exactly how to get press coverage for his theatrical protests. The truly old-fashioned and intransigent separatists of this era are largely invisible to history. If McIntire had really been as out of it as the neoevangelicals claimed, they would not have known of his existence. Instead, his petitions, rallies, and broadcasts made him a thorn in everyone's side.

Clearly, McIntire was more than just someone who was left behind as everyone else moved forward. In fact, I would argue that his voice of opposition actually aided and abetted the advancement of neoevangelicalism. Pyles argues that "After World War II a few Fundamentalist leaders such as Ockenga and Henry urged the movement to consider the social responsibility of the gospel, but they did not present a theological argument sufficient to capture Fundamentalists' attention. Their urging fell upon deaf ears until the late 1950s, when McIntire took up the issue,"[17] shortly after the Associated Press article appeared. Pyles does not develop this idea, and he further argues that new evangelicalism was pushed along by the social upheaval of the 1960s, which "demanded the attentions of the Fundamentalists/Evangelicals if they expected to survive and be relevant in American society,"[18] so he certainly does not give McIntire all the credit for the increasing discussion and debate over Henry and Ockenga's ideas. But Pyles is definitely on to something. With the merciless attacks he voiced on his radio show, in his *Christian Beacon* newspaper, and in interviews with the mainstream press, McIntire gave the neoevangelical cause enormous amounts of free publicity. As McIntire became a symbol of what neoevangelicalism was not, he himself provided people wavering over the issue an example of exactly the type of stridency that they might want to leave behind. Billy Graham often gets much of the credit for the eventual triumph of social engagement, for evangelicals finding, in theory, a way to be "in but not of the world." Graham provided a positive example of what neoevangelical engagement could be. McIntire provided a negative example of what neoevangelicalism was not, and, in doing so, inadvertently contributed to neoevangelicalism's triumph.

Ultimately, one of the major flaws of the oft-repeated story of McIntire's failure and neoevangelicalism's success is that it broadly and misleadingly describes McIntire as a "separatist." McIntire was a theological separatist, but not a political separatist. Indeed, on the cusp of Reagan's ascension to office, in a 1980 sermon entitled "Born-Again Vote," McIntire explained that it was imperative "for a born-again person to become deeply involved [in politics] and recognize his duty and his responsibility under God for the society where he lives."[19] McIntire complained that "the Bible-believing people, the Fundamental people, have had a tendency to withdraw and let things go. There are various reasons for that. One that I certainly take great issue with is that the Lord is coming soon, so why worry? That is a vicious repudiation of the Scripture."[20] It would seem that McIntire, so often referenced by historians as the prototypical fundamentalist, did not quite fit the mold insofar as he rejected the post–Scopes trial reluctance to engage publicly with the problems of the world.[21]

The notion that McIntire was a separatist represents a narrative told from the point of view of the neoevangelical victors. The neoevangelicals said that *they* were the socially engaged ones, and they won the separatism-versus-engagement debate. Thus, they—not the ultras—paved the way for the conservative Christian activism of the 1980s and 1990s. But if McIntire can be described as "not politically engaged" it is not because he didn't get involved in politics, but because his politics were seen by neoevangelicals and later historians as *ineffective*. His political gestures appeared largely symbolic, and he was better at demanding change than effecting change.

Technically speaking, McIntire failed at every political endeavor he undertook. He never elected anyone to office, won a court battle, helped pass a law, or engaged in a successful boycott, but McIntire did engage in a loud public battle over his radio station, publish his political views in the *Christian Beacon* for almost sixty years, briefly man a pirate radio station after the loss of WXUR,[22] picket meetings of the National and World Council of Churches for fifty years, organize several victory marches in Washington DC during the Vietnam War, arrange an American tour for the Republic of China's Christian ping-pong team, and—to the great embarrassment of Richard Nixon and Henry Kissinger—almost secure South Vietnam's vice president Nguyen Cao Ky as a speaker at one of his Vietnam Victory rallies. Nixon fled the US altogether shortly before the rally, while a reported one hundred thousand yippies plotted a counterdemonstration and promised to arrest Ky as a war criminal.[23] Someone in the Nixon administration finally dissuaded Ky from attending at the eleventh hour. McIntire then convinced Mrs. Ky to stand in for her husband, but her airplane en route to the US was conveniently called back to Paris with "engine trouble."[24] In sum, the whole thing was a bit ridiculous, but McIntire was in his element. The headlines were glorious (figure 19).

McIntire's activities were certainly a nuisance for Nixon, who, McIntire claims, put him under FBI surveillance.[25] McIntire felt that the president had betrayed America by trying to withdraw from Vietnam and by opening up relations with communist China. In 1972 his anger came to a head when Nixon welcomed the official ping-pong team of the People's Republic on American soil. This was a reciprocal gesture, as China had invited the American ping-pong team to visit the People's Republic in 1971. The

FIGURE 19. In his newspaper, McIntire reproduces a *Philadelphia Inquirer* cartoon poking fun at the reverend's battle with Nixon over the visit of South Vietnam's vice president, Nguyen Cao Ky. Flattering of McIntire or not, it was good publicity. *Christian Beacon*, 1970.

players were to engage in a few competitive matches and then perform a few exhibition matches in different cities. Journalists dubbed the friendly turn of events "ping-pong diplomacy." McIntire sprang into action, citing a *New York Times Magazine* feature explaining that Chairman Mao had furnished ping-pong tables to the masses in 1952 as part of his war against drug use. Mao advised players to "regard a Ping-Pong ball as the head of your capitalist enemy. Hit it with your socialist bat and you have won the point for the fatherland." McIntire organized demonstrations against these "slave players" at the sites of the exhibition matches. "Time is short!" he warned. "Let us send the message both to the White House and to Peking that there are those in this country who believe the Ping-Pong players are not here for friendship but to further the communist designs against the United States."[26]

McIntire arranged to have Free China's Christian ping-pong team come to the US to play a series of exhibition matches. Nixon rejected McIntire's request that he personally greet the Christian players, and, in protest, McIntire decided to play table tennis in front of the White House and to lead a team of Peking ducks past the gates. The ducks apparently did not pan out, and the US Park Service would not grant a permit to set up a ping-pong table. McIntire was, however, briefly allowed to play on a legless table carried by assistants. This was sufficient, since the point was to provide a great photo op for the press (they obliged) and to stimulate publicity for his cause (he did). He even made the best of the Park Service restrictions by announcing, "Ping-Pong diplomacy has lost its legs."[27]

McIntire's Victory Marches were also carefully staged media events, though it would be a bit of an exaggeration to say that the whole world was watching. In April of 1971, the National Peace Action Coalition had organized a march on Washington that drew two hundred thousand people. McIntire referred to this as "the hippies surrender march." Correctly realizing that staging his own "Patriots' March for Victory" just a few days later would maximize press coverage, McIntire led his march on May 8. McIntire explained the marchers' demands: "There must be no more withdrawals until the war is won and Vietnam secure, the POWs brought home first, Lt. Calley given justice and freedom, and the Red ping-pong participants exposed and rejected."[28] McIntire always predicted high numbers for his marches, and always disagreed with the official count (as most marchers do). He anticipated two hundred thousand for the October 1970 march, and about twenty thousand arrived.[29] Regardless of the numbers, McIntire's efforts were an ongoing irritation to Nixon. In a nutshell, McIntire's extremism was not an image that matched Nixon's idea of a mythical "silent majority."[30] How could Nixon imperiously fix America in the name of his silent majority if they suddenly got loud?

*    *    *

The picture of McIntire drawn thus far has been painted largely from the outside; I've argued for a new understanding of McIntire as a politically engaged figure who can be understood as a kind of missing link between fundamentalist separatism and neoevangelical engagement, a figure who fits neatly under neither the "fundamentalist" label nor the "evangelical" label. But what if we paint a picture of McIntire more from the inside? How did his own brethren understand him? His papers include fan mail from radio listeners, but such letters offer few insights into the exact nature of McIntire's appeal, as letter writers mainly just confirm that McIntire is right: the world is going to hell in a hand basket, and the evil United Nations, National Council of Churches, etc. are entirely to blame.[31] Rather than focusing on McIntire's devoted *fans* (the original "dittoheads," as Rush Limbaugh describes his own echo-chamber following), however, what if we examine McIntire's complicated relationship with his *organizational peers*, specifically those within the ACCC? This will produce a different picture of McIntire—not the "keeper of the fundamentalist flame" known to historians and religious studies scholars but, rather, McIntire the leader of men and opponent of apostasy, who founded the premiere organization of American fundamentalists in 1941, only to find himself expelled from that very group some thirty years later.

On the surface, the ACCC might seem to be just another symbol of McIntire's backward, fundamentalist intransigence. The more accommodationist neoevangelicals formed their own National Association of Evangelicals in 1942. Both groups were a response to the liberal, mainline Protestant National (then "Federal") Council of Churches, but the NAE sought a different image and officially stated, upon its founding, that the organization was "determined to break with apostasy but . . . wanted no dog-in-the-manger, reactionary, negative, or destructive type of organization." Moreover, it was "determined to shun all forms of bigotry, intolerance, misrepresentation, hate, jealousy, false judgment, and hypocrisy."[32] Now, the NAE did not support the civil rights movement any more than any other conservative American religious groups did in the 1950s and 1960s, so we certainly should not mistake such statements as expressing any kind of liberal political thinking. But expressing the intention to shun hatred and intolerance did indicate a basic willingness to engage with differently minded people.

The NAE symbolized the victory of Billy Graham and neoevangelicalism, an early step in bringing conservative believers toward an image of mainstream respectability. People like Jerry Falwell would later take the worldly engagement that began with the NAE in a more attack-dog direction, but by 1950 the NAE had already aligned itself with conservative politics (condemning civil rights legislation, national health care, etc.).[33] Still, we should not point to the NAE as having been initially formed simply in order to promote right-wing policies; the idea was to organize formerly separatist Christians as a reputable group willing to engage in discourse with the modern world. The NAE's founders were not so much friendly to secular society as they were unfriendly to the previously violent rejection of that society by the old-school fundamentalists. William Martin quite rightly concludes that with their founding statements against bigotry the NAE showed their determination "not to be like Carl McIntire and the ACCC."[34] The NAE would have surely materialized without McIntire, but there's no denying that he functioned as a kind of negative inspiration. If the NAE didn't want to be anything like the NCC, they also didn't want to be anything like the ACCC.

The ACCC, still hobbling along today, remains part of McIntire's legacy, and, like him, has consistently been better at making complaints than at effecting change. McIntire was the first president of the ACCC and remained on the organization's executive council thereafter. In addition to using the ACCC's name for his lawsuits against broadcasters, McIntire pursued other, more publicity-grabbing endeavors in the name of his group. In 1952, for example, the ACCC made headlines by voicing violent opposition to the new Revised Standard Version of the Bible, a translation the group claimed to be both communistic and the work of Satan. And in 1953, the ACCC "furnished the House Committee on Un-American Activities with considerable information alleging that Bishop G. Bromley Oxnam was a 'top Red clergyman' in America."[35] Bromley advocated liberal social action and ecumenism and was critical of McCarthy; a HUAC investigation found no evidence that he had been a member of the Communist Party. This was a failure for McIntire and his ACCC, but also a triumph insofar as they had succeeded in pushing HUAC to conduct the investigation. This one moment of glory was as close as the ACCC—or McIntire—would ever get to having true political influence. But we err if we simply see the organization and the man as one and the same thing. Indeed, as early as 1954 McIntire was already contending with ACCC members complaining about his "undemocratic" style, "hyperbolic exaggeration of statistics," and "erratic leadership."[36] It's really a marvel that it was only in the late 1960s that McIntire finally lost his grip on the organization. By then, the problems were multiple, though they ultimately boiled down to McIntire's dictatorial manner. Here's what happened.

To recap, the fundamentalist ACCC was formed by McIntire in 1941, in response to the liberal Protestant NCC, and the NAE would emerge just one year later. McIntire also founded the ICCC in 1948, in response to the

NCC's new international arm, the WCC, a liberal organization completely beholden to the communists, in ICCC's view. McIntire remained in charge of the ICCC until he died in 2002. If the ACCC was a mouthpiece for Mc-Intire for many years, the ICCC was even more of a McIntire operation. It's unclear how many members the group had, though it was certainly linked to many missionary operations around the world. In a 1967 brochure, the ICCC described its three arms as consisting of a missionary group, a relief group, and a youth group (International Christian Youth), and listed vice presidents from across the globe. Still, it remained in many ways a one-man show. The ACCC may have held annual conventions to do business, but McIntire didn't really need to meet with others to get his ICCC work done. Indeed, ACCC general secretary John Millheim actually contended that the only way McIntire was able to get good attendance for his ICCC conventions was by covering expenses for some of his dubious field missionaries to attend. So-called rice Christians had "converted" to Christianity only for material gain, and an all-expenses-paid trip to an ICCC conference was a pretty big payoff.

In 1960, the ACCC had agreed to set up an International Christian Relief (ICR) commission. As McIntire's relationship with the ACCC leadership became increasingly strained in 1968–69, he secretly transferred the ICR to the control of the ICCC, shifting $62,000 of ACCC/ICR money to a new bank account in ICCC's name. He also seized the ICR's mailing list and office equipment. Thereafter, he claimed that the ICR had always actually been a commission of the ICCC, a claim he might have really believed, since the ICR had largely been his idea in the first place. The ACCC first asked, then pleaded, for audited reports of ICR finances, which James Shaw, McIntire's man who ran ICR, refused to provide. ICR had not actually met as a group since Shaw was appointed executive director in 1961, and it had no board or any system of accountability built into it.

For all intents and purposes, McIntire had stolen $62,000 from the ACCC, and possibly more in similar maneuvers over the years. He was no garden-variety embezzler; he simply felt he could use ACCC funds as he saw fit. Having left $51.73 in the ACCC's old ICR account, McIntire (or Shaw) added insult to injury by closing out the account and sending the check for $51.73 to the ACCC, with a note on the back reading: "By endorsement of this check the ACCC releases ICR from any and all claims, and further agrees that this sum closes the account, and no further demands will be made upon ICR for books, records, accounting, bills, etc."[37] Needless to say, the check remained uncashed.

McIntire became increasingly difficult to handle at ACCC meetings, and the executive council now found itself depending heavily on a new Good Book: *Robert's Rules of Order*. McIntire consequently used his *Christian Beacon* newspaper and *Twentieth Century Reformation Hour* radio program to attack the ACCC for its efforts to silence and destroy him via the imposition of cruel protocols. To submit agenda items to be discussed at ACCC meetings in *writing*, and in *advance*, or to declare that speakers had to be *recognized*—in sum, to require any kind of parliamentary procedure—was understood by McIntire as nothing short of a conspiracy against him. McIntire was perennially late to ACCC committee meetings, and then he would demand that any decisions made in advance of his arrival be undone. Further, McIntire had made some problematic appointments to ICCC's Associated Missions subgroup, allowing both churches and missions out of line with official ICCC (and ACCC) positions to join. The ACCC in particular pointed to egregious instances of ICCC having *chainsmokers* in the mission field, a high offense for fundamentalists adamantly opposed to all smoking and drinking. (Wild rumors also floated about of Pentecostal missions being taken under the ICCC's wing—a grievous error for an organization that officially repudiated faith healing and speaking in tongues—and of McIntire tolerating polygamous missionaries.) Also, McIntire had a protégé he wanted to bring into the ACCC who believed in infant baptism ("baptismal regeneration"), which threw ACCC's Baptist members into apoplexy. McIntire simply insisted that the protégé did not believe in baptismal regeneration, regardless of voluminous proof to the contrary, including the protégé himself stating his belief in the power of infant baptism. From then on, McIntire gave over many pages of the *Beacon* (and hours on his radio show) to explaining the Baptist plot against him. McIntire was also unwilling to listen to concerns voiced by ACCC/ICR staff that McIntire's publications and radio programs were becoming a serious problem abroad. People of color learning of McIntire's racism were unwilling to collaborate with the ACCC or the ICCC, in the missionary field or elsewhere.

By 1969 McIntire appeared to have been virtually squeezed out of the ACCC. He did not attend the annual ACCC convention for the first time since he had created the organization. But in October 1970, he rallied, arriving at the ACCC convention with a group of followers and proceeding to take matters into his own hands. At a morning meeting, McIntire motioned that a business meeting be added to the docket (in advance of one scheduled that very afternoon), but the convention had not fully gotten underway yet, many delegates had not arrived, and the president himself was not yet in attendance. The ACCC vice president running the meeting was polite, but not sure if McIntire's motion was in order. "I'm not a parliamentarian, I'm a country preacher," he explained, with a hint of desperation. After eighteen minutes of debate on procedure, the meeting was recessed.

At this point, McIntire appropriated the microphone to declare the meeting not recessed, and his followers (not registered ACCC delegates) motioned to appoint him temporary chairman. Those shuffling out of the room for the recess stopped, some of them laughing. Surely this was a joke. Within two minutes, a new vice president, secretary, and treasurer had been elected; at this point, the proceedings sounded more like an auction than a business meeting. In the next two minutes, the reverend had himself nominated president and elected by unanimous voice vote of his bevy of followers. There was a moment of dead silence, followed by an uproar from ACCC members. Hotel management was called to ask him to step down, but to no avail. McIntire would not relinquish the podium or microphone. ACCC members began to shout "you are out of order, you are out of order, you are out of order," as McIntire, never fully raising his voice, retorted, "I am sorry sir, I am sorry sir, I am sorry sir, this is a duly constituted meeting." The two-and-a-half-hour takeover, recorded on reel-to-reel tape, and later available via mail order from the ACCC for $7.50, devolved into utter chaos, as the audience for McIntire's show became not just angry but also embarrassed. A flurry of voices cried out: "Carl, I never thought you'd do a thing like this . . . I expected something a little more sophisticated than this . . . Come on, Carl, don't make a jackass of yourself all the time . . . When are you going to realize that you can't always domineer everybody?" Most damning of all were comments such as: "What do you suppose the public is gonna take [out of] this kind of stupid thing? . . . This is a public spectacle that will be long heard around this country . . . This revolutionary takeover is piracy of the highest degree! . . . I'm afraid the rest of the press will be here shortly, and the television cameras . . . [and] Dear friends, this is going to be a shame to Christ if the police come in here and try to put Dr. McIntire out . . . If the police come, shame on all of us." [38] This was a horrible dictatorial spectacle, but, even more so, it was profoundly embarrassing. As other scheduled speakers rose, they stood beside McIntire, their papers balanced in their hands, attempting to give speeches while McIntire heckled them. He even injected negative comments when they were reading from the Bible! By the time of the 1971 conference, there was a court order against McIntire, and his ACCC days were definitively over.[39] The ACCC finally formally dissolved its association with the ICCC.

McIntire's final break with the ACCC was not surprising, in light of his domineering personality, but I believe the story of his difficulties with the organization is also of interest insofar as it lends nuance to our perception of what "fundamentalist" meant in the 1960s. First, thanks to McIntire's high-profile politicking, ACCC members had been forced to recognize that racism was a problem for them. Some, like John Millheim, were personally appalled by racism and took it as a moral issue. For many, though, racism was more of a practical problem. If you were trying to start up a new mission in a country in Africa (as the Associated Missions, a subgroup of the ICCC, was attempting to do), and the government of that country learned that the very vocal spokesman of your organization was ferociously agitating against rights for blacks in a widely disseminated newspaper and on over six hundred radio stations in the US (with some penetration overseas as well), the mission simply wasn't going to work out. In fact, you couldn't even hold a meeting: in 1963 an ICCC gathering that was to have been in Bangui, in the Central African Republic, was canceled when the government learned of McIntire's stance on civil rights.[40] Later, in 1975, McIntire would actually be deported from Kenya in the middle of an ICCC Congress, and would send out a shocked fundraising letter, asking how his missionary work could possibly be described as "neocolonialism" and then begging for money to help in "cleaning up the hotels and the food for these Blacks who came from all over Africa to that Congress." He further explained that his work saving these untidy Africans had been interrupted by an evil government composed of guerillas supported (of course, as conspiracy was always afoot) by the World Council of Churches.[41]

For American fundamentalists, missionary work was, theoretically, one way to be "in but not of the world." You could be a missionary and still be "separated" in your heart, eschewing engagement in worldly political issues. But McIntire's vocal assaults on blacks undercut the ACCC's idealized notion of separation, for, if you opposed civil rights on biblical grounds, weren't you being political, even if your intention was to avoid political engagement? Could you work with blacks in the mission field if you opposed civil rights in your heart, but didn't make a public stink about it? These were not questions the ACCC was comfortable asking or answering, but the upshot was straightforward: it would be difficult for the ACCC to do much of its international work while affiliated with McIntire.

By virtue of his alarming political declarations and demonstrations, McIntire threatened to pull the group away from a separatism that was on increasingly unstable footing anyway.

Second, the antimodernists of the ACCC were, post-McIntire, able to take the bold step of actually conversing with the NCC. In 1971, Millheim made a point of not *picketing* a NCC conference but, instead, *attending* and reporting back to the ACCC membership. Even before this, Millheim had told a *New York Times* reporter that "now is the time to become responsible critics, trying to understand, listening and not speaking at a distance. But we will not tamper with doctrine, nor will we ever move in a liberal direction."[42] It was a calculated attempt to reassure the ACCC's fundamentalist base while also signaling a new, post-McIntire attitude. If the neoevangelicals of the NAE had begun conversing with the wider culture in the early 1940s, while the fundamentalists of the ACCC insisted on maintaining a more bellicose stance toward anyone who was different, thirty years later the fundamentalists were briefly open to limited interaction with the fearsome liberal Protestant other. The shift was short lived, and the group would soon return to business as usual, but without their former fearless leader and his very public attacks on the NCC, the United Nations, and other worldly organizations. They had gone from McIntire's open hostility to polite engagement before finally sliding into the home base of separatism.

For years historians have casually referenced the ACCC as McIntire's angry anti-NCC and anti-NAE group, but once we see the struggles within the group it emerges as a collection of individuals who had, for some years, been held in the sway of a cult of personality, began to resist, and finally were able to find a new identity—one that was really quite old fashioned, for, ultimately, the upshot of McIntire's departure was a withdrawal from politics altogether. Post-McIntire, the ACCC publicly announced that "the issue of ecumenism would be [the] main concern of the council in the 1970s along with national moral decline."[43] Left to steer its own ship, it turned out, the group had little interest in publicly condemning civil rights or calling for the continuation of the war in Vietnam. To put it plainly, perhaps they were not the deeply negative force we have previously taken them for. On the other hand, the story of McIntire's being pushed out of the ACCC paints an even more negative picture of him than we have previously imagined. It's a strange pill to swallow, since even without the ACCC story there was already a clear picture of McIntire as dogmatic, authoritarian, and racist.

Of course, a follower of McIntire, lodged completely within his world-view and learning of his trials and tribulations from reading the *Christian Beacon*, would have had little sense of McIntire's own culpability in the ACCC split. A typical issue of the *Beacon* contains a long piece by Mc-Intire detailing exactly how his enemies are out to get him, explaining a new project to help defeat the agents of apostasy, or simply making an extended vituperative attack on civil rights, the NCC, the United Nations, UNICEF, the FCC, etc. This original prose would be accompanied by a few outrageous cartoons by former Disney comic book artist Vic Lock-man. In one three-panel cartoon, for instance, Little Red Riding Hood follows signs in the forest to "Civil Rights" and "Freedom." She herself has been labeled "Property Rights." Panel 1 notes that "Granny has a big heart." Next, we see Red in the bedroom with Granny (the wolf) peering over a blanket labeled "Civil Rights Bill" with her "big eyes." In panel 3, the Civil Rights Bill—which has a "big appetite"—devours "Property Rights." Aside from such cartoons and McIntire's latest diatribe, the rest of the paper was often filled with Photostats of articles from mainstream newspapers, with a note at the bottom reading, "reproduced for documen-tation purposes." So, for example, if the centerpiece essay by McIntire was on the evils of the United Nations, all the reproduced news articles would be on that topic, often with a few key phrases circled by McIntire to draw the reader's attention. The wealth of exact reproductions gives the paper a certain aura of accuracy; you might disagree with McIntire's *interpretation* of the facts, but the facts are pretty clearly laid out in articles from mainstream publications. One is given an impression of earnest and dogged determination on McIntire's part: if he is not always telling the truth, he seems to really think he is. It is only by reading the sad story of the ACCC battles that it emerges clearly the extent to which McIntire was an unapologetic—if self-deluded—liar. And it was only when his own brethren challenged him that the full picture of his duplicity emerged. Reading ACCC members' endless letters to McIntire refuting key details of *Christian Beacon* articles, one cannot help but conclude that the *Bea-con* included tremendous amounts of "information" that was, more than just misinterpretation, overtly misleading.

Ultimately, we might conclude that McIntire was rejected by the ACCC because he was not fundamentalist enough. This may sound contradictory, as I've already myself described him as the überfundamentalist, but the problems for the ACCC extended beyond personality conflicts and finan-cial improprieties to include a number of other key issues. First and foremost, McIntire protested like a radical leftist! In seizing the microphone and podium at the 1970 ACCC meeting he had acted like an anarchist, the ACCC complained in a press release.[44] Another press release despaired that McIntire's attempted coup was the kind of thing a hippy would have done.[45] This was not the way a Bible-believing Christian should act.

More generally, McIntire was losing sight of the importance of separation. At the climax of the attempted ACCC coup the reverend had finally lost his cool and bellowed, "You repudiated the March of Victory, and you're a bunch of softies! You won't fight for our freedom in this country! . . . The heart of this thing is where the fundamentalists are going to stand in the great militant battle in the march for victory! That's the issue, and that's the only issue!"[46] The ACCC had not actually repudiated one of McIntire's Vietnam Victory Marches, as he claimed, but they did fear it would bring them into contact with unbelievers. In other words, they remained fundamentalist separatists, uncomfortable with engagement in worldly disputes and encounters with outsiders. As one concerned ACCC officer noted, "the ICCC has been criticized strongly by many people across the country who are completely separatist in their convictions but who object to methods used by McIntire, the extreme statements he sometimes uses, and his involvement in political issues."[47] As we've already seen, McIntire had challenged Nixon himself by inviting Vice President Ky to speak at a Vietnam Victory rally, and, as if this wasn't enough, the vice president was a *Buddhist*. This was truly beyond the pale of fundamentalist acceptance. One frustrated opponent of McIntire asked, "Is the New Testament Church meant to become a Right Wing Political organization?" McIntire replied that "if the New Testament Church is doing its duty to God and country, as it should, it may be that it actually is being called to be a right-wing political organization." McIntire would make no apologies for staging rallies that drew not just devout Christians but also more "worldly" devout anti-integration activists and George Wallace supporters (figures 20–21). Disturbed by McIntire's contention that duty to God and country necessarily entailed right-wing activism, ACCC officers Paul R. Jackson and Robert T. Ketchum responded, "this we emphatically deny and submit the New Testament as evidence," yet Jackson and Ketchum also made sure to reiterate their rejection of "doctrinal, moral, and civic evils."[48] Their problem, in other words, was not necessarily with McIntire's right-wing beliefs per se, but rather with how he acted upon those beliefs in a public, political manner.

Further, the ACCC was wounded by McIntire's *public* statements on

FIGURES 20–21. A rally protesting the New Jersey State Board of Higher Education's actions against Carl McIntire's Shelton College drew a wide range of politically engaged characters, ranging from representatives of J. B. Stoner's National States Rights Party to ardent George Wallace boosters. Photos courtesy Gary K. Clabaugh, 1969.

*Twentieth Century Reformation Hour* and in the *Beacon*. A typically cruel
Vic Lockman caricature of the entire ACCC executive council was particularly devastating for them. In fact, the public nature of McIntire's attacks
seems to have stung even more than the loss of the $62,000. McIntire even
intimated that the ACCC had been infiltrated by communists, and actually
told radio listeners planning to bequeath money to the ACCC to change
their wills and leave their money to the ICCC instead. Airing dirty laundry
in such a way was simply improper: fundamentalists needed to work things
out in private, as per Matthew 18.[49] A Group Research report based on
interviews with Millheim concluded that Millheim "estimated that many
of them [in the ACCC] lacked his moral concern about McIntire's bigoted
and immoral activities. But above all they shrunk from getting involved in
public controversy no matter what the moral issue."[50] McIntire had alien-
ated and hurt his brethren most powerfully by the very act of going public
with his accusations of the ACCC's "conspiracy" against him.

Our longstanding stereotypical image of neoevangelicals as the "nice
guys" willing to make an effort to engage with modernity (Billy Graham,
for example, going on TV and reaching out to numerous denominations
to participate in his crusades),[51] in contrast to the surly old fundamentalists, may at least in part be a function of McIntire's having been such a
strong public face of fundamentalism for so many years. The point here is
not that fundamentalists were, as a group, simply a backward lot until the
ACCC threw off the yoke of McIntire, but rather that McIntire may have
almost singlehandedly held that backward *image* of fundamentalism very
firmly in place. Yet in rejecting the symbolic father who had ruled with
an iron fist, the ACCC, though saving itself from undemocratic domination, may have planted the seeds of its own destruction. For, interestingly,
after McIntire's departure the ACCC's numbers declined precipitously.
The ACCC organization remained officially opposed to engagement with
worldliness, but, clearly, members began to drift away following McIntire's
ouster. Is it possible that some ACCC members were curious about the
neoevangelical "apostasy" they had steadfastly opposed for so long? The
last bastion of fundamentalism may well have finally lost many of its members to neoevangelicalism.

In the past, the ACCC has claimed between one and two million individual members but has steadfastly refused to release proof of its size.
In 1949, the widely accepted estimate of ACCC membership was eight
thousand; by point of comparison, in 1946 the then Federal Council of
Churches had one million members.[52] In 1969, the NCC claimed forty

million individual members, while the ACCC claimed 1.5 million members.[53] Yet in 1974, four years after McIntire's departure, one reputable source estimated ACCC membership as between two hundred thousand and a quarter million.[54] In 2010, the ACCC had only eight member organizations, and attendees of the 2009 ACCC convention were all able to fit into a single church in Ontario, Canada. Fundamentalism has persisted as a "lingering fire" since Scopes, but clearly the premiere organization of American fundamentalists is now little more than a sputtering flame. From 1941 to 1970 the ACCC may well have kept afloat because of its overbearing leader who simply wouldn't give up. Given his level of engagement in worldly affairs, there were ways in which he simply did not fit the fundamentalist bill, yet his forceful presence obviously somehow drew and held rank-and-file ACCC members. Although the ACCC had always been much smaller than the NAE and the NCC, it would only truly decline once the organization embraced a truer separatism than what was possible under McIntire's rule.

*   *   *

As we've seen, McIntire's problems with the ACCC sprang not only from his very difficult personality but also from his relentless engagement in the world of politics. But what exactly were those politics, and *why* was McIntire so irate about the NCC, the FCC, and, especially, civil rights? While H. L. Hunt was fixated on promoting deregulation, patriotic advertising, and the oil depletion allowance, and Billy James Hargis was fixated on opposing communism, McIntire was closer to Smoot, though clearly lacking Smoot's intellect and smooth style of delivery. Both were bitter, but McIntire was simply uncouth. Still, like Smoot, McIntire was particularly focused on the issue of civil rights.

As previously noted, the growth of the civil rights movement in the 1960s was a major inspiration for the emergent right-wing movement in general, and for practitioners of right-wing broadcasting in particular. Many of the era's fundamentalists were drawn away from separatism and into politics by their opposition to civil rights. Interestingly, though, many described their reaction as merely reactive, focusing in particular on the issue of education. *Brown v. the Board of Education* had led to the creation of "segregation academies" throughout the South—new private schools created just for white children. In addition, previously established religious schools of all denominations remained a haven for segregation, even though some of their leaders spoke out in favor of integration.[55] In higher education, government accreditation standards were having a direct impact on Bible colleges struggling to make the grade. McIntire lost accreditation of his Shelton College in 1971, which meant losing the tax exemption on the rather large piece of property on which the college stood. He and other purveyors of small fundamentalist Bible colleges were dependent on tax exemption to survive, and accreditation was thus truly a matter of life and death. To top it all off, *Engel v. Vitale* had removed officially sanctioned prayer from public schools in 1962, and in 1963 *Abington Township School District v. Schempp* had outlawed Bible reading in public schools. As many conservative Christians began to get more political in the 1960s—creeping away from fundamentalist separatism and toward evangelical worldly engagement—outsiders would see their activism as purely belligerent, while the Christians saw themselves not so much as *fighting* but as *fighting back* against rapid, intrusive changes (figures 22–23). For conservative Christians who opposed integration on what they defined as religious grounds, civil rights legislation could only be understood as deliberate religious persecution.

As Quentin Schulze observes, "American fundamentalism from the 1920s to the present has been organized around media and schools."[56] It was through separatist schooling and fundamentalist radio that fundamentalists both maintained believers within the fold and built social networks for many years. So when schooling was seen as under attack in the 1950s and 1960s (never mind that *private* schools could have as much prayer and Bible reading as they wanted) it was not surprising that the other organizational cornerstone—radio—became the place where a counteroffensive was launched. Indeed, nowhere was protest against civil rights louder than on right-wing radio, especially on McIntire's *Twentieth Century Reformation Hour*. While some evangelists, like Charles Fuller, stuck to the old-time gospel message they had been preaching for decades, McIntire attacked the civil rights movement as unbibilical, immoral, dangerous, and communistic. A 1963 *Christian Beacon* cartoon aptly illustrates McIntire's bigoted point of view: the NCC was acting like a donkey's ass, teaming up with communists to foment a revolution under the phony banner of civil rights (figure 24).

If McIntire hated anything as much as civil rights activism, it was the NCC and the FCC. The NCC was key to the communist plot to desegregate America, he believed, and the FCC was key to the communist plot to eliminate free speech, and *McIntire's* free speech in particular. Vic Lockman

FIGURE 22. In the years following the Supreme Court decisions against prayer and Bible reading in public schools, and with sex education on the rise, many conservative evangelicals saw themselves as under direct governmental attack. A rally for McIntire's Shelton College was thus highly symbolically charged, with attendees voicing support for a wide range of causes. Photo courtesy Gary K. Clabaugh, 1969.

FIGURE 23. A rally for McIntire's Shelton College draws a large crowd and publicity. Note the camera operator in the foreground, with sound technician at his side. Photo courtesy Gary K. Clabaugh, 1969.

even pictured the NCC, FCC, a Russian priest, and Gus Hall, leader of the American Communist Party, in cahoots as a barbershop quartet seeking to emasculate "Uncle Samson" by cutting off his beard (figure 25). Notably, the FCC's regulation of religious programming shifted in 1960; if McIntire had been capable of seeing goodness in the FCC, he would have noticed a subtle turn of events that could have worked in his favor. Tona Hangen explains that in that year, "the FCC ended its policy of distinguishing between sustaining-time [free public-service time] and commercial programs in determining whether a station met FCC standards for service in the public interest."[57] Much sustaining time had previously been given over to religious programming, and the mainline Protestant, politically moderate NCC had been responsible for choosing which religious programs were distributed to stations via free, sustaining time. The NCC adamantly opposed paid religious programming, and the networks went along with them. Paid religious programming became a synonym for proselytizing fundamentalist programming, which would have brought controversy that the networks sought to avoid. Such programming, then, showed up almost exclusively on local, independent stations, while the

FIGURE 24. Former Disney comic-book artist Vic Lockman lampoons Eugene Carson Blake of the National Council of Churches for supporting communism, under the phony banner of civil rights. *Christian Beacon*, August 8, 1963.

NCC made sure the big networks only had access to less controversial, middle-of-the-road religious programs.[58]

Naturally, McIntire saw the NCC arrangement as communistic. The NCC and the networks, with the blessing of the FCC, were controlling what Americans could access on the airwaves. This was no free market, from his point of view. In fact, in the 1940s McIntire had brought numerous lawsuits against small stations refusing the ACCC either free or paid airtime, but he lost every time.[59] He also unsuccessfully attacked the FCC and the networks themselves. As described in a law journal in 1950, the legal decisions against McIntire showed that "the religious programs the FCC [was] favoring [were] those which serve[d] the public interest in receiving spiritual comfort through radio rather than any public interest

FIGURE 25. A *Christian Beacon* cartoon illustrates McIntire's insistence that the liberal commitment to "peaceful coexistence" with the Soviet Union is a communist plot. *Christian Beacon*, 1963.

in the dissemination of controversial ideas by religious groups."[60] The National Association of Broadcasters' Code of Good Practice echoed this, stating that "religious programs should place emphasis on broad religious truths, excluding the presentation of controversial or partisan views."[61] Without these legal cases and network policies, Christians seeking to bypass the blackout on right-wing religious perspectives would not have begun slowly to acquire their own radio stations in the 1920s, creating the future home for the right-wing programs like the *Dan Smoot Report* and *Twentieth Century Reformation Hour* that proliferated in the 1960s.[62]

During the cold war years, TV and radio broadcasters needed public-service programming to satisfy the FCC's requirement to serve community needs. A broadcast about PTA squabbles or local elections was one way to satisfy the FCC, but it also brought with it the risk of offending viewers. Broadcasting ecumenical religious services provided by the NCC, on the other hand, was a worry-free means of satisfying public-service requirements. In theory, NCC-sanctioned programming would serve everyone's needs and be inoffensive. And mainstream broadcasters didn't have to worry about losing much money: religious shows aired for free could be broadcast on Sunday mornings when advertising rates were abysmal anyway.

The Broadcast and Film Commission of the NCC was started in the late 1940s, producing programs such as *Let There Be Light* and *Frontiers of Faith*. *Frontiers* is a perfect illustration of the NCC's approach. In the 1950s and 1960s, this weekly half-hour television series split time between Catholics, Protestants, and Jews. The Protestants produced twenty-four episodes annually, the Catholics sixteen, and the Jews eight.[63] Only four episodes were produced by non-NCC groups. The *Catholic Hour* radio show had asserted that its purpose was "to affirm the dignity of all human beings,"[64] and it appears that this same purpose applied to most of the free public-service religious programs of the 1950s and 1960s. "Ecumenism" was the word of the day, and the liberal cold war understanding was that religion (at least on the airwaves) should be moderate and noncontroversial. America was a *Judeo-Christian nation*, where denominational differences should be minimized. The goal of religious radio and TV, therefore, was to inform and inspire, not proselytize. Asked about Episcopalians, Quakers, Catholics, and members of other faiths at the FCC's WXUR hearing, the WXUR station manager replied, "All I can do is go to the Holy Bible itself . . . and it says, 'Many name the name of Christians who are not really Christians.'"[65] Nothing could have been farther from the NCC's ecumenical approach. McIntire and his cohorts flew in the face of everything the

FCC, the NCC, and the rest of the liberal establishment believed to be the true purpose of religious broadcasting: explicitly, to make viewers feel good about themselves and promote a general idea that religion was good, and implicitly to do public relations for a few denominations.

The distribution of free time, allocated by the NCC, had given broadcasters credit when they renewed their licenses and had to prove that they served community needs. But once paid and free programs counted equally as public service, after the FCC's 1960 policy statement, the incentive to give away time through the NCC was gone. Thus, Hangen argues, "the 1960 federal policy statement allowed radio and television stations to claim their paid religious broadcasting as public service time, permitting the year to become a cultural milestone marking the 'virtual silencing' of mainline churches in mass media."[66] Hangen is a bit hyperbolic here, as it did take a few years for the sustaining programs to fizzle out, but it is reasonable to date the decline of mainline Protestant broadcasting to the 1960 decision. We can also date the roots of televangelism to this deregulatory moment. Ironically, while right-wing broadcasters like McIntire complained endlessly in the 1960s that there was an FCC plot against them because they were being shut down by Fairness Doctrine complaints, the FCC's own elimination of free sustaining time, quite inadvertently, not only contributed strongly to a virtual elimination of liberal religious programming but also created new opportunities for fundamentalist and evangelical broadcasting—though such programming would ultimately find a proper home for itself not so much on the network airwaves as via cable and satellite. Shut out by the NCC for years, the conservative, anti-ecumenical crowd had learned to operate their own radio stations, and they had learned how to fundraise. Now the 1960 policy statement opened up the real possibility of getting airtime on national networks. Years before the rise of Pat Robertson and the rise and fall of Jim and Tammy Faye Bakker, religious TV and radio was already slowly shifting away from the NCC's liberal approach and, if not toward McIntire's fully abrasive style, at least toward conservative evangelicalism of the Billy Graham variety. McIntire, of course, could not see any FCC action as operating to his advantage and failed to observe that the NCC's monopoly of the mainstream airwaves was waning.

While the next chapter will center specifically on McIntire's FCC battles, this context is crucial here, for we cannot understand McIntire's oppositional stance toward modernity—which for him broadly encompassed evangelicalism, ecumenism, and pluralism—without understanding how

crucial opposition to the NCC was to McIntire's confrontational politics.
The NCC was the enemy against which he defined himself, and his hatred
made him deaf to the NCC's own complaints about the FCC. Indeed, the
NCC was quick to point to the increase of paid religious programming in
the wake of the 1960 policy statement as the cause of the disappearance of
NCC-sanctioned programs from American television and radio. The NCC
could not survive in the free market with their bland, feel-good shows and
simply did not have what it took to compete in the new environment. They
didn't want to pay for broadcasting time from their own pockets, and they
also didn't have fundraising skills or, more to the point, the desire to use
radio and TV to raise money. To succeed in paid religious programming
would have required a compromising of NCC principles.

In fact, as Michele Rosenthal has shown, the mainline Protestant organization had had mixed feelings about media use from the beginning. Far
from the conniving communists that McIntire imagined were eager to monopolize the American airwaves, the NCC was ambivalent about the use
of media, and about television in particular. Fundamentalists, conversely,
the very believers who opposed "modernism" were the most eager to use
electronic media to spread the Word. As Rosenthal argues, "Just as evangelical Protestants turned out to be far more 'modernist' in their pragmatic
approach to technology than their theological rhetoric would indicate,
mainline self-defined liberal Protestants were far more ambivalent about
modernity than has been previously suggested."[67] And for these liberal
Protestants, broadcasting was a central symbol of modernity. By the time
the FCC changed its policy on paid programming, the NCC's Broadcast
and Film Commission had come to dominate public-service religious programming simply because the networks had allowed them to, but the NCC
itself remained uncertain about the use value of religious media.

It should hardly be surprising, then, that today the NCC is barely involved in media production, and "mainly views itself as an ecumenical
clearing house for media education and cultural critique."[68] Although Carl
McIntire is long gone from the airwaves, fundamentalism—or, rather, the
more modern evangelicalism—has a very strong presence on both radio
and TV, especially via cable and satellite. McIntire would probably see
much of today's born-again programming as utterly corrupt (so much faith
healing, speaking in tongues, and other apostate activity!), so it would be
an exaggeration to say that he won the battle to get "fundamentalist" views
on the air. He did, however, win (if indirectly) the battle to get explicitly
ecumenical, liberal, mainline Protestant views off the air.

*   *   *

Though McIntire was a political failure, he was not politically inconsequential. In some ways he was like Barry Goldwater, whose unsuccessful campaign for president was, in the long run, not a failure for the Right. The Goldwater campaign motivated conservative Christians and others on the Right to boost their political involvement, building the base for the eventual right-wing takeover of the Republican party.[69] Though hardly as major a figure as Goldwater, McIntire was also a "successful failure" insofar as he served as a negative model for the evangelical politicos who would become the New Christian Right. He was a "fundamentalist," while they were "modern." In her well-known essay on the mass media's narration of the Scopes trial, anthropologist Susan Harding argues that "the voices of modernity emplot the opposition between fundamentalist and modern in history, producing a naturalizing narrative of the progressive spread of modern ideas, at times lamentably thwarted by outbursts of reactive and reactionary fundamentalist fervor."[70] A similar naturalizing narrative underpins the common understanding of McIntire; he represents an outburst of reactionary fundamentalist fervor, confirming what many liberals already believe about fundamentalists: they are kooks.

The New Christian Right, as represented by forces such as Jerry Falwell, Pat Robertson, Gary Bauer, Paul Weyrich, and James Dobson, has bought into the narrative Harding describes. The narrative enables them, I would argue, to paint their own political endeavors as *conservative* but not *extremist*. The fundamentalists at Scopes were represented by *outsiders*, the mass media that disdained them, but the leaders of today's Christian Right (or "leaders in the faith community," as they have been euphemistically described) can control media spin and actually represent themselves, when it suits their purposes, as part of the "progressive spread of modern ideas."[71] At its peak in the mid-1990s, for example, the Christian Coalition's self-projected image was one above all of averageness. The group's baby-faced leader Ralph Reed appeared on television wearing sitcom-dad sweaters and a big smile. The coalition stood up for average Americans who wanted to express their faith politically, he explained. There was nothing kooky about it. Of course, feminists, AIDS activists, and the ACLU weren't buying this for a second. In fact, the image did not even hold up among many local branches of the Christian Coalition, where many members saw themselves as radical antiabortion activists, not friendly moderates.[72] If the new nonextremist image was not altogether convincing, it did nonetheless represent a fascinating historical revision. Reed's friendly face of evangelicalism was meant to blot out the embarrassing televangelists of the 1980s. And if politically engaged evangelicals of the 1990s wanted people to forget about Jimmy Swaggart and Jim Bakker, they certainly didn't want them to remember the Christian Right's roots in the extremism embodied by McIntire.

The nature of McIntire's political activism has made it easy for the New Christian Right to eliminate him from its own history. Contemporary activists like Dobson can claim to have mobilized followers to achieve concrete goals such as passing anti-gay-rights voter referendums. Since McIntire's political efforts were so often merely symbolic, conversely, it is easier to erase him from memory. Of all of McIntire's extremist contemporaries, it is only Billy James Hargis who has been readily acknowledged by the New Christian Right, probably because he was an innovator in computerized mailing lists, laying the groundwork for mechanized mass mailings focused on specific political issues and candidates. In the 1960s, Hargis was also, as we shall see in chapter 5, a major agitator against sex education, a movement that had long-term effects, drawing many conservative Christians into politics.[73]

Although this chapter has largely examined McIntire in isolation from other major right-wing figures of the sixties and seventies, he was not a complete loner. He did manage to cooperate with Hargis, Fred C. Schwarz, Major Edgar C. Bundy, and other right-wingers enough to organize numerous anticommunist seminars at his Cape May, New Jersey, Christian Admiral resort hotel. In fact, he jumpstarted Fred Schwarz's long anticommunist career, actually bringing him from Australia to America in 1953. Yet as Schwarz's popularity grew he sought to become a more mainstream anticommunist voice and avoided mention of the ACCC or fundamentalist doctrine.[74] (In a 1967 *Firing Line* interview, Schwarz even claimed that not only was his movement not right-wing, it wasn't even specifically conservative. The only position he was willing to claim was "anticommunist.") Similarly, McIntire brought a young Francis Schaeffer under his wing as a pupil,[75] but Schaeffer had a strong intellectual impulse, and the relationship could not last. McIntire also helped Hargis with a major project. In the 1950s the two preachers dropped a million balloons with Christian messages inside them behind the Iron Curtain. Whether this action led to any conversions is unknown, but journalists were eager to cover the event, and Hargis and McIntire were eager for the publicity. The balloon project marked the limit of McIntire's collaborative capabilities, but, of course, his radio station WXUR did spread the right-wing ideas of many ideologues, not just McIntire's ideas. There was, in other words, some kind of "coop-eration" insofar as McIntire was willing to program many different shows on WXUR, thus helping to spread the conservative ideology that under-pinned the post-Goldwater right-wing revival. McIntire was not involved in fundraising or organizing for Goldwater, but his station gave a voice to many who were, as well as to those supporting Ronald Reagan in his first political campaign in 1966—though Reagan smoked and drank and was divorced, so it is most likely that he was embraced more by WXUR's secu-lar right-wing news commentators than its fundamentalist personalities.

By the time the conservative revolution climaxed with the election of Reagan as president, though, McIntire had long since lost his radio sta-tion, and *Twentieth Century Reformation Hour* was barely on the air. Un-like later figures of the Christian Right, McIntire was virtually incapable of forming strategic alliances, so working for the 1980 Reagan campaign was never really an option. Reagan had many of the correct conservative credentials, but, as if being divorced and smoking and drinking weren't enough, he had worked in Hollywood, that den of iniquity. McIntire simply couldn't see past this kind of derelict behavior in order to make the kinds of compromises that politics requires. As Allan J. Lichtman so wonderfully puts it, what the many different factions of the emerging Christian Right needed to do was embrace "the idea of cobelligerence." McIntire's old protégé Francis Schaeffer, Lichtman explains, was "doctrinally rigid" but "tactically flexible," and he was the one who "introduced [Jerry] Falwell to the idea of cobelligerence among people of different faiths but com-mon morals."[76] McIntire had belligerence down pat, but "co" was another matter.

McIntire did have one thing in common with more successful political operators, though. Like later figures of the Christian Right, he was able to milk publicity from the mainstream media (figure 26). He was able to position himself as a poor victim of the government, and, at the same time, as God's warrior, a man who could not be defeated. He knew the value of framing the attack on him not as a legal response on the part of the FCC but as a government conspiracy, as unfair persecution of Christians. Such persecution rhetoric lives on, and, indeed, McIntire was not the only one to exploit it. Goldwater, Nixon, George Wallace, William F. Buckley, and, more recently, George W. Bush all made ample use of the language of victimization and positioned themselves as persecuted "outsiders." Nixon and Bush focused in particular on attacking the media. (Bush even re-named the media. To him it was "the filter," which he understood as a con-spiracy of liberals scrupulously weeding out facts and replacing them with

FIGURE 26. Always savvy when it came to milking coverage from the mainstream media, Mc-
Intire invited fellow publicity hound Gov. Lester Maddox (left, with McIntire's wife, Fairy,
right) to share the podium with him at a rally in support of Shelton College. Photo courtesy
Gary K. Clabaugh, 1969.

anti-Bush propaganda.) McIntire did not invent the populist language of
victimization, but he did make a science of fine-tuning it.

More than a footnote in the history of hard-line fundamentalism in the
twentieth century, McIntire's drama throws a wrench into our standard histories. He was a vocal *Northern* fundamentalist, which in itself is unique,
since both fundamentalism and evangelicalism are more typically thought
of as the product of the American South and Southwest. He was politically
active during a period when many have claimed that fundamentalists were
withdrawn from the world, their politics largely inconsequential. Furthermore, his struggle with the FCC laid bare the underlying assumptions of
cold war liberal policy; though officially neutral on matters of religion and
politics, the FCC created and enforced policies that affected fundamentalist broadcasters quite directly. As we shall see in the next chapter, far
from a neutral policy statement, the Fairness Doctrine as enforced in the
1960s was inspired by a liberal idea of fair and balanced public-sphere
debate, where fairness and balance (and the meanings of "controversial"
and "religious") were defined by authorities with little patience for—or
understanding of—the scorching flames of fundamentalist perspectives.

# A Story of "Epic Proportions"

## The Battle between the FCC and WXUR

Memo to: H. R. Haldeman
From: J. S. Magruder
Re: The Shot-gun vs. the Rifle.
Yesterday you asked me to give you a talking paper on specific problems we've had in shot-gunning the media and anti-Administration spokesmen on unfair coverage . . . The real problem that faces the Administration is to get to this unfair coverage in such a way that we make major impact on a basis which the networks-newspapers and Congress will react to and begin to look at things somewhat differently . . . The following is my suggestion as to how we can achieve this goal: 1. Begin an official monitoring system through the FCC as soon as Dean Burch is officially on board as Chairman. If the monitoring system proves our point, we have then legitimate and legal rights to go to the networks, etc., and make official [fairness] complaints from the FCC. — Cited by Rev. Carl McIntire in his testimony before the Senate Sub-committee on Communications, April 29, 1975[1]

His 1970 putsch having failed, by 1971 Rev. Carl McIntire had been definitively removed from the American Council of Christian Churches. In 1973, he would suffer his next great defeat, losing his radio station WXUR. McIntire had fought the FCC for years, but the regulatory agency had finally ruled against his retaining his license, a circuit court had upheld the FCC's decision, and the Supreme Court had declined to review the case. It was over. The decision was tough on conservative evangelicals living in the Philadelphia area: McIntire had a large devoted following, and the station was a major source of not only right-wing news coverage but also fundamentalist preaching. On the other hand, liberals rejoiced and thought the decision was quite just: McIntire had used the publicly owned broadcast spectrum to air one-sided political jeremiads, patently in violation of the Fairness Doctrine.

WXUR had survived longer than many other independent stations owned by fundamentalists. Most such stations featured right-wing commentary and were either unwilling to provide time for liberal rebuttals or simply unable to keep up with the notifications that the FCC required be sent out to those who were personally attacked on the air. So when WXUR was finally brought down, it was a major symbolic defeat for conservative, local radio. But even more symbolically important was the role that the Fairness Doctrine had played in McIntire's defeat. For conservatives, the doctrine itself became—and remains—a symbol of liberal persecution of conservatives (and, more specifically, Christians). In fact, the doctrine, suspended years ago by the Reagan FCC, has become something of a cipher for both liberals and conservatives. On the left, it is invoked as a needed measure, though how a regulation conceived to function in an environment of communications *scarcity* could possibly function in today's environment of communications *excess* is certainly open to question. On the right, it is invoked as a mythical evil force against free speech, and it is spoken of, with extreme paranoia, as if it were always just about to be reinstated. Anyone who follows such discussions has become used to hearing the doctrine discussed as a hypothetical, a big "what if?" The story of McIntire's prolonged encounter with the FCC provides a wonderful opportunity to see how the doctrine functioned when it actually did exist, and how, even then, liberals and conservatives fought over the doctrine's symbolic meaning.

Testifying before a Senate Subcommittee on Communications in 1975, the Reverend Everett C. Parker was a perfect spokesman to give the liberal perspective on the Fairness Doctrine. It was Parker and his organization, the Office of Communication of the United Church of Christ, that had succeeded in making legal a citizen's right to appeal FCC licensing decisions. The group's original goal was simply to challenge the right of radio and TV station WLBT in Jackson, Mississippi, to air overtly racist news programs. Such programming did not, they contended, serve the public interest, and therefore WLBT's license holders should be open to challenge at license renewal time. Parker had won this battle yet remained frustrated by the inability of citizens to provoke action from the FCC. As he explained to the subcommittee, "In spite of the thousands of hours of programming that are on the air daily, fairness complaints to the FCC are infrequent and are seldom effective, because of Commission bias in favor of the broadcaster. In a typical year [in the early 1970s], the FCC received 2,000 program complaints. The Commission followed up on 168 (8 percent) of them by writing letters to stations. They made 69 rulings, only five of which were adverse to licensees. So much for the terrible burden the Fairness Doctrine imposes on broadcasters!"[2] Citizens may have had the right to object to station practices as unfair, but the FCC was slow to respond and generally favored broadcasters over the public. Therefore, while Fairness Doctrine complaints were a legally valid means of fighting bigotry on the airwaves, they weren't particularly effective, Parker contended, clearly flummoxed by those crying foul play and insisting that the doctrine was the enemy of free speech. In fact, Parker may have been actually overstating the effectiveness of the doctrine: one study showed that Fairness Doctrine complaints in the 1973–76 period had about a one-in-one-thousand chance of succeeding.[3]

Not surprisingly, McIntire had a very different perspective. His testimony before the Senate, just one day earlier, quoted heavily from CBS newsman Fred W. Friendly's book exposing the Democratic National Committee's campaign, beginning in the Kennedy years, to shut down right-wing broadcasting by raising Fairness Doctrine complaints. Years later, Nixon would continue the plot against free speech, and McIntire proves it by citing a conspiratorial memo from Jeb Stuart Magruder to fellow Watergate felon H. R. Haldeman (a.k.a. "the President's son-of-a-bitch"). Far from a weak and barely enacted policy, the Fairness Doctrine was, in McIntire's mind, part of the vast liberal-communist conspiracy against him. *Nixon's* men involved in a liberal-communist conspiracy to monitor US media and file FCC complaints about any coverage they found disagreeable? That Nixon's right-wing credentials were not in order was confirmed by the fact that he didn't achieve victory in Vietnam and had opened up communication with China, the Right believed, and no one on the Left—or center, for that matter—could doubt Nixon's ability to conspire against his enemies. As far as McIntire was concerned, the Fairness Doctrine was the cornerstone of a deliberate plot against the radio ultras.

So, the Fairness Doctrine: virtually worthless policy with no real teeth to affect the broadcasting business, as Parker contends? Or tool for the annihilation of the First Amendment, as McIntire insists? Actually, there's something to be said for each position. The FCC never did effectively use the doctrine to truly make an impact on network practices. And the DNC, and later Nixon, did use Fairness Doctrine complaints to harass certain broadcasters. But there are holes in both Parker's and McIntire's arguments.

First, while the FCC only followed up on a rather small number of fairness complaints, as Parker complained, they were much more likely to go after the little fish than the big network sharks. This was in part because ABC, CBS, and NBC had lobbyists and political power, but also, of course, because the little guys—the independent, largely fundamentalist owned, right-wing radio stations—really *were* the ones operating unfairly in many instances. In any case, even if the FCC did not follow through on most fairness complaints, the doctrine frightened right-wing broadcasters and *did* affect their practices.

Second, to rebut McIntire, while the FCC did end up pursuing a number of complaints against right-wing radio, to a large extent the right-wing stations shut down *themselves* before they actually got involved with the FCC: most of them ended up canceling their most popular shows because they couldn't bear the expense of giving away free time for personal-attack responses, and they didn't have the staff to contact everyone who was attacked on the air. The fact is that relentless one-sided attacks were simply against the law. The way for the radio ultras to survive was to genuinely strive for balanced programming, and this was beyond their ken. Overall, the key thing to consider is that the FCC was exclusively *reactive* when it came to the Fairness Doctrine. They did not monitor TV and radio looking for violations but instead passively waited for citizens to file complaints, and they took no action on the vast majority of those complaints. If there were more fairness investigations of the superpatriots than there were of other broadcasters, this was not an FCC plot but, rather, a function of which stations were being complained about.

By contrasting Parker and McIntire's perspectives, we can come up with arguments both in favor of and in opposition to the Fairness Doctrine. It was a well-intentioned idea, and those who favored it were right to exclaim that in exchange for promising to be fair, broadcasters got a monopoly of the airwaves—a virtual license to print money.[4] Was this really asking too much? Use the scarce, publicly owned spectrum to sell your ads, and, in exchange, try to give balanced political coverage and not let someone like Father Coughlin take over.

On the other hand, in the case of the (mostly) liberal attacks on the ultras, the idea of "free speech" was used to shut down free speech. McIntire's WXUR was the main source of fundamentalist political and religious speech in the Philadelphia area. Was it fair for those who found those perspectives offensive to eliminate them? The Fairness Doctrine was never a policy measure that fully succeeded or was fully fair, and it seemed to work particularly well in having a chilling effect on right-wing speech. The doctrine stated that broadcasters had a duty to address controversial issues of public importance, and that when they expressed one point of view on such issues they were obliged to provide contrasting points of view. Needless to say, fundamentalists are not always adept at respecting multiple points of view, and it should hardly be surprising that two of the most important court decisions regarding the Fairness Doctrine, *Red Lion Broadcasting Co. Inc. v. FCC* (1969) and *Brandywine-Main Line Radio, Inc. v. FCC* (McIntire's court case, 1972), were decisions against fundamentalists.

Of course, the FBI relentlessly pursued the producers of left-wing speech in the cold war years, so it's not as if the right-wingers were the only victims of unfair government harassment. Pacifica and other stations were mercilessly plagued with obscenity charges and seen as "subversive" by both the FBI and HUAC.[5] Whether the harassment was against left-wing or right-wing speech, the ostensible goal of the harassers was either apolitical or politically centrist/neutral media. A key rationale for such centrism was the idea of scarcity—there was only so much room on the broadcast spectrum, and few citizens possessed a broadcast license, whereas most could, conversely, print up a flier or give a speech on a street corner. In a world without satellites, cable, or the Internet, the idea of trying to keep things "fair and balanced" on the limited number of TV and radio stations that existed made some sense. Still, it is unfortunate that both left- and right-wing speech were subject to censorship in the name of "fairness." The Fairness Doctrine meant well. But it didn't work well.

Rather than simply arguing for or against the doctrine, though, what I'd like to do is use McIntire's FCC case to explore the schism between liberal and conservative understandings of a policy that was, theoretically, neutral and apolitical. Specifically, how did the extended argument over the Fairness Doctrine between fundamentalist broadcaster and secular government agency play out? Could either side truly communicate with the other, or would they endlessly talk at cross-purposes? The neoevangelicals, as we've seen, wanted to communicate with the wider world, while the fundamentalist McIntire wanted to chastise that world with a picket sign and a bullhorn. Put on a FCC witness stand, could he stop hollering and make an articulate case for himself? And would his case make sense to those outside of the fundamentalist fold?

McIntire's battle against the FCC culminated in an unusually long hearing to determine whether his license to operate radio station WXUR

should be renewed. It was an encounter between "biased" fundamentalists and the "neutral" voices of modernity, an encounter in which neither
side could speak or understand the other's language. This cultural conflict between secularism and fundamentalism presented quite a dilemma
in the quasi-legal context of an FCC hearing. Focusing as they do upon
the presentation of testimony, evidence, and counterevidence, hearings
pivot on rational debate among parties assumed to be on a more or less
rhetorically level playing field. Today, conservative evangelicals are quite
adept at playing on this field, but McIntire was the product of an earlier
era. Analysis of his FCC hearing reveals a fascinating portrait of a specific
historical moment before the Old Christian Right acquired the rhetorical
savvy (not to mention funding, organizations, databases, and mailing lists)
that it needed to transform itself into the New Christian Right in the 1970s
and '80s. As we saw in the previous chapter, McIntire was engaged in
"worldly" politics back when fundamentalists, according to conventional
histories, were still apolitical separatists. Still, McIntire remained separatist enough that he was destined to lose: he and his cohorts simply could not
speak the worldly language of secular politics or even understand what a
nonfundamentalist conception of "fairness" might entail.

For example, John H. Norris stated during WXUR's FCC hearing that
he gave God's point of view on all issues. To obey the doctrine, he asked,
did he have to give free airtime to the Devil? McIntire had a similar one-
dimensional understanding of the doctrine. After WXUR came under attack the station tried to turn things around by going out of its way to satisfy
the FCC. Its most vociferously right-wing commentator was fired, and the
station hired an eccentric socialist commentator who was rabidly opposed
to capitalism. If the FCC was attacking the station for its pro-American,
anticommunist point of view, McIntire reasoned, the only response was to
hire an anti-American, procommunist. The Devil, in other words. That any
voice between these two extremes existed was inconceivable.

McIntire's stance toward communication and compromise is aptly il-
lustrated by his discussion of the Hegelian dialectic in *The Death of a
Church*, a book he wrote in response to the United Presbyterian Church's
Confession of 1967, which called for world peace, civil rights, and the end
of poverty. McIntire attacked the idea of "peaceful coexistence" among
nations, which the Confession discussed using the term "reconciliation."
Biblical reconciliation is the work accomplished by Christ on the cross, not
by man in the slums, McIntire contended. For the revisionist Presbyterians, McIntire claimed,

reconciliation of the nations . . . is brought about by compromise and concession, dialogue, rapprochement, and peace. This has nothing to do with the Cross. It involves simply the dialectic—two sides are in conflict; each side makes compromises, and they find unity in a new position. The new position then enters into conflict with an arising opposition. There is thesis, antithesis, and out of this conflict there comes the synthesis. Thus the process is repeated . . . and before long, society is a long way from where it first started under the original thesis. This is nothing but the Hegelian or Marxian dialectic.[6]

In sum, dialogue enables compromise and new ideas; new ideas erase old (better) ideas. This understanding of "dialogue" was hardly commensurate with the FCC's liberal notion of what it meant for a broadcaster to provide "contrasting points of view." Indeed, McIntire put a crazed socialist on WXUR to represent a point of view contrary to his own because he knew that this way dialogue with his own point of view would be impossible. No revolutionary synthesis would be spawned by this concession.

\* \* \*

McIntire premiered his *Twentieth Century Reformation Hour* in 1955, and by the mid-sixties the program could be heard nationally on over six hundred stations. After WVCH in Philadelphia cancelled the show in 1965, and no one else in the area would pick up the show, despite its apparently rather large audience, McIntire decided to acquire his own radio station. McIntire applied for a license to operate WXUR in Media, Pennsylvania, a Philadelphia suburb, and the FCC was immediately flooded with complaints from groups such as the AFL-CIO, the American Jewish Committee, the NAACP, the Philadelphia Council of Churches, the Catholic Community Relations Council, and the Women's International League for Peace and Freedom. Based on his claim that the station would feature a general format of news, music, and talk shows, the FCC ended up granting McIntire a one-year license instead of its usual three-year license. In his license transfer application, McIntire claimed that he would broadcast two daily one-hour religious programs and several religious programs on Sunday. He also "pledged to provide balanced programming in matters involving controversial viewpoints."[7] McIntire's actual programming, however, was dominated by right-wingers such as Clarence Manion, Billy James Hargis, and Dan Smoot, with no time devoted to liberal or left-wing responses. Further, WXUR commentators often made personal attacks in the course of their discussion of controversial issues of public importance, which meant that the station was required by the FCC to contact the person attacked and offer him or her free airtime to respond. The proper personal-attack protocols were rarely followed, and free on-air rebuttals were infrequent.

McIntire acquired WXUR at a key moment, shortly after the liberal, mainline Protestant NCC began to lose its grip on radio and television, pursuant to the FCC's 1960 policy statement. Furthermore, this was just a few years before the *Red Lion* decision, which supported the FCC's use of the Fairness Doctrine (specifically, its personal attack rules) against fundamentalist broadcaster John M. Norris, the father of WXUR's general manager John H. Norris. The senior Norris's station had run an attack on an anti-Goldwater book, without also supplying an anti-Goldwater spokesman to offer a "balanced" perspective. McIntire contributed $10,000 toward Norris's legal fees, but Norris ultimately lost.[8]

It was inevitable that McIntire, who was as rabidly right-wing as Norris, would also be challenged by the FCC for not abiding by the doctrine. Despite his tendency to play the innocent victim, McIntire must have surely seen that an FCC challenge was imminent. He had made some effort to invite those he had attacked onto his program to respond to his accusations, but he was routinely refused by liberal politicians and activists, many of whom felt that his invitations were not made in earnest. With his confrontational programming strategies, McIntire was obviously spoiling for a fight with the FCC over the Fairness Doctrine, a fight he expected to win because he was certain that the doctrine was unconstitutional. In fact, he thought that the FCC itself was unconstitutional since its policies were enforced like laws, even though it was an unelected body. A cartoon from McIntire's *Christian Beacon* newspaper summed it up: a farmer representing Congress is bewildered by the FCC's literally mushrooming power (figure 27).

WXUR's FCC hearing ran from October 1967 through June 1968. The transcript was almost eight thousand pages long, and there were many more pages of exhibits (that is, evidence submitted by both sides). It is easy, when wading through such a lengthy transcript, to be sucked into the surface narrative laid before the reader. The question officially at hand was: Did WXUR mislead the FCC in its license application by not delivering the programming it had promised and by not adhering to the Fairness Doctrine as promised? The drama built endlessly, as one side argued yes, the other no, and each repeatedly proved that the other was, without a

## A MUSHROOMING MENACE, SHADING OUT THE GRASS ROOTS!

FIGURE 27. McIntire saw the FCC as an illegal agency and its Fairness Doctrine as the archenemy of grassroots, right-wing speech. *Christian Beacon*, date unknown.

doubt, lying through its teeth. There were two sets of lawyers attacking WXUR, the lawyers for the Broadcast Bureau (that is, the FCC), and the lawyers for the Intervenors (the Philadelphia Council of Churches, ACLU, B'nai B'rith, etc.).

If one can pull away from the transcript's endless quibbling, name calling, and scrutiny of evidence, a subnarrative is readily apparent. In fact, one might go so far as to say that what makes this case interesting is not so much that McIntire lost his license and the doctrine was upheld, but rather that the FCC's lawyers spent almost a year in a hearing room with a bunch of fundamentalists, and neither side could altogether agree on what they were actually fighting about. To say that this was only a battle over "free speech"—the question being, does McIntire get it?—is to miss the interpretive battle that was played out over phrases like "personal attack" and "controversial issues of public importance." How to properly define "religion," "politics," and "racism" was also at issue, as was the question of what constituted "news."

Adding to the drama was the fact that McIntire's lawyer, Benedict P. Cottone, had been an advocate for the Fairness Doctrine when it was drawn up in 1949. He was now on the other side, a strong opponent of the doctrine. Like most converts, he was overcompensating for his past sins. He was also hostile and disruptive, always eager to make a scene in the hearing room.[9] The other interesting character in the drama was H. Gifford Irion, the FCC's hearing examiner, equivalent of the judge in a normal courtroom. It is hard to find much information about Irion, but we do know that he wrote an essay skeptical of *Brown v. the Board of Education*.[10] Though it might be jumping the gun to say with certainty that he was a conservative, he was, at least, not a liberal. Irion was also the author of *Windward of Reason*, a mediocre novel about a girl's loss of innocence during the Jazz Age. Interestingly enough, this forgettable novel would come to haunt Irion: it was eventually referenced by both the bureau and the Intervenors, who attacked Irion for the fanciful "literary" approach he took in his final report on the hearing.

Though the Intervenors contended that WXUR's programming was consistently racist, McIntire was adamant that he was not a racist. As was typical of many segregationists, McIntire contended that the civil rights movement was a communist plot. McIntire wanted to save blacks and other Americans from communism, as well as from the escalating violence besieging the country. He opposed everyone who broke the law, but "everyone" most often meant black militants and draft dodgers. If pressed, he might have included the white dynamiters from Birmingham and the people who beat up the Freedom Riders in his list of lawbreakers, but his modus operandi was to first point to the communists as instigators of violence, then turn to their American agents—civil rights activists. McIntire proposed that man's only hope for surviving such lawlessness was Jesus Christ. That this was "racist" was incomprehensible to him. Likewise, he did not understand how people could say that his station's programming in general was racist, though there was ample evidence to prove that it was.

One of McIntire's most overtly bigoted commentators, Tom Livezey, ran a call-in show called *Freedom of Speech*. Though he was consistently rude to liberal callers, like McIntire he did not perceive himself as prejudicial. (This was somewhat incredible, as he had been previously fired from another radio station because of critical comments he had made about the NAACP and the civil rights movement.)[11] In one transcribed on-air exchange included in the FCC hearing documents, Livezey chided a right-wing caller who referred to black people as "niggers" in a poem. Livezey appeared to find the word objectionable not so much because it was racist but because it was in poor taste.[12] On another occasion, a caller said that the police patrol dogs, which had been put in place following race riots, were going to be removed from the Philadelphia subways, and Livezey responded, "I think they out to leave the dogs down there and let them take some bites out of their black butts." The station manager, Robert Fulton, immediately stormed into the studio, "turned off the mike switch, substituting a sixty second commercial and advised Livezey that if he ever said anything of that nature again on the air that he would fire him."[13] Notably, Fulton had been an employee under the previous secular owners of the station, and WXUR's new general manager, the fundamentalist John H. Norris, had decided to keep him on. So it is not clear whether or not Fulton shared Norris and McIntire's religious and political agenda, but it is clear that Livezey's racist comments were considered inappropriate by the station's onsite manager.[14] Livezey's usual mode was to encourage callers to make prejudicial anecdotal observations. A caller claimed on one occasion, for example, that it was common knowledge that Jews ran the American pornography business, and Livezey did not deny it. Though McIntire enjoyed Livezey's consistently high ratings, he also seemed offended by the parts of the show that were in poor taste (overtly as opposed to implicitly racist), and Livezey was fired after five and a half months on the air.

Carl Mau, another commentator hostile to "un-American" voices, was not fired; he readily admitted that he liked to "rough up" guests with whom he disagreed, though a careful reading of the transcripts shows that after confronting his guests (asking a black woman, for example, if she would consider marrying a white man), he would, unlike Livezey, allow guests plenty of time to explain their perspectives. A white Quaker peace activist, Mrs. Allen Olmsted, complained that she felt uncomfortable on Mau's

show, but it is clear from the transcript of her appearance that Mau let her
explain her position and defend her points of view in great detail: at least
three-quarters of the program is given over to her remarks. Though apparently gracious and not deliberately insulting to Mrs. Olmsted, Mau was
also overt in displaying his own promilitary, anticommunist point of view
as he interviewed her. Even hearing examiner Irion, who so often gave
WXUR the benefit of the doubt in his final hearing report, acknowledged
that "Mau was anything but subtle. Where McIntire . . . wielded rapiers,
Mau was still swinging a stone-age ax."[15] In any case, though McIntire's
own bigotry was palpable, if consistently more subtle than Livezey's and
Mau's, it does seem that he agreed with the Intervenors that racists were
people who hated black people, and he had no idea why anyone would
use the word to describe *him*. As a Christian, he explained, he loved
everybody.

     If McIntire and his opponents could not agree on a definition of racism,
they had no more luck with "personal attack." McIntire's lawyer Cottone
contended that the Intervenors' idea of an "attack" did not square with
WXUR's. He questioned whether when WXUR's Pastor Bob read aloud
from a government report alleging that a person or group was communist,
he was making an "attack." It was simply a matter of public record, Cottone argued, that the report had made such allegations. Consider Pastor
Bob's introduction to reading aloud from a series of congressional reports
on the ACLU: "The American Civil Liberties Union as usual hastened
to the defense of those assorted beatniks, radicals, and communists who
carried on so terribly at the House Committee on Unamerican Activities
hearings recently. This brings to mind the fact that few Americans know
about this ACLU. Here's what others have said about the American Civil
Liberties Union. Notice, these are not my words, but the findings of others."[16] The vituperative Pastor Bob gave his discussion of the ACLU a
negative spin in his framing comments, but, Cottone insisted, should it
have been considered an "attack" to read from official government documents on the air?

     Of course, legal debates that do not involve fundamentalists also in-
clude technical debates over the meanings of words. What was unique
here, though, was that the fundamentalists involved in the case were paranoid data collectors, and their archival activities convinced them of the
truth value of certain "facts." To them, the news articles, press releases,
and congressional transcripts they had gathered, and the conclusions they
had drawn from them, were as transparent and impervious to alternative

interpretations as the Bible itself. The WXUR gang were clipping fiends who closely monitored left-wing publications. There were few people who read the *Daily Worker* more carefully than they did; their citations from the *Worker* were, at base, intended as attacks, but they were actually quoting from the communists' own publication, not just making wild, unsubstantiated statements.

Another twist in the debate over what constituted a personal attack was the fact that WXUR's insults were generally outlandish and enmeshed in a fundamentalist worldview. While politically moderate radio listeners would not agree that the NCC's progressive attitudes toward peace and civil rights made it an "apostate" organization, was it a "personal attack" to air those attitudes and then label them "apostate"? Perhaps this was simply a right-wing fundamentalist opinion. A 1963 *Christian Beacon* cartoon perfectly illustrates both McIntire's attitude toward the NCC and his characteristic rhetorical excess (figure 28). The cartoon pictures McIntire's "Prescription for Losing the Cold War." Metropolitan Nikodim of the Russian Orthodox Church foists a giant "phony peace pill" down the throat of a child seated in a church pew. Behind Nikodim we see Premier Khrushchev helping to position the pill. A book beside the child on the pew, where the Bible should be, is entitled "Social Gospel." This kid is obviously in cahoots with the NCC, which promotes peaceful coexistence and aid to the poor—obviously a communist conspiracy. In fact, the child's head is being positioned to swallow the bitter peace pill by NCC president Eugene Carson Blake. This kind of image clearly "attacks" those pictured, but it speaks from so far within a fundamentalist worldview that it should have been hard for an outsider to take it seriously.[17] Though many cold warriors might have agreed with McIntire's skepticism toward peaceful coexistence, the idea that the country's largest mainline Protestant organization was, in effect, in bed with the enemy would have seemed ridiculous to most nonfundamentalists. As a publication, of course, the *Beacon* was not subject to the Fairness Doctrine, but this cartoon perfectly illustrates the kind of insider address that characterized the rhetoric of *Twentieth Century Reformation Hour* and other programs aired on WXUR. The NCC was quite right to realize that WXUR was consistently attacking them, but were these attacks that anyone outside of the fundamentalist fold could take seriously, and should these often patently nutty attacks have had legal consequences? Even if McIntire and his cohorts often seemed crazy, the reality was that they were expressing many commonly held fundamentalist views. If this was a "lunatic fringe," it was one with an enormous constituency.

Rx PRESCRIPTION for LOSING the COLD WAR!

FIGURE 28. McIntire's "personal attacks" spoke from so far within a fundamentalist worldview that it should have been hard for most outsiders to take them seriously. *Christian Beacon*, March 1963.

Though the FCC was adamant that its opposition to WXUR had nothing to do with the station's religious perspective, it is easy to understand why McIntire's audience earnestly believed that the FCC's attack on WXUR was nothing but religious persecution. Like many fundamentalists, McIntire's listeners could not understand—or tolerate—an interpretive worldview outside of their own, which meant that in their minds, their secular enemies were only feigning interest in policy regulations and the provisions of the Communications Act of 1934 stating that broadcasters were required "to serve the public interest, convenience, and necessity."

In 1963 and 1964, the commission began receiving complaints from fundamentalists that the Fairness Doctrine required ministers to submit scripts of their sermons to stations. Though some stations may have made this request of controversial ministers such as McIntire, this was certainly *not* an FCC requirement. To clarify matters, in January of 1964 the commission issued a public notice, which contains this passage, worth quoting at some length:

> from time to time, licensees . . . have urged . . . that programs treating with [*sic*] "anti-communism," "pro-Americanism" or religion should not be governed by any obligation of fairness since the opponents of the views expressed on such programs must by definition be "procommunist," "anti-American," or atheistic. *The Commission knows of no substantial public controversy in this country concerning the merits of religion* and certainly the Commission did not hold that the broadcast of church services, devotionals, prayers, etc. invoked the "fairness doctrine." However, some of the programs described above as dealing with "anti-communism," "pro-Americanism," or religion often do express vigorous viewpoints on the United Nations Organization, the wisdom of foreign aid, how best to combat communism and a host of other genuinely controversial issues . . . [T]o the extent any program, regardless of label, deals with controversial issues of public importance, the "fairness doctrine" applies.[18]

Here, the commission neatly dispenses with the idea that religion is controversial by stating that there is "no substantial public controversy in this country concerning the merits of religion," rather absurdly implying that the only reasonable way for religion to be controversial would be if one were to argue for or against religion itself. "Normal" religion here consists of church services, devotionals, and prayers, which are (at least as presented in NCC-approved programming) inherently nonideological and noncontroversial. So, the Fairness Doctrine should, in normal circumstances, not apply to a church service, prayer, or hymn. If religious broadcasts are understood in these terms, McIntire's version of religion could only be understood as aberrant, since his sermons were packed with politically controversial statements. It was an objective fact, he claimed, that communists were behind civil rights agitation; only if we reject communism (and thus the civil rights movement) and turn to God can we correct the situation. McIntire saw this as a statement of religious, not political belief.

It would hardly have been in the FCC's interest to acknowledge that WXUR's one-sided personal attacks really were often expressions of fundamentalist religious beliefs, as applied to politics. This would have complicated things by destabilizing the definition of "attack," and the FCC needed "attack" to be a neutral legal term. That the FCC labeled WXUR's expressions of fundamentalist political/religious beliefs "attacks" clearly reflected the liberal perspective of a regulatory agency that perceived itself as *neutral*, neither secular nor religious in orientation. As commissioner Robert E. Lee—old friend of both Joe McCarthy and H. L. Hunt—noted in the FCC's final report on the hearing, "We are not concerned with the social, political, or religious philosophy of the licensee or any person using its facilities. Our interest is in the right of the public to a reasonable opportunity to hear contrasting views on controversial issues."[19]

The FCC's personal-attack rules required that a broadcaster notify and send a tape or transcript, within one week, to anyone attacked on a program during discussion of "controversial issues of public importance." Thus, if an attack were made during discussion of a topic that was not truly a controversial issue of public importance, the rules should not have applied. Here is another area where the FCC and WXUR could not agree on the terms of debate. It was easy for anyone at the time to see why the civil rights movement or Vietnam might be controversial. But, in general, who could be an objective arbiter of what counted as controversial? Controversial to whom? This was truly a fault line of the Fairness Doctrine.

For McIntire, the fluoridation of water was a controversial issue of public importance. Yet most people saw this as an issue of interest only to extremists, and, to the best of my knowledge, no one ever contacted McIntire demanding radio time to discuss the profluoridation position. McIntire also often freely criticized the United Nations, but then realized he had to censor himself to avoid FCC problems. As he explained during his FCC hearing: "I was not aware that the United Nations was a controversial question of public importance. I thought everybody was supposed to be for it. There are just a few of these so-called 'extremists' that are opposed to it around the country. But at that moment, when the FCC said [in an official statement] that the United Nations was a controversial question of public importance, from that point on I have not been able to talk about the United Nations on my broadcasts."[20] The FCC had mentioned the UN specifically as an example of a controversial issue in a public statement it made in response to the huge influx of letters it had received from distressed WXUR listeners. The meaning of "controversial" was precarious, and it was dangerous for a fundamentalist broadcaster to scream too loudly about an issue that he thought *should* be controversial, like the UN.

If his voice actually *succeeded* in making the issue controversial, he would then face fairness issues. After all, a one-sided perspective on a *non*controversial issue was not subject to the doctrine.

A few issues did clearly remain "controversial" only from within the right-wing fundamentalist worldview. The dangers of Halloween, for example, were not a pressing concern for those outside of the fold. Irion, the hearing examiner, went so far in his final report as to note that some "controversial issues" on WXUR would be laughable to nonfundamentalists. A show called *Conversion Center* tried to save Catholics by converting them to fundamentalism. Irion observed that "there is certainly nothing wrong in this from any legal point of view but the production of a program called *Conversion Center* which addresses itself to converting nuns, monks and priests from the Roman Catholic faith to what these individuals considered Christianity has a comic character which escapes all legal analysis. Insofar as this opinion is concerned, the verities which were expressed have nothing to do with the case but in the context of the Fairness Doctrine—which cannot ignore philosophical disputations—they are at worst harmless." A small, independent radio station's attack on the behemoth of the Catholic Church might be regarded as unfair by some, but Irion saw this as farfetched. "No one can ignore the fact," he argued, "that the Roman communion is a vast and respected institution, unconnected with the blissful vagaries of a five hundred watt station in Media, Pennsylvania."[21]

One *Christian Beacon* cartoon in particular aptly illustrates Irion's point that, though McIntire was eager to aim his slingshot at various Goliaths, most would not have felt his sting. In a cartoon discussed in chapter 3, Gus Hall, leader of the American Communist Party, is pictured in a barbershop quartet with Eugene Carson Blake of the NCC, Metropolitan Nikodim, and a figure representing the FCC. They are singing joyfully of "peaceful coexistence" and are about to cut the hair of a wary "Uncle Samson." The idea that the American Communist Party was directly politically aligned with the FCC, the NCC, and the Russian Orthodox Church is one that all four parties would find quite laughable. It is hard to imagine any one of these parties could feel genuinely threatened by such a ludicrous contention. But the NCC was, at least, quite irritated by McIntire's endless potshots, and though it is doubtful that McIntire's formulaic attacks constituted a true threat to the NCC, the group was nonetheless eager to see him off the air.

One problem with the NCC, FCC, and others attacking McIntire for his one-sided political diatribes was that McIntire did not share his opponents' definition of "politics." The Intervenors and the Broadcast Bureau lawyers contended that religion and politics were separate categories, while McIntire et al. contended that they were inseparable and that, really, everything they said on the air was religious speech. Which it was. As a politically engaged fundamentalist, McIntire had no understanding of religion and politics as separate spheres. Indeed, McIntire and his fundamentalist brethren on WXUR never condemned civil rights, communism, the United Nations, or Social Security on strictly secular grounds. Medicare, McIntire explained at the hearing, was wrong not for political reasons but because "the Bible says that the body is the temple of the Holy Spirit; that God has created the body, and that the individual is responsible to God [not the state] for his care of his body."[22] Similarly, the War on Poverty was immoral because of the proverbs of Solomon.[23]

On the other hand, WXUR did carry numerous secular right-wing programs, where political arguments were not justified on biblical grounds. These programs were a particular point of contention in the Intervenors' case. In their license application WXUR had pledged three hours per day of news programs. Shortly after they were granted their special one-year license, they started airing numerous right-wing non-religious programs such as the *Dan Smoot Report*, *Manion Forum*, *Life Line*, and the *John Birch Society Report*. These were all programs that had been labeled "Hate Clubs of the Air" in the *Nation* in 1962, and that had even been attacked in the pages of *TV Guide* in 1967. WXUR claimed that they had no choice but to turn to such programming, because as soon as they went on the air local advertisers began a boycott. The objections of local advertisers should not have been a problem for such shows, since many brought along their own national sponsors (e.g., D. B. Lewis and *Dan Smoot*, HLH Products and *Life Line*). In any case, WXUR could never effectively prove that they were being boycotted. For example, they claimed that the Towne Restaurant, where Carl Mau hosted his live show, cancelled its sponsorship to avoid controversy. But the opposition said the Towne cancelled because a right-wing war veteran threw a steak knife at a pacifist who was on Mau's program. In any case, the FCC wisely noted that WXUR began broadcasting the Hate Club shows only a few days after McIntire took over, presumably too soon to feel the effects of a boycott.

In addition to claiming that they were responding to a boycott, WXUR's management justified its broadcasting of the Hate Clubs by insisting that they were *news* shows. When the Intervenors and the Broadcast Bureau said the station had lied by not providing exactly the programming it had promised, WXUR countered that they had promised three hours a day of news, but that they were providing *even more* with all of their "informational" programming focused on topics such as the dangers of foreign aid, civil rights, Social Security, and the UN. How could WXUR get "the death penalty," Irion asked in his sympathetic final hearing report, for, in effect, providing *too much news to the public*? Neither the Intervenors' nor the Broadcast Bureau's lawyers ever addressed the possibility that the Hate Clubs really were news shows. Instead, they simply said that the programs had not been listed in WXUR's license application, and that the programs presented only one side of controversial issues and therefore violated the Fairness Doctrine. This was absolutely accurate, and WXUR had further blundered in informing the hosts of the shows that it was *they* who were responsible for contacting people who had been attacked and offering them free rebuttal time. Contacting attacked people was legally WXUR's responsibility. The costs of monitoring programming were too high, though, and this is why the Fairness Doctrine finally succeeded in putting small right-wing radio stations out of business.

What is particularly interesting here is not simply that WXUR was really guilty as charged for not properly following Fairness Doctrine rules, but rather that the liberals attacking WXUR were unable to understand the fundamentalist belief that the Hate Clubs actually were news shows— biased, certainly, but still reportage of current events. From a cold war liberal perspective, appropriate news gave balanced perspectives on issues, never from a Far Right or Left perspective. So these putative informational programs about world events were not "news." Indeed, in discussing WXUR's personal attacks in their final report repudiating their own hearing commissioner, Irion, the FCC noted that "none [of the attacks] were on bona fide newscasts, bona fide news interviews, or on-the-spot coverage of bona fide news events."[24] This was an important point, because if the Hate Clubs had been "bona fide" news shows, WXUR would not have even been obligated to comply with personal-attack rules. But the FCC simply rejected the programs as phony news.

From the ultraconservative point of view, though, it was the mainstream news that was actually horribly biased and slanted. The radio extremists were interested in covering stories rejected by the network news shows, or in making new interpretations of stories that the networks had interpreted in their own "definitive" way. Anyone to the left of Barry Goldwater would probably agree that the Hate Clubs got their news interpretations horribly wrong. On the other hand, the right-wing extremists were arguing a reasonable point: the news pretended to be neutral, but actually gave only very narrowly defined "diverse" views on issues. The mainstream news of the 1960s typically omitted perspectives of both the Far Right and the Far Left, but, as the FCC explained, McIntire's station went further than this: "Broadcasters on WXUR repeatedly took the position that the major news media in this country are communist propaganda outlets."[25] Leftist communist extremists like Walter Cronkite, in this paranoid worldview, dominated the news media.

Interestingly, McIntire did have one voice of the Far Left on his radio station. Martin Burak, an avowed socialist and agnostic, had a commentary show called *Radio Free Philadelphia*. Burak readily proclaimed himself a genius, and he was introduced at the beginning of each program as "Radio's Boy Wonder Fool." Burak was an eccentric personality, to say the least, and the Broadcast Bureau argued that his presence did not constitute a genuine attempt on WXUR's part to present contrasting points of view on controversial issues of public importance. McIntire did not understand: if the problem was that he was a "right-winger," he thought he had offered balance by hiring a "left-winger." Clearly, though, this was not what the FCC meant by "balance." Balance meant an even-handed, overall mix of liberal and conservative perspectives, not a seesaw of extremism from show to show. Hearing examiner Irion, however, understood why WXUR imagined Burak as an evil twin to its own worldview: "Just as Dr. McIntire placed all his ideas in the frame of reference of the Bible, Burak related everything to his faith in the superiority of socialism over capitalism."[26] The fundamentalist Christian McIntire had tried to satisfy the FCC by putting a fundamentalist socialist on the air. Only Irion understood that McIntire could not perceive any middle ground between right- and left-wing extremism.

Though Irion was clearly incompetent when it came to interpreting FCC policy (and the law in general), he was the only person involved in the WXUR case who seemed able to comprehend McIntire's fundamentalist perspective. Irion thus showed great sympathy for WXUR in his final hearing report, recommending license renewal. In a highly unusual move, the FCC overturned its own examiner's recommendation, savaging Irion's account in particular for its literary pretensions. In the introduction to his 116-page initial decision, in which he recommended license renewal, Irion candidly acknowledged the narrative dimensions of the case. "The story to be told has what may be described without exaggeration as possessing epic proportions," he awkwardly declared.[27] WXUR's story, he further explained, "is one of fitful efforts and frequent frustrations but it is not wholly lacking in moments of courage and even humor. It presents a spectacle which must be painted on a vast canvas so that each detail can be seen against the whole. Inasmuch as the actors will appear and reappear in different context, it will be a service to those who wish to understand the case to begin with a recitation of the station's history and to identify the actors as they perform in the drama."[28] If this language was not enough to set the FCC commissioners' teeth on edge, a few pages later Irion observed that "while it is not customary for an opinion of this sort to indulge in the nature of personalities, a complete understanding of WXUR and all it stands for . . . could not be obtained without some insight into the individuals involved. There will be and, indeed, must be considerable restraint in such a diversion, but vignettes will be drawn of the major figures."[29] "Vignettes"? This is not the standard language of FCC documents, and the commissioners skewered Irion for the fanciful literary language he used throughout his report.[30]

In the Broadcast Bureau's report of its "exceptions" to Irion's final report in favor of WXUR, Irion was found incompetent in every way for misinterpreting or ignoring various facts of the case, and his understanding of the case as a narrative with characters was singled out in particular as evidence of his incompetence. In its final decision overturning Irion's recommendation for renewal, the FCC itself also noted Irion's errors, observing dryly that "the Examiner neither tied his view that WXUR had put on all shades of the political spectrum to the station's treatment of particular controversial issues nor made a distinction between the pre- and post-renewal date programming," the latter point being particularly relevant, because many of WXUR's attempts to satisfy the FCC came *after* the Intervenors brought their case against the station—too late, from the FCC's perspective.[31] Though it is clear that Irion was incompetent when it came to interpreting much of the evidence before him, he was willing to consider the nuances of character, to think through the nature of the fundamentalist worldview, and to identify the moments of humor in the case. He even wondered about the nature of political conservatism, noting that philosophical and popular conservatism were not the same thing: "[T]he Ku Klux Klan (and Livezey had favorable views about this [group]) is popularly conceived of as a conservative group but the Klan has no more relation to the philosophical conservatism of Edmund Burke or his modern apologist, Russell Kirk, than Marxist socialism has to the 'liberal' tenets of Jefferson or Lord Acton."[32]

Unlike both the FCC and Carl McIntire, Irion did not think in absolut-
ist, black-and-white terms. Throughout the trial, he frequently seemed
like the only one in the room who actually understood the nature of the
collision between secular liberalism and fundamentalist conservatism.
But the FCC needed a hearing examiner who could make a sound legal
decision, not a sociologist with a keen sense of drama and a florid sense
of prose. The FCC demanded an objective ruling against McIntire, not
one "telling a story . . . in which there are various heroes," with a "happy
ending" in which the station's license was renewed.[33] The kind of ruling
the FCC demanded would not address, as Irion did, what fundamentalists thought of the King James Version of the Bible, why McIntire and his
compatriots could not understand that ideas they thought were purely religious would be seen as political by nonfundamentalists, or how the KKK
differed philosophically from Edmund Burke.

The Broadcast Bureau lawyers had seemingly produced just such a
"neutral" document in their own proposed findings report, but WXUR
begged to differ, complaining that the bureau had the right to be offended
by examiner Irion's style, but that "it is *not* its right or privilege to falsely
accuse the Examiner, because of his occasional use of colorful expressions,
of having corrupted his quasi-judicial role in order to aggrandize himself
in the literary world. The bureau itself appears to have been intent upon
developing a 'plot' for a story by tailoring the facts of record to meet the
needs of the plot and to support a tragic rather than a happy conclusion."
In the bureau's report, WXUR's defense contended, each event "was made
to sound like WXUR villainy, and each WXUR character was made to
look like a villain," and, though the bureau had avoided colorful language
and adopted a more neutral-sounding style, it had, WXUR complained,
even "without such literary expression succeeded in writing a fairy tale
with WXUR 'monsters' as its characters."[34] WXUR claimed, in other
words, that it was Irion's more fanciful, literary account that was actually
nonfiction, and that it was the objective-sounding Broadcast Bureau's account that was fictitious. Though the bureau's account was not pure fiction
by any means, it is true that Irion's account—though *completely* unaccept-
able from the legal angle, and, I would add, rightfully overturned—was
the one that more accurately understood the fundamentalist perspective.

In Irion's view, WXUR was more incompetent than malevolent. The
station's management certainly ignored or misunderstood the Fairness
Doctrine and personal-attack protocols, shunting off duties onto individual announcers that were actually the duty of the station itself. The
owners and operators of WXUR simply weren't very good businessmen.

According to Irion's report, at one point the liberal Institute for American Democracy (IAD) made a tape to respond to right-wing radio attacks, and the tape was to be bicycled according to IAD instructions. "Bicycling" is a common radio industry term for quickly shuttling a single tape from station to station, but Pastor Bob, who clearly knew nothing about the business of broadcasting, took deep offense to the word and absurdly attacked it on his show as "plainly and disgustingly sarcastic, rude, discourteous, insolent, arrogant, bigoted, and intolerant. Such low expressions are not much above barbarism."[35] This was hardly a professional response. Similarly unprofessional, the absent-minded general manager Norris, when asked about important correspondence or documents, would typically reply that he wasn't sure whether it could be found at WXUR, at WGBC (his other radio station), or in the trunk of his car. Norris seemed more scatterbrained than defensive in his testimony. Indeed, if he occasionally squirmed in his seat on the witness stand, this could be chalked up not to anxiety but to an unnamed health problem that prevented him from testifying on several occasions. The Broadcast Bureau's report finally revealed the mystery ailment: hemorrhoids.

There is no doubt that McIntire and the WXUR managers were inept and did not fulfill their Fairness Doctrine obligations; there is also no doubt that on numerous occasions they actually did try very hard to satisfy the doctrine. McIntire in particular invited practically everyone he attacked, from Lyndon B. Johnson down, onto his show. Invitations to Gus Hall, U Thant (secretary general of the United Nations), vice president Hubert Humphrey, and the US Post Office were routinely denied or ignored. No one, it seems, wanted to engage in an argument with a bitter fundamentalist on a Podunk radio station in Pennsylvania. FCC commissioner Henry Hyde went so far as to tell McIntire that he would not come on the show to rebut comments about the Fairness Doctrine because it was *not* a "controversial issue of public importance"—a patently ludicrous contention. Unfortunately for WXUR, this meant that fundamentalist views could not exist on the airwaves, because if opponents refused to make rebuttals, there could be no "balance" and no possibility of satisfying the doctrine. When it finally denied WXUR's license renewal, the FCC contended that people declined WXUR's invitations to rebut personal attacks because they did not feel comfortable appearing on the station. It was not *their* fault for declining but rather WXUR's fault that it did not provide a more hospitable climate. Irion's attitude, conversely, was that invitees needed to have thicker skins.

Admittedly, it would be hard to imagine anyone with a skin thick enough to deflect some of the rapiers and Stone Age axes of WXUR commentators. For example, the infamously anti-Semitic and phony *Protocols of the Learned Elders of Zion* was cited repeatedly on WXUR, and Norris didn't understand why anyone thought it was anti-Semitic to discuss this "historical" document: "After all a study of the incest and murderous tendencies of numerous former royal personages of England is not considered to be anti-British."[36] In a letter to WXUR's station manager, Norris exhibited irritation with the Anti-Defamation League of B'nai B'rith's refusal to appear on the air and, incredibly, offered this solution to B'nai B'rith's complaints about WXUR's anti-Semitism:

> Mr. Gaber [B'nai B'rith regional director] is *not* so ignorant, that he does not fully understand that there is one universally accepted and positive method that will absolutely, completely, and for all time: defame, stigmatize, discredit, and forever destroy any effectiveness of the "Protocols of the Learned Elders of Zion" if they are indeed, as he pleads, a forgery. Neither Mr. Gaber, nor any other of the many who have cried "forgery" through these many, many years, has been willing to exterminate and obliterate the so-called "forgery" by submitting the GENUINE article.[37]

Norris was seriously contending that the way to debunk the *Protocols* as forgery was by producing the real anti-Semitic documents. No wonder Gaber was reluctant to appear. Norris's insistence that "no one can be a follower of Jesus Christ, and be at the same time, Anti-Semetic [*sic*]" was hardly convincing, even though McIntire himself had clearly stated on the air that he understood the *Protocols* to be fraudulent.[38]

Still, WXUR was *trying* to have the right people on the air. There was not much they could do if they had already repulsed their invitees to such an extent that they refused to engage in debate. As WXUR's lawyer Cottone asserted in his oral closing arguments, "It was quite clear that whether you believe there was an economic boycott here, that we were being subjected to an ideological boycott. There were nineteen Intervenor organizations. They were invited time after time. They refused."[39] The FCC countered that McIntire's invitations were not sincere; he read his invitations over the air mainly to publicize his own cause and boost his ratings. The FCC implied that he knew his invitations would be ignored. My own reading is that McIntire really did want his invitations to be accepted. He was itching to fight with liberals on the air. When he was rejected, it simply reinforced his paranoia.

But, to paraphrase Woody Allen, just because McIntire was paranoid doesn't mean the liberals weren't out to get him, for, if there is no doubt that WXUR was incompetently run and flagrantly disrespectful of FCC requirements, there is also no doubt that the station was targeted because many members of the local Philadelphia community found speech expressed on WXUR offensive and therefore wanted it censored. The doctrine had been designed to enforce diversity of opinion, but as lawyers Thomas G. Krattenmaker and L. A. Powe Jr. write, "prior to his purchase of WXUR, McIntire's type of voice was unavailable in Philadelphia and it became so again after the FCC ruled adversely to him. Denying WXUR renewal thus served none of the affirmative purposes of the Fairness Doctrine while in fact reducing both the amount of controversy and the range of available opinion on the air."[40] Krattenmaker and Powe's argument is troubling in its elision of the fact that the "type of voice" featured on WXUR was often racist and anti-Semitic. At the same time, though, the authors are correct to conclude that eliminating McIntire's voice reduced the range of opinion on the air, and, I would add, eliminated a fundamentalist voice in an area where religious broadcasting was dominated by mainline Protestant voices. McIntire was correct when he asserted so vociferously that the doctrine infringed upon free speech. His case forced examination of competing speech interests, and the fundamentalist radio audience lost to the majority, who found fundamentalist speech repugnant. Any serious examination of American media and legal history, then, must consider McIntire's case as an example of censorship in the name of fairness.

In fact, as CBS newsman Fred Friendly has documented, the DNC used the doctrine throughout the 1960s to limit the speech of the radical Right and drive financially unstable stations off the air. In 1964, the DNC claimed 1,700 hours of free response time from stations carrying right-wingers like McIntire who attacked Democratic policies. A DNC report explained that "most of the stations are 'small rural stations . . . in desperate need of broadcast revenues . . . Were our efforts to be continued on a year-round basis, we would find that many of these stations would consider the broadcasts of these programs bothersome and burdensome (especially if they are ultimately required to give us free time) and [they] would start dropping the programs from their broadcast schedules.' "[41] McIntire was undoubtedly eccentric. He held a UFO conference in 1975, he dreamed of creating a Vietnam theme park in Florida, and he thought that Nixon, Kissinger, and Billy Graham were hopelessly liberal and soft on communism. But his contention that he was under liberal attack was not simply boilerplate paranoia. The DNC was indeed using the Fairness Doctrine specifically to eliminate right-wing speech. After an excerpt of Friendly's book was published in the *New York Times Magazine*, McIntire released a supplement to his *Christian Beacon* entitled "What's Fair on the Air?" in which he reproduced Friendly's article. The cover of the supplement pictured the Fairness Doctrine as a looming Frankenstein monster (figure 29). Friendly's piece was published in 1975, a full two years after WXUR had been shut down, and offered McIntire vindication for the conspiracy he had been claiming for years. For once, he made no complaints that the *New York Times* was nothing but a tool of the liberals.

Throughout the long hearing, McIntire's loyal listeners had deluged the FCC with complaint letters, all assuming that the FCC's action against McIntire had nothing to do with the Fairness Doctrine and everything to do with a liberal (communist) attack on fundamentalism. Though the FCC did build its case on Fairness Doctrine violations—and was hardly a bastion of communism—McIntire's followers were on to something insofar as FCC Fairness Doctrine violations at the time were disproportionately weighted against right-wing fundamentalist speech. This was perfectly "fair" insofar as one-sided, right-wing diatribes were, from a legal standpoint, a misuse of the limited broadcast spectrum. One can certainly understand the anger of the citizens who took their complaints to the FCC (for, indeed, the FCC's actions against WXUR really were a result of Philadelphia citizens' complaints, not simply a DNC and/or Nixon conspiracy). Letters written to the FCC by McIntire's opponents take particular offense at the station's anti-Semitism, and a number of the writers identify themselves as Jews and draw parallels between McIntire's station and Hitler's propaganda machine. Many local listeners, in sum, took deep personal offense at the bigotry they heard on the station, and part of the FCC's mandate was to make sure that local listeners were properly served by radio.

But this ultimately meant that the needs of fundamentalist local listeners didn't count. The Broadcast Bureau reported that the voices of WXUR used the station as "their *personal* propaganda vehicle to advance their sectarian and political views . . . The needs and interests of the community and the various groups which make up the community were generally totally ignored."[42] It did appear that fundamentalists—who, the WXUR controversy seemed to be proving, were intolerant, bad citizens—were not considered part of the community. Their radio listening needs were not addressed on other area stations targeting the "general" community,

The Sunday magazine feature of the New York Times by Fred W. Friendly is an atomic bomb. It shows the conspiracy inside the Kennedy Administration to get at "right wing" extremists. It was a plot, clear and simple. The same thing also continued into the Nixon Administration, and the plot against Station WXUR was a continuation of the action against Station WGCB. The article is photographically reproduced.

FIGURE 29. After an excerpt from CBS newsman Fred Friendly's anti–Fairness Doctrine book was published in the *New York Magazine*, in 1975, McIntire released a supplement to his *Christian Beacon* in which he reproduced Friendly's article, with this new illustration. *Christian Beacon*, 1975.

and WXUR, the only station to address their needs, was faulted for exclusively addressing their needs. McIntire's loyal listeners seemed ensnared in a Catch-22. Strangely enough, letters written to the FCC by McIntire's distraught supporters are often as touching as those from his distraught detractors. None that I've read spew vitriolic racism or anti-Semitism, though they are not lacking in more subtle racism. (Nor are the liberal letters—some include complaints that WXUR was dangerous because it was upsetting Negroes, and surely violence would erupt if WXUR didn't stop.) Most supporters begged the FCC not to take away the only patriotic Christian radio station available in the area. One writer goes so far as to declare, "an anti-Semitic station does not broadcast truth. Station WXUR broadcasts truth."[43] And several bemoan the modern tunes ("crazy jazz and beatle [sic] music") dominant on other radio channels, expressing not so much right-wing bigotry as anxiety about the counterculture and the Generation Gap.[44]

Though the FCC claimed that WXUR did not properly gauge community tastes, it was clear that the station did serve a small, underserved part of the community.[45] The Philadelphia Council of Churches, which was in charge of parceling out religious programs to some sixty stations in the area for its member churches, was made up exclusively of liberal or moderate Protestant groups.[46] The council, in effect, made sure that there was a moderate Protestant monopoly on the area's airwaves. Without WXUR, there would be no radio programming available presenting fundamentalist perspectives on religion and politics.

After the FCC overturned Irion's opinion, McIntire immediately went to the courts to challenge the legality of the FCC's decision against renewing his license. The District of Columbia Circuit Court ultimately ruled that the denial of McIntire's license was legitimate—not specifically because McIntire had violated the Fairness Doctrine but more generally because he had misrepresented his programming plans in his initial license-transfer application. The 1972 *Brandywine* ruling explained that the owners of WXUR, "with their hearts bent toward deliberate and premeditated deception, cannot be said to have dealt fairly with the Commission or the people in the Philadelphia area. Their statements constitute a series of heinous misrepresentations."[47] McIntire appealed the circuit court's verdict to the Supreme Court, which declined to review the case in 1973. McIntire, then, suffered a double defeat: he not only lost his license, but he also never got his day in the Supreme Court to fight the Fairness Doctrine. This provided ample fuel for his already exaggerated persecution anxieties, and he continued to produce and distribute *Twentieth Century Reformation Hour*, giving much of his airtime over to attacks on the FCC. But the number of stations that would broadcast the show dwindled rapidly under the threat (real or imagined) of Fairness Doctrine enforcement.

Having finally lost his license in 1973 after eight years of legal wrangling, McIntire came up with a new plan to spread his message through the ether. He purchased a World War II minesweeping ship, which he set up three miles off of the New Jersey coast in international waters. (Journalists were eager to observe that he seemed to be modeling himself after British pirate-radio operators—hippie kids who had done the same thing a few years before when the BBC was too stuffy to broadcast rock and roll.)[48] Before hopping a jetty to the ship, McIntire posed for journalists wearing a pirate hat and an eye patch. WXUR had been a five-hundred-watt station. The pirate-radio ship was a ten-thousand-watt station, which, McIntire claimed, his engineers would operate without interfering with other broadcasters. But stations in Delaware and New Jersey were immediately affected by McIntire's broadcasts; even a station two thousand miles away in Salt Lake City reported interference. After less than an hour on the air, the floating station was shut down by the FCC.

\* \* \*

Before dying in 2002 at the age of ninety-five, McIntire must have taken some satisfaction in the late twentieth-century renaissance—à la Rush Limbaugh, Sean Hannity, Bill O'Reilly, and Fox News in general—of right-wing broadcasting, a renaissance directly enabled by the Reagan FCC's suspension of the doctrine in 1987. The networks had argued that they were hamstrung by the doctrine, but its demise seemed to enable the Right more than the mainstream. Still, the doctrine had been a headache for the Big Three. Skilled professional broadcasters felt that they could discern what constituted responsible, balanced reporting on their own, without the interference of government agencies or pesky activist groups. And while they complained most loudly about the doctrine's possible effects on news coverage, also of great concern was the FCC's ruling in 1967 that the doctrine applied to cigarette ads.[49] If anyone could claim "equal time" to rebut advertisements, the very economic foundation of American broadcasting was in danger. So the network suits were probably almost as disappointed as McIntire when the Supreme Court declined to review his case; they wanted the doctrine eliminated as badly as he did.

Communications scholar Patricia Aufderheide has argued that, although the networks claimed that the doctrine had a chilling effect on
speech, suspending the doctrine did not induce the anticipated thaw. To
some extent, she is right. Certainly, investigative TV and radio reporting
did not suddenly become more politically hard-hitting after 1987. Aufderheide contacted seventeen stations that had participated in the National
Association of Broadcasters' 1985 filing against the doctrine and asked
each to provide a single example of recent controversial programming that
it would not have aired when the doctrine existed. Only one broadcaster
was able to come up with an example. Another noted that his programs
had not changed but that "we do have less concern now that we'll have to
pay money for the kind of frivolous complaint[s]" suffered in the past.[50]
For this broadcaster, and presumably others, the doctrine was an insult
more to the wallet than to free speech.

Since Aufderheide published her findings in 1990, TV news has become
increasingly entertainment driven, taking on a definite advertorial quality.
*Dateline: NBC*, for example, "devoted five hours of programming to the
season finale of *The Apprentice* and series finales of *Friends* and *Frasier*
during the May 2004 sweeps."[51] If this is now what constitutes "news,"
then the question of balancing controversial points of view is simply not
at issue. We certainly cannot blame the demise of the Fairness Doctrine
for the rise of ratings-driven news and the decline of hard reporting. After
all, the doctrine disappeared just as cable began to spread and as the entire communications industry was deregulated, enabling many programming changes. The Reagan FCC may have been responsible for the rise
of Limbaugh, but it was also responsible for the rise of the infomercial,
not to mention toy-based kids' shows like *He-Man and the Masters of the
Universe* (syndicated, 1983–85) and *My Little Pony* (syndicated, 1986–87).
If TV news is less hard-hitting than ever, this certainly has much more
to do with the triumph of cable over broadcast and with network news'
struggle to survive than it does with the presence or absence of the Fairness Doctrine. We can, in other words, only point to the demise of the
doctrine as one factor among many to help us understand the current state
of affairs. Even so, it is certain that Limbaugh and other "biased" commentators (not all of them speaking from the Right) could only thrive in
a postdoctrine environment. As radio historian Jesse Walker observes,
"it's clear that the repeal of the Fairness Doctrine actually precipitated a
renaissance of opinionated, controversial speech, in the form of the talk
radio boom."[52]

Liberal activists incensed by O'Reilly and other pundits have fought to have the doctrine reinstated. On the Right, conversely, a "marketplace mentality" continues to declare the doctrine an infringement on broadcasters' rights. Neither side is altogether honest in this debate. The Right does not really believe in a truly free market, otherwise it would not try to censor popular and profitable "immoral" media. There is hypocrisy, then, in its rejecting the doctrine on the grounds that it allows for censorship. The Left tells its own misleading stories, claiming that the doctrine was never censorious and that no one ever lost a license over it. With both sides bending facts to make their arguments, it is unlikely that the theoretical debate over the Fairness Doctrine will be settled any time soon. On the practical front, though, it is clear that the free-market forces have emerged victorious.

If *Life Line*, the *Dan Smoot Report*, and other popular extremist shows sank shortly after McIntire lost WXUR, this was only a short-term defeat for the Right. For, as the neoevangelicals mutated into the New Christian Right and Reagan won the White House, the call to eliminate affirmative action, defeat communism, and raze the federal regulatory structure took center stage. The old extremists' language was softened, but many of their underlying ideas were intact in what had become mainstream conservatism. Thus today, in the wake of not only the 1980s deregulation that killed the doctrine but also the conglomeration enabled by the 1996 Telecommunications Act, the FCC has largely dropped its public-interest mandate. We should not let the occasional panic over a "costume malfunction," followed by huge fines and a sudden FCC interest in punishing f-word slipups on live programs, blind us to the much more typical, industry-friendly operations of the FCC.

The FCC has always been industry-friendly. But in the past they also operated with the working assumption that the Fairness Doctrine protected the speech of *nonbroadcasters*—citizens whose ideas deserved representation via a precious medium that they could not directly access. The doctrine's greatest strength was that it was designed to ensure a diversity of expression that is not guaranteed by the free market. From that perspective, McIntire's one-sided broadcasts against minorities were implicitly seen as infringing on those citizens' speech rights; someone on radio had to express their side. In today's climate, it is not listeners but rather Limbaugh and others of his ilk whose speech rights are deemed paramount. Like Limbaugh, McIntire consistently projected a right-wing populist attitude; the doctrine couldn't apply to him, he reasoned, because

he already served the public interest. Or, more precisely, *his* public's interest. Still separatists, and a long way from today's sophisticated Christian
Right, the WXUR fundamentalists were doomed from the moment they
set foot in the FCC hearing room—not, as they thought, because the FCC
simply hated them for being fundamentalists, but because they couldn't
speak in terms comprehensible in a secular legal context.

Today of course, conservative evangelicals (who long ago rejected the
old-fashioned fundamentalist label) are quite adept in the courtroom. In
fact, Pat Robertson has established his own Regent University School of
Law so that there will be more evangelical lawyers—and, more importantly, *judges*—to fight right-wing legal battles. The Reverend Jerry Falwell
likewise created a law school at his Liberty University.[53] Today's conservative evangelicals have learned how to speak a language understood by the
secular world. In fact, they have become particularly skilled at using the
language of identity politics and multiculturalism to make their case, a
rhetorical shift that would have chilled Carl McIntire to the bone. When
evangelical politicos are criticized for their theocratic intentions, they express shock at such bigoted attacks on "people of faith." WXUR, on the
other hand, is emblematic of an earlier period, and McIntire's hopeless
struggle to keep his license thus gives us a picture of what fundamentalist
activism was before the emergence of the New Christian Right.

Clearly, today's Religious Right has adapted pragmatically to use the
language that works. They have learned how to fight for a theocracy based
on their version of biblical principles without actually quoting from the
Bible. Evangelicals reentered politics in the 1980s with the idea in mind
that they could be "in but not of the world."[54] But, of course, as they have
tried to change the world, it has changed them as well. Their expertise
in media spin and public relations, their willingness to manipulate secular media forms like rock and roll and heavy metal, and their increasing
strength in the courtroom all illustrate this new worldliness.[55]

By the time the doctrine was suspended these newfangled, worldly
born-agains already had a strong infrastructure in place on cable and satellite, distribution technologies that were beyond the purview of the doctrine, and there was little practical reason for the Christians even to notice
that the FCC had urged Congress, in 1987, not simply to "suspend" the
doctrine but to eliminate it from the books altogether. The Democratic
Congress retaliated by trying to elevate the doctrine from FCC *policy*
into *law*. President Reagan vetoed the law, and further attempts to bring
back the doctrine were torpedoed by a veto threat from President Bush in

1989. Efforts in 1993 failed, at least in part, because Limbaugh inveighed heavily against reinstatement of what he egomaniacally called the "Hush Rush Law." Later, the Democratic Party called for reinstatement of the doctrine in its 2000 platform. Democrats keep revisiting the doctrine, even as the number of expressive venues continues to expand via digital cable, satellite radio, and the blogosphere. Needless to say, abundance is not the same thing as diversity, and there is no reason to believe that the increase in media outlets simply obviates the need for governmental concern about citizens being fairly served by media. But reexamining media-ownership regulations is a more realistic way to try to address such concerns than reinstating the Fairness Doctrine. Frankly, liberals are starting to look silly for beating this very dead horse.

In any case, once the doctrine was suspended, McIntire's obsessive clipping files on broadcasting tapered off to a small trickle. What was the fun in monitoring broadcasting without the specter of government conspiracy? Over the course of the 1970s, 1980s, and 1990s, as the Republican Party moved ever rightward, and the Christian Right gained power, McIntire persisted in seeing enemies everywhere. He was too dogmatic and obstreperous even to consider collaborating with the New Christian Right. That his Christian Republican "enemies" were fighting against abortion, feminism, gay rights, and evolution did little to temper his vitriol. But with enemies like that, who needed friends?

## CHAPTER FIVE

# Everything Old Is New Again

## *Billy James Hargis, Extremist Tactics,*
## *and the Politics of Image*

Dr. Billy James Hargis, founder of Christian Crusade out of Tulsa . . . arrived in a streamlined, air-conditioned bus with two bedrooms, two baths, a living-room, and a radio-telephone. He stayed long enough to condemn, as the Houston *Chronicle* reported, "communism, liberalism, the National Council of Churches, federal aid to education, Jack Paar, federal medical care for the aged, Ed Sullivan, the recent Kennedy-Khrushchev meeting, Eleanor Roosevelt, disarmament, Steve Allen, and the Freedom Riders."—Willie Morris, *Harper's Magazine*, October 1961[1]

In 1960, a suave, middle-aged man with political aspirations delivered a speech to potential supporters. Though there is no filmic record of the event—only audio recordings—one imagines the standard banquet room full of round tables with cheap floral centerpieces and the classic "rubber chicken" meals typical of such events. There was no time allotted for Q&A afterward; this was a disquisition, not a town hall meeting. The speaker began by expressing anxiety about communist infiltrators and then worried his way through a list of complaints about federal spending. Government payment for medical care was "disguised as humanitarianism." VA hospitals were filled with servicemen suffering from diseases unrelated to their military service. And now there was a dangerous proposal for the federal government to provide health care for the elderly, an inevitable step toward socialized medicine. Social Security, relief programs, and federal aid for education were speedily pushing America down the road to socialism, and the progressive income tax was the handiwork of Karl Marx.[2] These conservative bromides could have been uttered by H. L. Hunt or Dan Smoot. The speech sounded a little bit like Billy James Hargis and

Carl McIntire too, although the Almighty was not invoked. In point of fact, the speaker was not a right-wing broadcaster, although he had been on TV quite a bit. He was a mildly talented movie actor named Ronald Reagan.

Six years later, Reagan was campaigning to become governor of California. He still denounced federal spending, and he came down particularly hard on the War on Poverty, proposing that we could solve the problems of health, education, and poverty "without compulsion." But now Reagan did not evoke the specter of Marx, and he included no anticommunism talking points. Reagan still sounded conservative, but he hit fewer extremist notes: his politics had a different spin, as he consciously used rhetoric to both attract ultraconservative voters and distance himself from the old cold warriors. That labels like "right-wing" were on his mind was clear as he moved toward his concluding comments: "For too long we have been Republicans complete with descriptive adjectives and hyphens before the word Republican. Moderate Republicans, liberal Republicans, conservative Republicans . . . The truth is we've been sucker Republicans. Those adjectives and those hyphens were given to us by our opponents, and the time has come to bundle them up and give them back. If you have to have to hang onto the hyphen, just be a good-[Republican] or a Republican-Republican."[3] In other words, the Grand Old Party wasn't deviating from its course by veering right. The right just happened to be where you were standing if you were a "good Republican." The strategy worked. As historian Lisa McGirr aptly puts it, "Reagan picked up Goldwater's mantle, sheared it of its more menacing elements, and was catapulted into the governor's mansion of the most populous state in the nation."[4]

Reagan knew he needed to create a modicum of distance from Goldwater, but his conservative agenda overlapped with the proposals issuing at the same time from the Far Right. The would-be governor did not want to be linked with either the brazen ultras embodied by Billy James Hargis—a rotund, right-wing anticommunist radio preacher from Oklahoma, who despite his wealth would never shake his low-class image—or the more respectably middle-class ultras of the John Birch Society. In excising paranoid comments about communism and Karl Marx, Reagan conveyed that he was no extremist nut. If Carl McIntire served as a negative example for the neoevangelicals, he and anticommunist fellow travelers such as Hargis and the Birchers also served as negative models for conservatives like Reagan angling for mainstream respectability. All on the Right wanted to raze federal spending. By 1966, if your position was couched strictly in terms of communist conspiracy you risked remaining at the political margins. But if you could make your proposals sound rational and deliver them with conviction but without Sturm und Drang you might, like Reagan, forge a respectable career for yourself.

Hargis and the other cold war ideologues were decidedly not respectable. Hargis disdained higher education and any pretense of "sophistication," declaring that "the wisdom of this world is foolishness with God . . . I think it is ignorant people who are going to save this country."[5] A political consultant today might observe that Hargis had an "image problem." Journalists and authors of books with titles like *Danger on the Right* not only attacked Hargis throughout the 1960s for his opposition to civil rights, the United Nations, and Earl Warren, they also mocked his Southern drawl, criticized him for his affluent lifestyle, and always found an excuse to mention his shaking jowls and "porcine" appearance. Hargis was unmistakably Southern, well appointed, and fat; those who called attention to these facts did so in order to mock him and dismiss him as an ignorant lunatic. But what if we take him seriously? What role did he play in the cold war Right, and what can we learn from his story? How far do the "bawl and jump" preachers of the postwar Old Christian Right really stand from the slick operators of the New Christian Right?[6]

As we will see, Hargis, like Reagan, was engaged in a complicated rhetorical dance. Although he and the other radio and TV ultras would never escape their right-wing extremist image, they learned quickly to speak of property rights and states' rights rather than racial supremacy. They *tried* to solve their image problem, but with little success. The violent white supremacists of "Bombingham," Alabama, had no compunction about publicly referring to "Martin Lucifer King" and "Martin Luther Coon," but a number of the high-profile right-wing broadcasters attempted to bite their tongues. Hargis would freely note that the US was outvoted in the United Nations "by a group of Africans not far advanced from savagery," but he would try—though he was not always successful—to avoid such language in discussing African Americans.[7] For Hargis and other radio/ TV extremists, it was a question not only of futilely staking a claim for a more moderate image in order to gain political power (or at least to gain contributions from listeners and viewers), but also of hoping to avoid Internal Revenue Service harassment and of maintaining their tax-exempt, ostensibly nonpolitical educational and religious organizations.

Today, conservative evangelical political leaders often speak of America's historically "Christian roots" and reference the 1950s as an era of strong religious sentiment and high moral standards. That the loudest politically engaged fundamentalist voices of the cold war years spoke out against the civil rights movement, on hundreds of independent TV and radio stations all over the country, is now seen as something of an embarrassment. Thus, most figures of the Old Christian Right—including the many high-profile radio and TV broadcasters of the 1950s and 1960s—have been conveniently left out of the nostalgic histories spun by the New Christian Right. Only Hargis has found a small place in evangelicals' historical narratives, where he is described as an ardent anticommunist and, more importantly, as a pioneering politically engaged Christian from the years when fundamentalist separatism was more the norm. His opposition to "racial mixing" is less often remembered.

McIntire, as we have seen, was unwilling to temper his extremist discourse. Though an outspoken activist in his own right, he was largely incapable of collaborating politically with other fundamentalists. Therefore, he was unable to make the transition from the Old Christian Right of the 1950s and 1960s to the New Christian Right of the 1970s and 1980s. After losing his radio station, McIntire tried to remain in the public eye, but by the time the Moral Majority came along in 1979, he was just treading water. Hargis too had his share of troubles in the seventies, and by the next decade his Christian Crusade was barely hanging on, as pleas for funds became more and more desperate, and TV and radio outlets declined. Still, Hargis remained a kind of link between the Old Christian Right and the New. His tactics lived on, and his innovations undeniably laid the groundwork for later Christian right-wing political activists, but he was never able to fully move beyond his anticommunist tunnel vision to embrace the causes that fueled the new politically active born-agains: opposition to gays, with roots in Anita Bryant's famous campaign; opposition to women's rights, with powerful woman Phyllis Schlafly at the helm; and opposition to abortion, which would bring about a politically advantageous alliance with conservative Catholics—probably unthinkable for Hargis.

Ultimately, Hargis's legacy is fourfold. First, he was an innovator in direct mail and mechanized and computerized mass mailings focused on specific political issues, and he was an early master of the bathos of fundraising rhetoric. Second—on a related note—he was an innovator in using TV and radio to raise money, and he also sold and rented a wide variety of 16mm films, recordings, filmstrips, and other media. He's remarkable not only as what one might call a prototelevangelist but also as an early version of James Dobson, one of the most successful evangelical mail-order

media distributors in the US. Third, in the 1960s and early 1970s, Hargis
was a major agitator against sex education, a movement that created controversy that drew many conservative Christians into politics, creating a
base (and a mailing list) that could later be tapped into to pursue other
political goals. The sex-ed campaign was part and parcel of his broader
objective of forming coalitions between a variety of right-wing organizations. Given the strong individualist drive of these disparate groups, this
was no mean feat. Hargis was at the forefront of coordinating conservative
efforts in the 1960s, though he was not able to push his efforts to their logical conclusion to create a coherent conservative *movement*. And, finally,
Hargis was particularly adept at masking the racist foundations of his cold
war activism. This makes him a useful figure for contemporary Christian
conservatives, who prefer to ignore the racist elements of cold war fundamentalist activity and claim that racism is no longer a serious issue. Hargis
did not create the Moral Majority, the Christian Coalition, or other organizations of the New Christian Right, yet he remains an interesting historical link between the old cold war Right and the New Right that gained
steam following Goldwater's defeat and reached the boiling point with the
"Reagan Revolution" of the 1980s. An explanation of the post-Goldwater
conservative surge and the complicated relationship between conservatism
and extremism that emerged in these years provides the context we need
to understand Hargis's role as a cold war political player.

*   *   *

Strategic innovators of the New Right such as Paul Weyrich have asserted
that today's leaders bear "no resemblance to the reactionary southern
icons of the past," but researchers insist that links between old and new
are strong.[8] Some historians argue that the links are rhetorical, with careful use of "racially coded language" functioning as the key bridge over
the years, while others, like Kevin Kruse, argue that "the connections
between the Old South and the New Right run much deeper than mere
rhetorical appeals to racism."[9] Kruse specifically argues that we need not
only to examine electoral politics and other "top down explanation[s] of
political transformations" but also to study how the Old Right and New
are linked on the ground—in the case of his research, the literal ground
of city streets: Kruse studies the phenomenon of white flight to the sub-
urbs in the 1960s. Like McGirr, Kruse is interested in the conservative
grassroots. Examination of a figure like Hargis contributes to the ongoing

process of uncovering the linkages between the Old Right and the New, and between the politicians at the top and the grassroots players on the bottom. Hargis was not as powerful or important as an elected politician, yet neither was he a typical conservative "man on the street." He was a politically engaged pundit disseminating his ideas on hundreds of radio and television stations. Hargis was a crafty political operator on the occasions when he ventured beyond raising money for the Christian Crusade, but he never lobbied for office and only occasionally translated talk into action. He thus exists in a grey area between the politicians who drive histories by people like Dan T. Carter and William C. Berman and the engaged citizens studied by Kruse and McGirr.

Historians trace the conservative resurgence of the 1980s back to Goldwater and, of course, to Reagan's entry into California politics in the 1960s.[10] A mere two years after Goldwater's 1964 defeat, "conservatives so dominated Congress that Lyndon Johnson couldn't even get up a majority to appropriate money for rodent control in the slums."[11] But what if we begin the narrative of conservative ascendancy a few years earlier and consider Hargis as a character? After all, the right-wing extremist broadcasters—of whom Hargis was one of the most powerful and shrewd operators—put forth many of the ideological arguments that would come to a head, though in modified form, during the Goldwater campaign.

Many Americans in 1964 feared Goldwater for his "extremism in defense of liberty," and it is disconcerting to consider that he might have represented a tempered conservatism. Certainly, many of the followers of Hargis and other right-wing broadcasters supported Goldwater, recognizing in him some version of their own anticommunist, anti–civil rights beliefs. Yet Goldwater didn't sound like George Wallace or Strom Thurmond. Nor did he sound like Billy James Hargis or Carl McIntire. This was not someone who would go as far as Wallace and declare, "Segregation now, segregation tomorrow, segregation forever." Goldwater ratcheted his language down several notches; he supported the Birchers but not the Ku Klux Klan.

In *Brunch with Barry* (1964), a twenty-five-minute advertisement for Goldwater disguised as a discussion show, Goldwater sat down for a tightly scripted chat with a group of five women and moderator Margaret Chase Smith, Maine's longtime Republican senator. Smith opens by referencing a meeting ten years earlier with Winston Churchill; the prime minister had explained to her how "weakness invites attack." Goldwater observes that before the Second World War Churchill had been called an extremist, but that we now know that "the way to preserve peace is through strength." He further explains how he has consistently supported Social Security and also that we need to send new, better planes to our boys fighting in Vietnam. He also notes his strong opposition to "segregation by compulsion," but argues that "integration by compulsion" is equally bad, begging the question of how segregation could be challenged without legal recourse. From *Brunch with Barry*, Goldwater hoped to emerge as the picture of reasonable conservatism, perhaps just to the right of Eisenhower. Aside from his rejection of compulsory integration, it was a fairly convincing show of non-extremism; Goldwater's praise of "the value of women in politics," his inclusion of a successful corporate lawyer on the panel of women, and his estimation that women were actually more politically informed than men might have even struck some viewers as overtly liberal.

Naturally, a very different image was drawn by the Democratic National Committee's attack ads against the senator. The infamous "daisy ad," in which a little girl pulling the petals off a flower is cut short by nuclear annihilation, was certainly the most notorious of the anti-Goldwater ads. This advertisement depended on emotional impact by implying that Goldwater was a dangerous and unstable man with his finger on the proverbial button. Another less well-known anti-Goldwater advertisement, however, strikes me as much more interesting for going beyond the emotional one-two punch of declaring Goldwater an extremist eager to detonate the bomb in order to focus instead on the psychological repercussions that the candidate was causing among moderate Republicans. Entitled "Confessions of a Republican," this unusually long advertisement, a four-minute dramatic monologue, featured a nervous Republican explaining why he was frightened by Goldwater and felt his party had made a mistake in nominating him. The actor offers a nerve-wracked performance, as the camera slowly pulls in during the ad's single long take. The confessing Republican (brilliantly portrayed by actor William Bogert) stutters a bit, cleans his glasses, lights a cigarette, before finally bringing the spot to its dramatic climax: "When the head of the Ku Klux Klan, when all these *weird* groups come out in favor of the candidate of *my* party, either they're not Republicans or I'm not." Numerous Johnson ads referenced Goldwater's apparent willingness to engage in nuclear warfare and his desire to cut federal programs, but only this ad made the explicit link between Goldwater and the "*weird* groups"—the ultras (figures 30–31).

Like Goldwater, Hargis, McIntire, Hunt, and Smoot all claimed distance from the Klan and other violent groups. They were not "weird"

FIGURES 30–31. An ad for the Johnson campaign opens with a dramatic title, after which a Republican (brilliantly portrayed by William Bogert) reveals his deep anxieties about Senator Goldwater and his appeal to "weird groups" like the Ku Klux Klan. MacDonald & Associates, 1964.

themselves and could hardly be blamed if some of their fans included violent lunatics. As with Goldwater, for the radio and TV ultras "extremist"
was always what someone else was. Hargis, in fact, explained that he was
actually a moderate. The Far Left consisted of fascists, communists, socialists, liberals, and Nazis. These were the forces demanding excessive
government control. The Far Right was embodied by anarchists, who demanded no government. Since Hargis accepted limited government, he
reasoned, he was a moderate.[12] After all, he didn't want to eliminate the
Supreme Court; he simply wanted its current members impeached and the
court's mission redefined so that it would exercise no control over states'
rights.

Goldwater was a candidate who would scare many Americans (he did,
after all, suffer a resounding defeat) but who could also pull conservative
votes both throughout the South and across the suburban Sunbelt. He
appealed strongly to white Southerners, who, in the course of the 1960s,
as Kruse argues, "were forced to abandon their traditional, populist, and
often starkly racist demagoguery and instead craft a new conservatism
predicated on a language of rights, freedoms, and individualism. This
modern conservatism proved to be both subtler and stronger than the
politics that preceded it and helped southern conservatives dominate the
Republican Party and, through it, national politics as well."[13] Goldwater's
platform resonated strongly with both the middle-class, white, conservative suburbanites who would emerge as the core of Nixon's silent majority
a few years later and, at the same time (and in greater number), with those
"weird groups" prone to extremist talk and, sometimes, violent action.

Senator Goldwater and Governor Reagan didn't say no to votes from
the Far Right, but they didn't go out of their way to call attention to the
fact that this was part of their base. And make no mistake about it: this was
quite a base. But it was an embarrassing base. When hardcore Goldwater
booster and segregationist Lester Maddox—a "psycho," the editor of the
*Atlanta Constitution* privately warned LBJ—was elected Georgia governor
in 1966, he certainly tapped many of the same voters whom Goldwater
had drawn two years earlier. How crushing for Maddox, then, when Goldwater publicly referred to him as "a fellow that belongs back in the Stone
Age."[14] Both politicians thought that federally imposed desegregation was
unconstitutional. That Maddox felt this way for explicitly racist reasons
while Goldwater did not was important, but it did not alter their shared
objective of preventing federally legislated integration. Goldwater was not
a psycho, but opposing civil rights for arguably better (or, at least, less

racist) reasons than a psycho did not redeem him in the eyes of those who perceived him as an upscale version of Maddox.

In *America's Right Turn: How Conservatives Used New and Alternative Media to Take Power*, Richard Viguerie explains how conservatives gradually took over America in the years following Goldwater's failed campaign. Who were the "real" conservatives *before* Goldwater? Not racist extremists, Viguerie contends. He groups the cold war anticommunist Right under one umbrella term: they were the grumblers. The most important conservative voice was that of William F. Buckley. Viguerie explains that liberalism reigned supreme in America in 1955, the year that Buckley founded the *National Review*. The grumblers had small-time communications networks of books, magazines, and newspapers, but they couldn't organize a coherent movement. As for broadcasting, for Viguerie it is as if the right-wing broadcasting that thrived all over America—mostly but not exclusively on independent stations—never happened. Viguerie concedes only this: "There were conservative grumblers on the radio—John T. Flynn, Clarence Manion, and Fulton Lewis Jr. come to mind—but they had to pay for their commentary time by obtaining sponsors, usually small businesses. They didn't enjoy the federally granted monopoly of the TV networks, and they had nowhere near the same sized audience."[15]

It's a flimsy narrative at best. Perhaps Hargis did not reach as wide an audience as Walter Cronkite, but he blanketed small broadcasting markets all over America and had a strong presence on the fourth radio network, Mutual.[16] As we saw in chapter 1, Buckley himself appeared on H. L. Hunt's TV panel discussion show *Answers for Americans* in the 1950s, a show that was, like many right-wing programs, shown for *free* in many areas as a "public service" on network TV. In the 1960s, the White Citizens' Council TV and radio programs also saturated the South as free public-service programming on ABC, CBS, and NBC. And, of course, Hunt's *Facts Forum* was also on network TV in the 1950s.

What is really important is not so much the details but rather the big picture: Viguerie, a major figure of the New Right, virtually spins cold war extremists out of existence, claiming that they were victims of the liberal media monopoly and weren't good movement builders. What gets left out is their embarrassing, rabidly anticommunist, anti–civil rights, pro-states'-rights ideology, an ideology that would be presented in a tidier, less extremist-sounding package by Buckley and later conservatives. Hargis was loud and fat and had a Southern accent. He feared "mongrelization of the races" and a federal government that would force integration, both of which would result from communist infiltration. Anticommunist ideas sounded more reasonable delivered with Buckley's patrician accent and in a coded language about individual rights and the evils of tax burdens. This was a style of politics that respectable, middle-class, non–Bible thumpers could get behind. As Buckley himself explained, the objective of the *National Review* was "to articulate a position on world affairs which a conservative candidate can adhere to without fear of intellectual embarrassment or political surrealism."[17] The *Review* would finally explicitly distance itself from the Birch Society's Robert Welch for implicating Eisenhower as a communist. Buckley and Welch were pals, but Buckley could not afford to be linked with Welch's surrealist turn.[18] Still, it took Buckley a few years to concede that not just Welch but also his followers were an embarrassment to respectable conservatism.

Buckley succeeded over the long term because he was smart, wealthy, well organized, and capable of presenting a free-market, anticommunist philosophy in rational-sounding terms. His was not the paranoid style described by Richard Hofstadter. The image differences between Buckley and the ultras can perhaps best be summed up by simply comparing the titles of Buckley and Hargis publications, both on the evils of liberalism in education. Buckley made his name with *God and Man at Yale*; one of the Christian Crusade's biggest hits was an anti-sex-ed screed entitled *Is the School House the Proper Place to Teach Raw Sex?*, authored by Hargis's educational director and relentlessly promoted by Hargis (figure 32).

With such a title, Hargis clearly wanted to push book sales, with no high-class pretensions. Indeed, he sold 250,000 copies of *Raw Sex*, which was both published and distributed by Christian Crusade. "Anytime I fail to ask for an offering" while preaching, he explained, "you'll know I must be sick. And anytime the people don't come up and buy my books after I have finished talking, I know I have failed to put my message across."[19] Hargis certainly knew how to get people to take out their wallets. Though he was successful at selling Christian Crusade books and pamphlets as well as distributing John Birch Society literature and popular right-wing manifestos such as David Noebel's *Communism, Hypnotism, and the Beatles*, where he really excelled was through direct-mail fundraising.

Viguerie, the self-declared "funding father of the conservative movement," has taken much credit for innovating direct mail as a tactic to raise money and mobilize political support. Drawing inspiration from Walter H. Weintz, "direct mail guru for *Reader's Digest*"[20] and author of *The Solid Gold Mailbox*, Viguerie helped raise funds for the 1964 Goldwater cam-

IS THE SCHOOL HOUSE
THE PROPER PLACE
TO TEACH RAW SEX?

50¢

By
DR. GORDON V. DRAKE

CHRISTIAN
CRUSADE
PUBLICATIONS

FIGURE 32. Billy James Hargis used his sensationalist *Raw Sex* book to both attack the California public school sex education curriculum and promote his own organization. Christian Crusade Publications, 1968.

paign and later for Reagan's first presidential campaign and for the Moral Majority. In the sixties, he also raised funds for a number of anticommunist groups, as well as the National Right-to-Work Committee and the National Rifle Association. Renting lists of names and addresses was unheard of when Viguerie started out, and he contends that "although it's true that other conservatives were using direct mail, when it came to broadly funding a mass *movement* through direct mail, I pretty much had the field to myself from 1965 to 1978."[21]

At the exact moment that Viguerie was mobilizing for Goldwater and Young Americans for Freedom, Hargis was also engaged in direct-mail fundraising campaigns. In fact, although Hargis did not weather the long term, being largely politically defunct (plagued by both health problems and a sex scandal) by the time of Reagan's ascent in the 1980s, throughout his prime in the 1960s and '70s he was every bit as successful as Viguerie at raising funds through direct mail and at building up donor lists. If anything, Hargis was *more* successful insofar as he specifically targeted *fundamentalist separatists* and asked them to get involved in politics, even if "getting involved" often only meant writing a check to Hargis.

As we've seen, withdrawal from worldly affairs was a foundational aspect of fundamentalist identity, and thus the most basic self-perceptions of this group were challenged by Hargis's call to mobilization against communism. Jerry Falwell himself had denounced Martin Luther King as a minister inappropriately engaged in politics and declared that "Believing in the Bible as I do, I would find it impossible to stop preaching the pure saving gospel of Jesus Christ and begin doing anything else—including fighting communism or participating in civil rights reform."[22] Though Falwell was prosegregation in his early years, and likely saw King's activities as communist backed, it is interesting that he opposed *any* kind of church involvement in political activity, whether on the anticommunist or procommunist (i.e., civil rights) front. Only twenty years later would Falwell finally give his born-again following a strong push into politics. It's no wonder that Hargis is held up by contemporary Christian activists as a key early innovator. Recall the John Birch Society film discussed earlier, in which the Reverend Tim LaHaye, who would later become a very powerful player in the New Christian Right, explains his decision finally to get involved in politics, clearly aware that Christian viewers might be skeptical of his words. This was the kind of typical resistance that Hargis was fighting against among his fundamentalist brethren. And he used not only fiery radio and TV speeches but also a finely tuned system of direct mail to pull resistant fundamentalists toward worldly engagement.

Hargis was more directly engaged in political action (and *coordination*) than H. L. Hunt and Dan Smoot, but like both of these broadcasters he perceived mass communication itself as a form of activism. Lacking a personal oil fortune or a wealthy benefactor, Hargis's mass communications operation had humble beginnings. He had broadcasts on only three radio stations and was equipped with little more than "some old mailing equipment" when he introduced himself to L. E. (Pete) White, an advertiser who had previously worked for Oral Roberts, a maverick in Christian television.[23] A 1963 study of Hargis explains the ad man's strategy: "'We set up Hargis along the same pattern as Roberts,' White says. From $40,000 worth of commissionable radio-TV time and advertising in the first year, Hargis now has billings of between $400,000 and $500,000."[24]

With White's management muscle behind him, Hargis was now armed to use mass media to reveal the truth about communism and communist infiltration in the US, his primary political objective. Although Christian Crusade direct mailings sometimes pulled for specific policy objectives, more often they made a plea for funds to continue spreading the anti-communist message: "We feel our mission to be God-given: to awaken our fellow citizens to the twin dangers of communism and/or socialism and religious apostasy. We use mass communications (radio, television, publications, campaigns) to awaken the Christian people of America to the dangers within and without our nation."[25] Hargis's job, as he saw it, was to reveal communist plots. Once these secret plots were revealed, their power would be diminished. However, there were always new plots brewing, so fighting the communist threat (and raising money to fight it) was a constant battle.

Though Hargis was first and foremost a broadcaster, he also perceived film as a useful weapon, and the Crusade rented and sold a wide range of audiovisual material. A Christian Crusade pamphlet from the early sixties advertises some seventy 16mm black-and-white films. A series of twenty-six Hargis lectures, each running exactly twelve and a half minutes, included matter-of-fact titles such as *Education, Supreme Court, United Nations, National Council of Churches*, and *Air Force Manual*. These were probably designed with the possibility of TV in mind, as fifteen minutes was, of course, a common length for public-service programs. (The extra two and a half minutes of Hargis's films could have been given over to station identification and ads.) As we've seen in discussing Dan Smoot, local news often ran for fifteen minutes, and a fifteen-minute public-service feature could then fill out the remainder of the half-hour block of time.[26] Hargis also distributed ten 16mm Technicolor cartoons produced by the National Education Program of Harding College. Harding College promoted its free-market philosophies with an animated series entitled "Adventures in Economics," which were drawn in the Disney style; short sections of the films can be spotted in some of Disney's World War II propaganda films. The National Education Program films were probably conceived for school rental, though their address seems crafted to appeal to both children and adults, like Disney's cartoon shorts. Hargis also distributed thirteen films in the "American Adventure" series, from an unknown producer; a small number of "color film strips of Europe, studying social, economic, and political conditions under varying types of the Socialistic Welfare States" in counties such as Norway, Italy, and Germany; and a variety of exposés apparently not produced by Christian Crusade, such as *How Do You Feel?* (on socialized medicine), *The 2 Berlins*, and *Red China—Outlaw*.

It is almost certain that Hargis reaped some financial benefit from distributing others' films, but it is quite remarkable that he did so at all. Hunt, Smoot, and McIntire only distributed their own books, newsletters, audio recordings, and 16mm films, and this was typical of the fiercely individualist right-wing broadcasters of this era. Hargis was only matched by the John Birch Society in the distribution of a wide variety of right-wing media created by others. However, his first priority was his own media. Hargis had airtime on over 227 radio channels and a dozen TV stations in 1962.[27] He was on 400 radio stations by 1963. And, according to his 2004 *New York Times* obituary, at his peak he "broadcast sermons daily or weekly on 500 radio stations and 250 television stations, mainly in the South and in other countries."[28]

In 1972 Hargis made his first venture into *national* network television broadcasting with a Sunday afternoon show called *Billy James Hargis and His All-American Kids*, a program featuring students from his American Crusade College singing religious songs followed by a Q&A session in which the students asked Hargis about contemporary politics. Before this Hargis had run daily radio shows across the country, but his television programs had been aired locally and sporadically using a piecemeal distribution strategy. The possibility of national distribution in 1972 was surely a result of the FCC's 1960 revision of its policy on paid religious programs. The new venture appeared on nearly one hundred television stations, and Hargis sent out urgent letters to constituents asking for help to cover the $50,000 monthly cost of the new TV endeavor. Hargis candidly admitted that the Crusade had been forced to pay for broadcast time upfront and that he had taken out loans to do so. (Whether or not he really took out loans is inconsequential; it is the paying up front that is interesting, since he was used to often doing radio broadcasting on credit—and not always coming through with the money.) What was left out of the desperate letters was a tally of how much money the broadcasts themselves had already raised. In other words, Hargis explained how much the broadcasts cost,

FIGURE 33. Hargis carried his first-person, emotional address over from radio to television, promising "the answer" in exchange for contributions. Christian Crusade, 1979, Columbia University Rare Book and Manuscript Library.

but neglected to mention that every broadcast also included numerous solicitations for funds. By the end of the first thirteen weeks of broadcasting, Hargis did admit, he had received "approximately 50,000 inquiries for free anticommunist and Christian literature" from viewers.[29] This in and of itself made the show worth its weight in gold, because requests for free literature came with return addresses, and those addresses would go right into the Christian Crusade fundraising rolls. Free literature now meant donations later (figure 33).

In his letters to constituents Hargis was amazingly inventive in spinning monumental crises that could only be solved by immediate, large cash contributions. Throughout the 1960s, Hargis opened his letters with "Dear Christian Crusader" or, in a more urgent tone, "Dear Patriots Whose Children and Grandchildren Are Being Threatened by Communism." By the early 1970s, though, Hargis's letters opened by addressing recipients by name, which was not a simple task in an analog era of typewriters and filing cabinets. Like Clarence Manion, who also had a successful radio program and was a driving force behind the Goldwater campaign, in the fifties Hargis likely used "a Robotype machine—a clattering behemoth that could spew forth hundreds of identical copies of a form letter, each with an individual address and salutation that the machine read off a punched tape, player piano-style."[30] By the sixties, he had probably switched to using Addressograph/Scriptomatic metal plates.[31] Moreover, Hargis was one of the very first people in America to use a signature machine to make his letters appear personally signed.[32]

Americans are now so accustomed to receiving "personalized" junk mail that it is hard to believe that there was a time when personally addressed fundraising letters were a rarity. In one letter soliciting funds for the new TV broadcasts, Hargis took his personalization to a new level. After addressing the receiver by name, Hargis explained that "I have asked you for help so often, I honestly hesitate to come to you now . . . Last night at devotional time in our home, Betty and I discussed writing you. We both agreed that we should write to you. After all, we have no one else to whom we can turn for the funds and spiritual strength to carry on this ministry." Hargis went so far as to add, shamelessly, "this letter is only going to my 'inner circle of friends.' "[33] Later fundraising letters would come from Hargis's wife or children, supposedly writing secretly to surprise Hargis for his birthday, or to raise his spirits because of his ongoing struggle with "sugar diabetes."

Hargis was a skillful—if unscrupulous—fundraiser who provided a template for later Christian activists and in particular for televangelists, who, like Hargis, understood the potential impact of direct address via mass media. By addressing people intimately and emotionally and explaining your crisis du jour, you could raise a lot of money. Televangelists Jim and Tammy Faye Bakker embraced this tactic on their PTL network in the 1970s and '80s. As with Hargis's Christian Crusade, though, fundraising became the tail wagging the dog; PTL's broadcasting and real-estate empire became harder and harder to maintain, finally collapsing under the weight of financial and sexual scandals. They had imitated Hargis *too* closely. More savvy broadcasters like James Dobson would learn from both Hargis's victories and his mistakes.

Hargis is not usually listed among the key early innovators in American religious broadcasting. The major figures according to most accounts are Oral Roberts, Rex Humbard, and Billy Graham, and, judging by numbers alone, Hargis was never in a league with the big three. Graham, of course, never had his own regular TV and radio program, but in 1957, William Martin explains, Graham's "real breakthrough" came "when ABC set aside its policy against selling time to religious broadcasters and aired, on seventeen successive Saturday nights, live services from his crusade in Madison Square Garden."[34] Graham aired the crusades nationally throughout the fifties, sixties, and seventies, pulling in respectable ratings. Teaming up with ABC instead of the less prestigious local TV and radio stations more often affiliated with the ultras gave him cultural cachet and helped to mainstream and legitimate his image, and the modern neoevangelical image in general.

Roberts and Humbard were closer to what one would later call televangelists, with their own broadcasting empires, regularly scheduled radio and television programs, and a somewhat déclassé image. In 1971, Humbard's weekly *Cathedral of Tomorrow* was aired on 650 television stations and 700 radio stations.[35] By 1976, *Oral Roberts and You*, with its seven million viewers per week, was "the most watched syndicated religious program in the United States. The show was carried [on] over 349 local and satellite stations, thirteen of which were in Canada and nine overseas."[36] Roberts and Humbard had a lower-class image than Graham, though, and Roberts was controversial (and ridiculed) for his on-air faith healing. Graham had escaped the fundamentalist stigma, but Roberts and Humbard had not. Hargis, too, was rejected by the middle-brow audience, many of whom were offended not just by his politics but also by his patently low-brow image.

Although he was successful with his daily fifteen-minute *Christian Crusade* radio program for years, Hargis never came close to reaching as wide a television audience as Humbard and Roberts did weekly and as Graham did with each of his crusades. Arguably, Hargis was not a "religious broadcaster" at all, insofar as his Christian message was always inextricably bound up in (and often overshadowed by) dramatic anticommunist rhetoric. In the 1950s, though, Hargis seemed briefly to be in a league with Graham. Graham prioritized the old-fashioned message of salvation in his televised crusades, but he also made clear that love of God and country was a crucial strategy for holding the red menace at bay. Graham was vocally anticommunist in the fifties, but by the sixties he had toned down his old cold war emphasis; later commentators have speculated that Hargis never moved into the mass media mainstream like Graham did because he was stuck on anticommunism.

If Hargis was a prototelevangelist, then, he was one with limitations. Hargis was on the bottom floor of religious-political broadcasting and was on the cutting edge when it came to fundraising, but he could not expand his TV and radio empire and catch up with Roberts, Humbard, and other successful on-air preachers. By the early 1980s, it was relative newcomers Pat Robertson and Jerry Falwell who stole the limelight. These were the broadcasters who veered away from the old-time, largely apolitical Gospel message pioneered on radio by preachers like Paul Rader and Charles Fuller[37] and moved toward explicit politicking. Dobson, as well, gained visibility in the 1980s with his self-help radio programs, and plenty of political maneuvering on the side.

To make a long story short, Hargis lost the battle for his own version of right-wing Christian broadcasting; Roberts, Graham, Humbard, and others who stuck to a salvation message (with plenty of music and singing thrown in to entertain) seemed way ahead of him at their peak. But Hargis's approach—politicized religion—was ultimately victorious. In the wake of the collapse of the Fairness Doctrine and the rise of cable and satellite transmission, politically inflected Christian broadcasting was reborn in the 1980s, thriving into the 1990s and the new millennium. Apolitical Christian broadcasting continues to be popular—Joel Osteen's tremendous success is indebted to his feel-good message, not hatemongering—but many viewers and listeners are drawn to more overtly political operators like Robertson who emphasize the dark forces attacking Christians on all sides, and National Religious Broadcasters president Frank Wright is emphatic that "Christian truth" is under constant attack by "calls for diversity and multiculturalism," by hate-crime legislation (supposedly a tactic to silence Christian viewpoints), and, of course, by the looming, hideous threat of a revived Fairness Doctrine.[38] Hargis not only lead the way in fundraising and political coordination in the 1960s (as we will see shortly), he also proved definitively, like the other radio ultras and Father Coughlin years earlier, that positioning God-fearing Christians as victims in a world of soulless enemies worked.

Hargis's wild, overwrought diatribes on Christian victimization and creeping communism attracted more mainstream media coverage than restrained and respectable preaching would have. Indeed, like movie mogul Louis B. Mayer, Hargis seemed to believe that there was no such thing as bad publicity. Hargis initially came to national attention in 1953 with his infamous Bible balloon project. His official biographer, a Cuban American named Dr. Fernando Penabaz, tells Hargis's version of the story in *Crusading Preacher from the West*. First, Hargis wrote to President Eisenhower to inform him of his plan to send thousands of hydrogen balloons over the Iron Curtain with biblical pamphlets and extracts attached to them. He received a "courteous answer" from both the president and the State Department, assuring him that he would receive "support and consideration" from US State Department representatives in West Germany, where the launch was to take place.[39] The State Department in Germany was initially receptive but then waffled. Meanwhile, Hargis consulted with several Radio Free Europe employees, presumably experienced in propaganda dissemination. He also consulted with the General Mills cereal company, which, curiously, had offered Hargis "technical information that would serve to make the launching of the balloons successful. The company had hired meteorologists and engineers of the highest type to test weather conditions, determine the best kind of balloon and locate the best place to carry out the launching successfully." Hargis "had the balloons specially manufactured so they would have a range of from 3,000 to 4,000 miles in favorable winds," and he had his biblical extracts translated into Slovak, Czech, Russian, German, and Polish. The State Department continued to ignore Hargis, and he determined that "the godless communists, the off-springs of the devil, were at the bottom of his trouble." Luckily, "[T]he Lord a long time ago had taught him how to deal with the enemies of truth. Turn the light on and publicize the things they were doing and they would desert their posts and flee . . . [H]e would publicize the whole affair from beginning to end."[40]

By the grace of God, Carl McIntire just happened to be lecturing in Sweden. Ever the publicity maestro, McIntire wired Ike, received no answer, and then flew to Amsterdam and called a press conference. At this point, the State Department back home issued a statement that, actually, no approval or clearance was needed. In other words, as anyone but Hargis would have logically deduced, the whole thing was a bit embarrassing, and it was better to say that Hargis did not need approval than to give or withhold approval. But Hargis's team joyously interpreted the statement as "official permission," and ten thousand balloons were launched.

Where did the balloons land? Who read them? What were the results? No facts whatsoever were forthcoming, but no matter—all could be spun in a positive light: "The impact of the floating Bibles was terrific" because people living in communist countries now knew that they had not been abandoned by the outside world.[41] Furthermore, Penabaz insisted, "the communists rapidly became aware of the harm the Bible Balloon Launchings were doing to their cause."[42] The project continued for four more years, though only one event surfaced showing that the balloons had, theoretically, made an impact. A 1956 revolt in Hungary had failed, Penabaz explained, because the West hadn't lent assistance, but a Hungarian refugee

showed up shortly thereafter in New York with five of Hargis's Bible extracts hidden in the lining of his coat. Thus, the pamphlets had inspired the
Hungarian rebellion.

Hargis no doubt believed that the airborne word of God would inevitably do good, but his only tangible triumph was clear: his venture had
received massive publicity, his name was globally recognized, and his
radio and TV presence would only grow thereafter. Hargis's other publicity
coup occurred in 1960, with the surfacing of an Air Force training manual
that, in discussing communist infiltration, specifically singled out the
National Council of Churches. The author of the manual had gotten the
NCC information from a pamphlet by Hargis. The manual was withdrawn,
the Air Force apologized to the NCC, and Hargis had won by losing again.
The publicity from the scandal far exceeded the impact that the manual
alone could have had if it had not become a news event. Hargis described
the scandal as "the best break we ever got."[43] But this was a onetime event.
Sending balloons over the Iron Curtain, by contrast, could be repeated. In
fact, Hargis was able to use his ongoing balloon project to raise funds for
several years. In both 1955 and 1956 the Crusade received eleven thousand
dollars in donations to be used for balloons, but they only spent five thousand on balloons in 1955 and two thousand in 1956.[44] It is no stretch to say
that, in these years, Hargis's urgent fundraising letters declaring that the
Crusade was teetering on the edge of financial disaster were all hot air.

Though Hargis was a terrific fundraiser, he could never quite keep up
with his bills—which is not to say that he was broke. Christian Crusade
consistently had unpaid debts, but it was not consistently operating at a
deficit. In fact, the organization's tax returns (or, rather, its "returns of
organization exempt from income tax") showed profits of over one million
dollars in 1963, 1964, and 1965.[45] Hargis simply chose not to pay all of his
bills. In one fundraising letter he even admitted that he was behind on
payments to at least forty of the two hundred radio and TV stations playing his daily and weekly broadcasts; he then reasoned that some stations
were starting to cancel him not because of these financial issues but because they were "running scared" from the harassment of local press and
liberal clergymen.[46] However, a 1964 report from Group Research, a liberal organization that monitored the Right from 1962 through the mid-
nineties, noted that "There is disillusionment among the radio clergy
with . . . Hargis, whose Christian Crusade does not include paying past-
due bills for radio time." Dr. E. M. Mortenson, president of the Christian Broadcasting Association of Canton, Ohio, called Hargis "a lowdown

crook." Mortenson had run Hargis's show on his radio station for six months without being paid. When he went to Hargis's offices to complain, "he was sent away with syrupy promises of payment. A few days later Hargis cancelled out."[47]

Part of the problem was that the nature of Hargis's enterprise made it easy to rip stations off. If you buy a car and don't make the payments, it can be repossessed. But if you buy airtime and use it, the messages you've sent out cannot be pulled back. Once Hargis had used the airwaves, there was no incentive to pay except the threat of cancellation. An unscrupulous broadcaster couldn't get away with this on a national network like CBS. In fact, Christian Crusade was required to pay in advance for its broadcasts on Mutual—a struggling network willing to air controversial programs from the Left or the Right to boost ratings. (Although CBS, NBC, and ABC did not accept paid religious programming, Mutual was willing to run Hargis at a reduced "religious rate.")[48] But since right-wing programs ran most often on small independent stations, if you burned one radio station you could move on, and your bad reputation could take a while to catch up with you. Also, Hargis and other less-than-honest religious broadcasters could often depend on a fundamentalist station owner initially to give them the benefit of the doubt. Mortsenson carried Hargis for six months without seeing a dime, he explained, because Hargis "was a man of faith."[49] At the same time, Hargis could exploit his anticommunist credentials for free air time. In 1961, seventy radio stations ran Hargis for free to satisfy the FCC's public-service requirements.[50] Of course, the distribution of free *religious* programs was controlled by the liberal National Council of Churches, but Hargis could push his anticommunist programs as "news" or "public affairs" rather than religion, all the while claiming that his organization was strictly religious when it came time to pay taxes.

Finally, the financial advantage of radio (and, on a smaller scale, TV) for Hargis was that he was constantly raising money on the air. As we've seen with Dan Smoot and H. L. Hunt, by the early 1960s the financial configurations of right-wing broadcasting varied widely. Right-wing programs were either aired as public service, sometimes without ads, or the producers paid the stations to show their programs, and then the producers themselves procured advertising. Smoot found some local sponsors but mainly had his wealthy dog food manufacturer to provide funding, while Hunt advertised his own canned goods, then wrote off much of his broadcasting venture as an advertising expense. Neither solicited funds on air. Hargis,

McIntire, and other fundamentalists, however, were constantly passing the hat. The Crusade's gross receipts in 1952 were about $25,000, but thanks to Hargis's expansion on radio, with Pete White's help, by 1957 gross receipts reached $170,000, and they were up to $595,000 in 1960. By 1963 Hargis was earning a solid $12,000 salary, above and beyond the cars, tour bus, and home that he received for free, in a creative accounting twist, from his own organization.[51] It was all thanks to *Christian Crusade* listeners and viewers. Each broadcast was basically a license to print money.

Hargis's successful fundraising was not simply the result of technological innovation, savvy marketing, and emotional rhetoric. Hargis learned to sell fear to his constituents by honing in on inflammatory political issues. The 1962 American Supreme Court decision against school prayer was a particularly important issue for him. Indeed, the removal of school prayer was a singularly important event that pulled many fundamentalist separatists toward political engagement. Partly in response to the decision, Hargis held a "Conference for the Coordination of Conservative Efforts" in Washington DC. In a press release, Hargis sent an interesting mixed message. First, he argued against the centralization of conservatives into a cohesive movement. He had already met with conservative congressmen in August 1961, and the group had agreed that conservative groups needed to unify their "aim and purpose" and that the leaders of the organizations should hold monthly or quarterly meetings to coordinate their political efforts. The general agreement, however, was that "it would not be in the best interests of conservative forces . . . even to suggest an actual union or amalgamation of anticommunist groups." It was best, Hargis believed, "to have 2,000 individual organizations fighting communism, rather than just one . . . With 2,000 such organizations, if one is rendered ineffective, there are still 1,999 left to carry the message of freedom."[52]

Having argued against *centralization*, Hargis next argued for *coordination*, which was also what Viguerie was pulling for in his use of direct mail to create a coherent conservative movement from the numerous fragmented conservative groups of the 1960s. "I have frankly been told by many," Hargis explained, "that we will never get a working relationship and fellowship of anticommunists because we are all rugged individualists. I do not hold with this viewpoint." He then announced the Coordination of Conservative Efforts conference, which would "be a working meeting, planned to prepare the ground for further periodic sessions with an ever-expanding list of conservative legislators and an ever-increasing list of conservative organizations."[53] This was a dramatic move, because the "rugged individualism" of the hundreds of separate anticommunist organizations was a well-known fact. Conservative activism would later coalesce around the Goldwater campaign, but there was simply no one working as hard as Hargis to get the born-again anticommunists to talk to each other—and to politicians—in the early 1960s. Indeed, while McIntire, in his typical separatist mode, limited his membership to his own organizations (the American Council of Christian Churches and the International Council of Christian Churches), Hargis was an early member of the John Birch Society, Liberty Lobby, We, the People!, and the National Indignation Convention.[54]

The Christian Crusade was a blatantly political organization. Yet in 1961 Hargis shamelessly told a *Nation* journalist that "We, The People! is political. It gives me a chance to do something in the political area. But the Christian Crusade is strictly religious." The *Nation* writer observed that "donations to the Christian Crusade are tax deductible; those to We, the People! are not."[55] We, The People!, a Chicago-based organization of which Hargis was president for several years, was the product of the collaboration of a number of right-wing groups in 1955. Upon its founding, the organization called for the impeachment of the Supreme Court and issued a twenty-one-point program. Without actually mentioning race, the first two points clearly indicate that the group's inspiration came from opposition to civil rights, and specifically the 1954 *Brown v. Board of Education* Supreme Court decision: (1) "Return to the states the rights that have been usurped by the Federal Government" and (2) "Amend the US Constitution, restricting the power of Washington to control interstate commerce." We, The People! met jointly for several years with the National Committee for Economic Freedom, which Group Research identified as "the chief pressure group for abolishing the Federal income tax." Even so, Hargis told a reporter for the Washington *Daily News*, "I have never advocated repeal of income taxes. I know nothing of economics. I'm a radio preacher, fighting liberalism and communism. What we are doing is creating a climate of conservatism."[56] It would be hard to disagree with this last claim, and, further, it is not unlikely that Hargis knew nothing about economics. The first sentence, though, is a bit hard to swallow given Hargis's position as president of We, the People! and its relationship with the National Committee for Economic Freedom. To put it more simply: Hargis was lying. Regardless, Hargis's association with We, The People! raised his public profile and was therefore successful for the Crusade's endless fundraising efforts.

I do believe that the roots of the New Christian Right, which would emerge in the 1970s under the leadership of Paul Weyrich, Jerry Falwell, and others, must be traced at least in part back to Hargis's organizational efforts via We, The People!, his coordination conferences, and his TV, radio, and direct-mail activities ten years earlier. The "rugged individualism" of all the separate groups at that time cannot be understated, and Hargis's efforts to get Christian leaders to overcome their individualist tendencies—especially in his special anticommunism training seminars— were important early steps toward the kinds of group efforts that would culminate in the later rise of the New Christian Right.

The limitation of the training seminars, however, was that they were long on talk and short on action. There are no detailed records of the events, but some flavor is conveyed by surviving reel-to-reel tapes of their featured speeches. At one Hargis seminar, Dr. Frederic Curtis Fowler spoke on the topic "The Prodigal Nation." After one and a half hours of complaining about the Supreme Court, rock and roll, Tito, TV quiz shows, and, of all things, crooners, Fowler finally ended by proposing what he considered to be a concrete course of action:

> Let me close with five definite things we can do. First, let us recognize that we as individuals must demand with united voice that the government—city, state, national—put away deceit and put away cowardice and act with integrity and courage now and hereafter. Second, we must abandon all hope or thought of mending the condition that faces us simply by discussion and conferences— talk, talk, talk! We must witness and act as those responsible and accountable to almighty God. Third, let us press home the claims of Christ for immediate decision . . . Fourth, let us do all that we can to awaken the membership of our churches to their individual responsibility to be God's witnesses. And fifth, lastly but not least, let us pray. Pray continually . . . We must repent, repent. The only safe place for America is on its knees.[57]

It would be arrogant to contend that praying was not a course of action— to Fowler's audience, it was. But these five steps in and of themselves were too vague to translate into direct political *intervention*.[58]

Still, it would be accurate to say that the seminars and the Crusade in general had political *objectives*, and, thus, the Kennedy administration had more than a little legal justification in pursuing the long process (finally successfully concluded in 1972) of repealing the Christian Crusade's 501(c)(3) status. An American 501(c)(3) not-for-profit organization cannot support specific legislation or endorse specific candidates for office. But Hargis's organization was a propaganda machine supporting proposed laws that would have reinstated school prayer, and he was not shy about announcing which congressmen voted "like Christians" and which voted "like communists." The Crusade's most successful political effort was its national campaign against sex education, which began in 1969 and which was successful one year later, when the SIECUS (Sex Information and Education Council of the United States) curriculum was officially dead in the water in California. The SIECUS curriculum spoke frankly about birth control and venereal disease; it was in part a response to the sexual revolution and adult anxieties that kids were "doing their own thing" having received little or no sex education at home.[59] The ultras promptly attacked the creators of the curriculum as communists, "ultra-liberal one-worlders," and promoters of "perversion, adultery, teen-age sex, and premarital sex."[60] Crazy rumors ran rampant, and opponents of the curriculum proclaimed with certainty that liberal sex educators had actually demonstrated the sex act in the classroom. The Crusade began the anti-sex-education campaign on its own but was later joined by the John Birch Society and many other right-wing organizations.[61] Liberal organizations like Group Research pointed specifically to the sex education campaign as proof that the Crusade did not deserve its tax-exempt status.

Hargis's TV and radio broadcasts against sex ed snowballed into a movement that drew many evangelicals into politics, creating a base of supporters that could later be exploited for other political goals. SIECUS's curriculum for the Anaheim public schools was to have been a pilot project for the rest of the nation, so Hargis had accomplished no small task. And, notably, he accomplished this task in California, though his own organization was based in Oklahoma. It is hard to imagine many other fiercely individualistic, regional, and generally paranoid anticommunist groups successfully pursuing political activities so far away from their home bases. Here is where being a broadcaster made Hargis necessarily less insular, for the nature of his anticommunist ministry was to cross state lines, and even, occasionally, national borders. (The balloon venture was, from this perspective, simply a material version of what he had been doing all along with radio and TV.) Right-wing broadcasters tended to be insular in their thinking, yet their voices were far-reaching. Their programs sometimes *felt* local because they were aired on small, non-network stations, yet these stations were scattered all over the United States. Hence, right-wing broadcasting was simultaneously a *national* and a *local* movement. Hargis could ride his personalized tour bus in from Oklahoma to spearhead a California campaign and not seem like an "outsider" because the locals already knew him from radio and TV. If these were "imagined communities," as per Benedict Anderson, they coalesced into something solid, practical, and real every time Hargis made a whistle-stop appearance.

Undoubtedly, the triumph over sex education added to the government's case that Hargis's Crusade was political, not strictly religious. Ever the pragmatist, Hargis was able to use the 1972 revocation of his tax-exempt status as a fundraising tool, since he contended that the Crusade's loss of 501(c)(3) status was nothing short of a tremendous victory! The government was persecuting Christian Crusade, he contended, precisely because the organization was powerful and the feds were afraid of it. If the Crusade hadn't stopped the teaching of raw sex in public schools, there would have been no need for the government conspiracy against the organization.

Ultimately, how effective was the Christian Crusade? Outside of the anti-sex-education campaign, which was a clear victory, it is a difficult question to answer. Hargis didn't measure his on-air success by ratings; he measured it by contributions, and his detailed financial records are unavailable. But his massive organization did stay afloat for a good thirty years solely based on contributions and self-distributed books and films, and it was high profile enough that he was a regular target of liberal watchdog groups fearing the rise of fascism on American soil.[62] Hargis's fundraising letters spoke often of concrete objectives such as coordinating various conservative groups, expanding the number of stations the Crusade broadcast on, sending Crusaders specific lists of ways they could fight communism locally, and training young people in anticommunist leadership seminars. He held a number of such youth seminars over the years, but it's unclear if any of his other plans ever came to fruition. There were no follow-up letters detailing how financial crises had been solved, and if activities listed in previous urgent letters were revisited it was generally in order to ask for even more donations. It is difficult to fully gauge, in other words, how much of Hargis's talk about political organizing was bolstered by real activity and how much of it was just fundraising rhetoric. In fact, it's not even clear if Hargis himself could have discerned the difference between genuine political mobilization and nuts-and-bolts fundraising. There was a certain incoherence in his objectives, notwithstanding the absolute moral certitude he projected. Where the Crusade ultimately succeeded and where it failed will always be a bit fuzzy.

The Crusade did finally succeed in solving its image problem when, years later, the New Right and New Christian Right acknowledged Hargis as an important conservative (not "extremist") political figure. Today's conservative evangelicals generally contend that cold war evangelicals opposed civil rights simply because they felt that religion and politics shouldn't mix. This is certainly how Jerry Falwell repeatedly told the story. But Hargis did not use radio and TV to argue that Christian engagement in politics was wrong. He argued—like McIntire and the other broadcast extremists—that Martin Luther King was a communist (and a "stinking racial agitator")[63] and that desegregation was a horrible and dangerous violation of biblical principles. In fact, opposition to desegregation played some role in virtually *every* political issue that lured fundamentalists back into politics in the fifties and sixties, a fact that was conveniently deleted by many later Christian activists, and by Hargis himself.

In a pamphlet entitled "The Truth about Segregation" Hargis summarized how many fundamentalists felt:

> The entire problem that confronts America today was bred in the pits of communist debauchery and conspiracy . . . Segregation is one of nature's universal laws . . . No-intermingling or cross-breeding with animals of a widely different characteristic takes place except under abnormal or artificial conditions . . . Ancient Israel achieved a mission and accomplished a good which would have been impossible had they abandoned the principle of segregation and became integrated with the nations which hemmed them in on all sides centuries ago . . . It is my conviction that God ordained segregation.[64]

Significantly, Hargis did not use this kind of language consistently. Indeed, several exposés written at the peak of Hargis's popularity note that he had repudiated the "Truth about Segregation" pamphlet.[65] Erling Jorstad quotes Hargis in 1964 as stating, "You can't produce any writings of mine against the Negroes or any minority race." Jorstad also observes that in 1965 when he contacted the Crusade for pamphlets on civil rights he received "The Truth about Segregation."[66] Hargis may have been consciously lying about the availability of his racist writings, but it is equally possible that he simply did not perceive the pamphlet—or the anti–sex ed campaign—as anti-Negro, though clearly both were.

For Hargis, the SIECUS curriculum was part of a communist plot to indoctrinate children in "one-worldism," and miscegenation would be the inevitable result. Sex education would teach kids that sex was all about instinct and therefore it was OK to have sex with *anyone*. Sex education was thus part of the communist-driven civil rights conspiracy, but Hargis didn't always say this in public. He understood the value of cloaked language. For example, Hargis traveled with a film called *Pavlov's Children* (William and Lillian Drake, 1969) to sell his anti-sex-ed campaign. The film's narrator explained the problem with sex ed: "By reducing morality of all to the standards of the most immoral, people will no longer unite behind a shared outlook and religious, ethnic, or racial groups. The next generation will then be ready for homogenization into the faceless masses of an atheistic world tyranny. And unless the forces of evil are checked every mother in America will hold in her arms Pavlov's child."

Interviewed thirty years later about the sex education campaign for a PBS series on the Christian Right, Hargis reveals his political savvy. He doesn't tell viewers that he opposed sex ed because it was bound up in the "mongrelization" of the races that desegregation would produce. Instead, he tells us about the *Raw Sex* book and the road show he did with the book's author, Gordon Drake, to sell both their movement and copies of the book. "I gave [the book] the name, and I put the red country church on [the cover], and I sold one million of them. And then I hit the road with him. And we had two [speaking engagements] a night."[67] Looking back on his accomplishments, Hargis leaves the race issue aside and instead boasts about how he *marketed* opposition to sex education in public schools. His entrepreneurial pragmatism served him well and must have inspired later generations of Christian activists who would, like Hargis, nimbly revise the past and claim that cold war evangelicals opposed political involvement in general, when actually many took a strong political stand (sometimes strictly rhetorical, other times backed up by activist activity) against civil rights. When activists like Falwell and Robertson have told the story of the rise of the New Christian Right, they mention Hargis as an early player, specifically tagging him not as an anti–civil rights fanatic but as an anticommunist hero. Notwithstanding the negative connotations of McCarthyism, the blacklist, and so on, it is a canny move, for what could be more mainstream—perhaps conservative, but certainly not eccentric, marginal, or extremist—than opposing communism during the cold war?

It is probably too simplistic to put it this way, but I do believe that Hargis remains a historical reference point for the New Christian Right, and was a tactical beacon for them, because he was a terrific liar. He was simply shameless. McIntire, the only other fundamentalist cold war broadcaster as politically involved as Hargis, was also a lying scoundrel, but he never obscured his anti–civil rights activities, even if he did claim that such activities were actually "religious" in nature. He never repudiated his opposition to civil rights, or implied that opposing civil rights had been only a minor issue for evangelicals during the cold war. As an unrepentant racist activist of the 1950s and 1960s, then, McIntire could not be acknowledged by the New Christian Right of the 1970s and 1980s. He could not soften extremist rhetoric and give it a phony moderate spin. Hargis had no problem making such concessions to changing times.

In the forefront as a fundraiser and televangelist, Hargis even led the pack when it came to sexual misconduct. In 1974, years before the Jimmy Swaggart and Jim Bakker imbroglios, Hargis was brought down by a sex scandal. As the story has been told repeatedly, a man and woman from his American Christian College in Tulsa, Oklahoma, were married, and on their wedding night each revealed having had a previous sexual partner, none other than Reverend Hargis.[68] Hargis had allegedly coerced sex from a number of his "All American Kids," boys in particular. Hargis was dismissed by the school's board of directors and publicly disgraced. It was a salacious story, often recounted with homophobic overtones by the mainstream press. The part of the story that is less often remembered is the financial side. Hargis only resigned after forcing his trustees to cash in its $72,000 life insurance policy on him and to give him the money. He also secured a $24,000 annual salary. At this point, he finally declared that he was retiring for health reasons, and he absconded with the school's massive list of fundraising addresses.[69] Even at his lowest point Hargis remembered that money was the name of the game; deprived of the names and addresses of donors and potential donors, his indignant trustees would find it in their hearts to forgive him, he wagered. It was a bet that he won: Hargis was soon invited to return to the college. He did, but he did not restore complete access to the precious address lists. By 1977, the American Christian College was shuttered. Hargis had extracted his revenge.

He was back in power, but by the early 1980s his fundraising letters sounded more desperate than ever. He tried to exploit the prophesy craze that Hal Lindsay had sparked with his bestselling *Late Great Planet Earth* by claiming in one letter that changing weather patterns would soon bring pestilence, famine, plague, and finally the end of the world. The new weather was, he explained, "the result of deliberate manipulations by Soviet Russia," for the country had been sending "major weather changing signals . . . into the inosphere [*sic*] since 1978." Throwing in a pinch of anti-Semitism, Hargis exclaimed that "the INTERNATIONAL BANKERS [i.e., Jews] know that this is happening and they intend to capitalize on it."[70] Even for Hargis the weather conspiracy sounded a bit nuts.

In another particularly lunatic missive, Hargis seemed actually to make love to his readers:

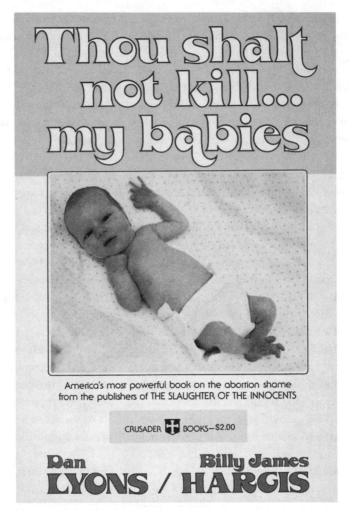

FIGURE 34. Hargis's coauthored antiabortion book was already in its third printing one year before the founding of the Moral Majority. Christian Crusade Publications, 1978.

Last night I sat here in my chair until late in the evening, holding your name and address in my lap. I just kept looking at it and praying for you. I thought to myself that if I had you here in my home I would get up out of this chair, walk over to you and, with tears rolling down my cheeks, throw my arms around you and tell you just how much I love and appreciate you . . . I want to help you so much that I just ache way down deep inside. I really feel this . . . I have to help you wherever you are hurting.[71]

Whether all this long-distance loving actually made checks arrive in the mail is unknown, but it was clear that Hargis was desperate. His real problem was that "the late 1960s and early 1970s witnessed the reorientation of the conservative movement away from its earlier focus on anticommunism,"[72] and what was Billy James Hargis without a communist enemy? Switching targets just wasn't an option for him. But his dreams of getting the rugged individualists coordinated were coming to fruition. Years later, the founders of the New Christian Right would acknowledge that Hargis had started it all with his anticommunist TV and radio shows and his victory over sex education. But in the early eighties, as the new-fangled activists fought abortion (and were probably eyeing Hargis's mailing lists hungrily), Hargis simply couldn't fit in.

Interestingly, he did seem to have cannily spotted abortion as an issue for born-agains early on. In 1978, one year before the founding of the Moral Majority, his coauthored antiabortion book was already in its third printing (figure 34). Hargis had founded a group called Americans Against Abortion ten years earlier, he explains in the book's preface, in order to both spread information (via books, films, pamphlets, and TV) about the evil of abortion, and to get people praying for passage of anti-abortion legislation. Predictably enough, Hargis next informs readers that the organization just can't keep going if it doesn't receive more contributions, and he invites readers to buy more copies of the book. If he had figured out how to *mobilize* people around the abortion issue, perhaps he could have been a major player in the 1980s. But he had merely seized upon abortion as a fundraising tactic. It was classic Hargis.

\*   \*   \*

Billy James Hargis, like H. L. Hunt, Dan Smoot, and Carl McIntire, did not leave behind an organization that could continue without him. He created no enduring think tanks and elected no one to office. In many ways, he is a dinosaur, an example of the old-school approach to melding fiery preaching and fiery political discourse. But his approach to political machinations is not altogether extinct. After all, the Christian Coalition also pretended not to be a political organization and was also wounded by the loss of its 501(c)(3) status. Further, its formerly indestructible leader

Ralph Reed, who was hired by Coalition founder Pat Robertson explicitly in order to soften the image of the organization and make it more appealing to the mainstream, has suffered from his own political indiscretions. Robertson himself attempted to convey a moderate image of himself in the mainstream media when he ran for president in 1988, but on his own *700 Club* TV program he advocated theocracy and "characterized the separation of church and state as an 'atheistic communist' ideal."[73] Anyone with a cable subscription and a remote control could see that the "mainstream" image Robertson tried to project when appearing on a network outlet was as phony as a three-dollar bill.

If Robertson is the contemporary figure who comes closest to mirroring Hargis's failures, we might point to James Dobson's Focus on the Family as a successful version of the Crusade. Focus has replaced opposition to communism with opposition to "antifamily" special interest groups— gays, lesbians, feminists, prochoice people, and liberals in general. The group has maintained its tax exemption for many years and, like Hargis, has had huge success on radio and has made a fortune from distributing books, films (on VHS and DVD instead of 16mm), and audio recordings (with cassettes and CDs replacing Hargis's records).[74] Dobson is a cannier operator than Hargis, though. He's not a *preacher* but rather a Christian *psychologist*, and he uses self-help rhetoric instead of the old "bawl and jump" strategy. He's a Christian Dr. Phil offering conservative lifestyle advice in a folksy, commonsensical manner. Dobson was a player in the Reagan years (serving on Edwin Meese's antipornography commission) and in the George W. Bush White House. In fact, he has had the ear of Republican presidential candidates since Reagan was first elected because he can rally a large constituency of conservative Christian voters. Dobson— head of Focus until 2005—has in the past been willing to bend his message to make it appear more moderate. Until 1991, Focus advocated for theocracy in its Community Impact seminars, but since then it has pushed instead for a return to the nation's "cultural heritage of religious values."[75] Religious pluralism is a "sociological fact" that Christians must respect, Focus maintains, though profamily lifestyles are the only "natural" way to live.[76] This is a deliberate attempt to distance Focus from its earlier, more extremist rhetoric, while ultimately pulling for the same policy changes.

Further, Dobson maintains like many in today's Christian Right that racism is no longer a social problem; it is an individual problem. People who have suffered under racism can be "healed" by forgiving the racists and finding inner peace, because (as Reed used to say) "American has a sin problem, not a skin problem." Following this logic, affirmative action is simply unnecessary, and opposing it is positive for everyone. It is a confusing effort to spin opposition to affirmative action as "moderate" and completely disconnected from racism. In later years, Hargis had similarly smoothed over his racist edges and, in effect, pretended that he had not been an extremist in his anticommunist effort. Clearly, this kind of pretending is always precarious. It only fools some of the people, some of the time. Indeed, Dobson himself is not completely comfortable with the tactics of moderation, a point to which I will return in this book's conclusion.

That the Bible was once used to oppose civil rights is now as embarrassing as the fact that this same book was also used to justify slavery. Angela Dillard argues that currently, "among conservatives in general the 1954–1965 phase of the [civil rights] movement is generally characterized as a heroic attempt to reform American democracy and to secure the civil and political rights of all Americans regardless of race." After 1965, however, conservatives claim that the "Civil Rights Establishment" rejected "the movement toward color blindness as well as the doctrine of individual equality of opportunity in favor of group-based equality of results."[77] The second part of the argument is no surprise, but the first part is quite interesting since during the actual 1954–65 period so many conservatives— Christian or otherwise, including many one would not necessarily classify as "right-wing" or "extremist"—characterized civil rights as a communist conspiracy, or at least as being influenced by communists.

Even Pat Buchanan now concedes that "the civil rights movement was liberalism's finest hour . . . If they have stumbled and blundered terribly since, they knew what they were doing then. And what they were doing was right."[78] Yet the actions, attitudes, and repercussions of the old-school segregationists have not simply disappeared. When North Carolina Republican senator Jesse Helms finally retired in 2003 he still maintained that the South should have been left on its own to solve its problems without federal government interference, implying vaguely that the South would have peacefully desegregated itself if left alone. Helms had never recanted his states' rights racism, and it had done nothing to prevent him from being reelected for decades.

Like Helms, the prosegregation and unrepentant senator Strom Thurmond of South Carolina was also elected again and again. At his hundredth birthday party, House Majority leader Trent Lott brazenly asserted (and not for the first time) that the country would have been better off if this Dixiecrat had been elected president in 1948, when he had run as the States Rights Party candidate. Shortly afterward, Lott was no longer House Majority leader. Thurmond died, and his secret daughter, whose mother had been the Thurmond family's black maid, stepped forward to tell her story. The man who had been one of the country's most fervent opponents of racial mixing had been caught with his pants down. This was a salacious story that the media milked to death, but discussion of this intransigent segregationist turned into an interesting opportunity to remember the civil rights movement, to discuss its legacy, and—with the fiftieth anniversary of *Brown v. Board of Education* in 2004—to ask where the movement had succeeded over the long term and where civil rights advances had not yet been made. Certainly, the contested issue of states' rights remains in play today, and not only around issues of race. If the New South has embraced a postracist rhetoric, it has also simultaneously tenaciously clung to old ideas about the evils of federal government intervention in state affairs.

Though media coverage of *l'affaire* Thurmond mostly treated the desiccated senator as an anachronistic throwback who had long ago lost any political influence he might have exercised, it is worth bearing in mind that, although Thurmond never quite accomplished anything lasting as senator, he was an outspoken opponent of the Fairness Doctrine for years after the civil rights movement had peaked. Thurmond understood that Democrats favored using the doctrine in the 1960s and 1970s to shut down the ultras, and he repeatedly entered newspaper and magazine articles on McIntire's long battle against the FCC into the official congressional record and wrote supportive notes to McIntire and other ultras; he also spoke at their rallies and seminars. That one of the most ardent segregationists in Congress was also one of the most ardent opponents of the Fairness Doctrine was no coincidence. Thurmond's conception of what it meant to "serve the public interest" matched up quite well with the work that McIntire, Hargis, and Smoot were doing.[79] That African Americans, Jews, union members, feminists, and liberals might be part of "the public" was irrelevant to Thurmond, because these were exactly the radicals who had an iron grip on the mainstream media. To his mind, it was only through alternative, grassroots, right-wing media that the real public interest could be served.

Today, of course, right-wing media need no longer function at the grassroots margin. Rush Limbaugh, Sean Hannity, and Bill O'Reilly have thrived on mainstream advertising support, high ratings, and the absence of regulatory speed bumps. Listening to talk radio and watching Fox News today, it is hard to disagree with Richard Viguerie's claim that conservatives have successfully used media to make many Americans "turn right."

# Conclusion

## *From Birchers to Birthers?*

Two recurring arguments of this book have been that the broadcast ultras were the embarrassing nuts who had to be left behind for a more legitimate and effective conservative movement to emerge in the 1970s and '80s, and that contemporary conservatives, while sharing some of the anxieties and presumptions voiced by the cold war extremist broadcasters, are generally much better at couching right-wing ideas in more moderate-sounding rhetoric. The first claim would be hard to deny, but the latter contention may seem a bit more open to debate, especially in the wake of the election of President Obama in 2008 and the ensuing rise of "Tea Party" conservatives in 2009. The Tea Party, a most immoderate (and certainly not unified) group, initially grabbed headlines by marching with picket signs portraying President Obama as Hitler (or the Joker, or a Muslim), calling for a new American "revolation," and decrying abortion as an American "Hollowcost." Angry, white, and mostly male and over forty-five years old, this group—egregious spelling errors aside—has somewhat higher education and income levels than the average American.[1] Tea Party supporters are adamantly opposed to government bailouts specifically, and federal spending in general, although by hollering things like "keep your government hands off my Medicare check!" they sometimes reveal a shallow understanding of what federal spending actually encompasses. There are, of course, also people involved in this grassroots uprising who know how to organize, strategize, and fundraise. This new movement is no laughing matter: it is potentially a powerful force to be reckoned with.

As far as media goes, the Tea Party presented an interesting challenge for Fox News in 2009 and 2010. Commentators like Sean Hannity had nothing but good things to say about these common folks dressed up in Thomas Paine outfits, and the more outrageous picket signs magically failed to appear in Fox's coverage. The right-wing news network embraced the movement, while trying not to draw attention to its more lunatic elements. It would appear that even Fox—which gladly boosts ratings by picturing Glenn Beck metaphorizing Obama's damage to America by pouring fake gasoline all over some poor college student intern, then lighting a match—draws the line somewhere, deliberately avoiding showing Tea Party folks who look *too* unhinged. In light of the fact that one poll found that 63 percent of Tea Partiers "watch Fox News for most of their news" (compared to 46 percent of US Republicans, 8 percent of Democrats, 18 percent of independents, and 23 percent of all adults), it is hardly surprising that Fox News would labor so hard to keep its Tea Party coverage almost exuberantly positive.[2] Setting aside the question of whether or not these "revolationaries" will accomplish their objectives, as a *media* phenomenon, they seem to confirm that extremism is alive and well in America, moderate-sounding rhetoric be damned.

But such extremism, as I have argued, is a double-edged sword. It gets people riled up, it gets them media coverage, it gets them voting. But at some point that momentum needs to be redirected into political action committees and lobbying, and the hard extremist edges need to be softened. At least that's what needs to happen if the Republican Party is going to tap into the Tea Party momentum. To quote Rick Perlstein again, "the crazy tree blooms in every moment of liberal ascendancy, and . . . elites exploit the crazy for their own narrow interests."[3] How will the elites—in this case, the Republican Party—exploit this particular blossoming of craziness? Or will it be Tea Party supporters who end up exploiting the Republicans? In 2010 Tea Partiers made one move in the right direction, image-wise, to mainstream themselves. The *New York Times* reported that "at the inaugural National Tea Party Convention [in 2010], gone were the [2009] placards that protesters carried . . . with Mr. Obama's face wearing a Hitler mustache or superimposed on the Joker . . . Organizers said that anyone 'looking too crazy' would have been tossed out."[4] As the founder of the Tea Party Nation social-networking site noted, "The movement is maturing."[5]

Yet, interestingly, such maturity did not entail inching toward the "legitimate" GOP. In fact, the Republican Party was not embraced with open arms in 2009–10, and Republican National Committee chairman Michael

Steele was noticeably excluded from Tea Party events. Instead, even as almost half of the Tea Party supporters surveyed claimed that Sarah Palin was unqualified for the presidency, she remained the group's totemic hero, with Glenn Beck almost as highly esteemed.[6] But Palin was not in charge, and the party continued to lack hierarchy and centralized leadership.[7] It remained a "sprawling rebellion," its agitators ranging from survivalists and militia members, to anti-immigration and anti-gun-control groups, to garden-variety populists more concerned about reducing government spending than about hoarding food and water.[8] In 2010, the group seemed united only by "a narrative of impending tyranny."[9] Jonathan Raban succinctly conveys the collage of viewpoints he observed at the 2010 Tea Party Convention: "At Opryland, devout, abstemious Christians were breaking bread with followers of Ayn Rand's gospel of unbridled and atheistic self-interest. The convention, designed to unite the Tea Party Movement, was helping to expose fundamental differences of belief and mindset between people who, before Nashville, had appeared as interchangeable members of a single angry crowd."[10] At the September 2009 Tea Party march on Washington DC, Raban had spotted t-shirts declaring "Obama Spends—Jesus Saves," but also shirts declaring "I am John Galt" and "Atlas Shrugged." Even with their fierce individualism and wide range of idées fixes, the cold war right-wing broadcasters were not quite this heterogeneous! And, although they were never quite able to unify as a political force, the most successful ones certainly understood how to centralize power (on their own turf, at least) and to get things done, even if that entailed nothing more than fundraising to keep their own propaganda organizations functioning.

H. L. Hunt, Dan Smoot, Billy James Hargis, and Carl McIntire had to be shunted aside, along with folks like the John Birch Society's Robert Welch, for conservatives to move forward in the 1970s. Is Sarah Palin our own Robert Welch, an extremist who gets followers motivated, but without a long-term future within the American political machine? The short answer is no: Welch was much smarter, wealthier, and better organized than Palin, if decidedly less photogenic and entertaining. A more helpful answer is: it is impossible to predict the outcome of the Palin or the Tea Party phenomenon, but the question itself is likely misguided. It's just too simplistic to make the comparison, given the fifty years between Welch and Palin, the John Birch Society and the Tea Party, and the kinds of changes, in terms of both politics and the media landscape, that America has undergone since the cold war years. Although we can perhaps apply lessons from the Birchers to our understanding of the Birthers, we shouldn't assume a direct lineage or that, as the old cliché holds, history will repeat itself.

Still, the claim that the extremist forces that persist in America are often those that find more moderate means of public expression does, I think, remain valid. Once Far Right ideas take root and their advocates turn into organizations and think tanks, the extremist ideas that persist tend either to become reframed or to go underground.[11] This is more pragmatism than conspiracy, and it doesn't always go smoothly. Fox News may have strategically averted its cameras from revealing some of the more eccentric Tea Partiers, but that didn't keep those same eccentrics from proclaiming their ideas on YouTube. The muting of radical-sounding ideas can be a messy and flawed process, especially when not all of the players agree that it's a good idea to "mature."

Take Focus on the Family. As noted earlier, twenty years ago Focus began to shift its tactics, replacing words like "biblical" with "faith-based" and describing America as a pluralistic country, though defining pluralism in a rather narrow manner: America is home to many different, wonderfully diverse kinds of people, all of whom would be better off if they embraced the specific values that Focus holds dear. In 2005, Jim Daly replaced aging founder James Dobson as leader, and he pushed to further modernize and temper the organization's image. There's clearly a growing generation gap between the graying (and balding) New Christian Right, as symbolized by Dobson, and those new, younger conservative Christian players who are trying to steer away from the anti-everything image that the New Christian Right has long conveyed.

Meanwhile, though, before Daly's ascendancy Dobson had established an offshoot organization, Focus on the Family Action, which could be overtly political without endangering Focus on the Family's 501(c)(3) status. In October 2008, Family Action released an alarmist "letter from the future," dated 2012, predicting what the US would be like after two years of an Obama presidency. In a nutshell, there would be: a liberal Supreme Court, zero tolerance for prolife doctors, no more Boy Scouts of America, a general homosexual takeover, and, of course, a reinstatement of the Fairness Doctrine in order to destroy all Christian radio. Yet in real life, in 2010, Daly praised Obama as a positive example for African American fathers, celebrated the president's attention to the issue of human trafficking, and "expressed a willingness to work with Democrats."[12] Daly was even willing to direct Focus energies toward issues like social services—not *attacking* the governmental provision of social services in a reactive manner but, instead, being proactive and getting involved in a nongovernmental program that encourages adoption of kids who've been in foster care. Focus's "I Care about Orphans" initiative is "an educational resource for adoptive families."[13] It's doubtful that Focus intends to help out same-sex couples, but it's simply not an issue that comes up on the strikingly apolitical and optimistic I Care about Orphans Web site. While one can be certain that Focus has not gone liberal, the difference between the collapse of civilization predicted by Focus Action in 2008 and the constructive attitude that Focus on the Family tried to project in 2010 is striking. This is clearly an organization that wants to be perceived as "conservative" and positive, not "extremist" and negative.

It doesn't sound like Dobson's style. Indeed, he left Focus on the Family in February 2010. Focus was already on shaky financial ground, and it remains to be seen if it can stay afloat without Dobson on the radio raising funds and selling advice books. There were rumors that Dobson left because his son Ryan is divorced and so would not be able to take over the organization. Much more likely, though, is that young Dobson was not slated to fill his father's shoes because he's out of touch with the more mainstream conservative style that Daly and others see as Focus's future. Ryan Dobson is perhaps best known as author of the inspirational tome *Be Intolerant: Because Some Things Are Just Stupid*. That's a title that would have made Billy James Hargis chuckle with glee. It's certainly not an attempt to appear moderate. It appears that some politically engaged evangelicals, like those Chris Hedges encountered at the 2005 meeting of the National Religious Broadcasters association, militantly "call for Christian 'dominion' over the nation and, eventually, over the earth itself,"[14] even as others, while still identifying as conservative, are also increasingly concerned about global poverty, environmental issues, and human trafficking, and are not framing their efforts to alleviate suffering as a bid for Christian global domination. In sum, there is no clear, across-the-board drive toward moderation of image among the many entities that make up the Christian Right.

Even Fox News, which features so many over-the-top commentators, sometimes has a sense of the value of trying to appear rational, centered, non-extremist. In fact, there is concern among a number of Fox News employees that the ever-excessive Glenn Beck is making them look bad. His "antics are embarrassing" to some Fox journalists, and "his inflammatory rhetoric makes it difficult for the network to present itself as a legitimate news outlet."[15] Notwithstanding Beck, it is the *liberals* who are extremists, the more tempered voices at Fox proclaim. Consider the network's short-lived attempt to undercut *The Daily Show* (Comedy Central, 1996–present). In 2007, Joel Surnow, outspoken Hollywood conservative and creator of the protorture and highly rated series 24 (FOX, 2001–10), devised a new comedy series for Fox News, the *1/2 Hour News Hour*, designed explicitly as a counter to the *Daily Show*. Since the *Daily Show* is willing to mock anyone who behaves foolishly, from former President Bush to Secretary of State Clinton, only an ideologue could attack the show as leftist propaganda. It certainly has liberal leanings and was consistently critical of the war in Iraq ("Mess O' Potamia"), yet the program is eager to show that power-hungry Democrats are just as likely to metaphorically (or literally) drop their pants at inopportune moments as power-hungry Republicans are. But to Surnow, the *Daily Show* is just typical agitprop courtesy of the "liberal-dominated media."

The premiere episode of the *1/2 Hour News Hour* opened with a short skit starring "President Rush Limbaugh," with "Vice President Anne Coulter" at his side. (Only seventeen episodes aired, with Limbaugh, a good friend of Surnow, appearing in eight of them.) Next, the show's news anchors ran through their shtick, making fun of global warming, politically correct children's books, and electric cars. The laughtrack was very loud, which did little to compensate for the fact that this was a painfully unfunny program. Several moments of the show do stand out, though, as germane to our examination of cold war right-wing broadcasting.

First, the anchors reported that House representative and former presidential candidate Dennis Kucinich had recently called for the reinstatement of the Fairness Doctrine, which they explained was a measure to eliminate conservative broadcasting. Punch line: since he made his statements on Air America, nobody heard him. Once again, we see the Fairness Doctrine described as the keystone of the Democrats' plan to destroy all conservative media, though it is unclear why the liberals need the doctrine if they already control all the print media and all the TV news (outside of Fox), as the right-wing pundits claim. Given how little overall impact the doctrine actually had when it existed—in effect, Carl McIntire was the only one to be trounced by it, and, given his derelict behavior and general incompetence, he probably could have lost his license for any number of other violations—it is rather amazing how the left and the right persist in their attempts to use it as a political blackjack.[16] As Chad Raphael aptly summarizes, "perhaps no broadcast regulation has been as hotly debated—yet had so little impact on the industry—as the Fairness Doctrine." Of course, it *did* negatively impact grassroots right-wing broadcasting, but this was not "the industry."[17] In the cold war years, the doctrine frightened the little guys (and there were many of them), while having little genuine impact on the big players in the American media business.

In any case, the suspension of the Fairness Doctrine in 1987 was only one small piece of the deregulation of the communications industry that began under Reagan and culminated with Clinton's Telecommunications Act of 1996, and re-regulation seems more than a little unlikely given the power of the communications lobby in Washington DC. The doctrine was truly the product of a limited-channel environment. In a world dominated by only three national networks, and a smaller upstart fourth radio network, the ultras could only survive by banding together on small independent radio stations. Today we have digital cable, satellite radio, and the Internet; telecommunications venues have never been more numerous, even as fewer and fewer companies own the venues. The doctrine would only apply to *broadcast TV and radio*, which is now hardly more than the tip of the iceberg. So, clearly, the doctrine is a symbolic issue more than a practical one. It's simply not coming back—and even if it did, it would not change the world much. Like Howard Stern in 2006, Limbaugh could always hop to satellite if things got too hot for him on network radio. Given the doctrine's current symbolic status, it is best described as a low-stakes poker chip occasionally tossed back and forth by Democrats and Republicans. It showed up on the 1/2 *Hour News Hour* mostly to establish the show's credentials as conservative . . . and paranoid.

On the other hand, the quip about Air America was not bad. It is undeniable that many liberals are infuriated by right-wing talk radio but that they have had difficulty coming up with a financially successful left-wing alternative. Right-wing broadcasting has done best under the leadership of cultish personalities, and the Left has been mostly unable—or perhaps unwilling—to create its own media demagogues, though Michael Moore has served as talking head, and Rachel Maddow and Keith Olberman have succeeded with liberal MSNBC viewers. Maddow and Olberman hardly balance out the huge number of successful right-wing radio and TV commentators, though the *Colbert Report* strikes a blow for "truthiness" in brilliantly satirizing O'Reilly et al.

Conservatives frequently complain about the oppressive liberal media, but the 1/2 *Hour News Hour's* Air America punch line is a tacit acknowledgment that they (or at least Surnow) know that they have won, even if they have not quite mastered the art of news parody. Air America was short-lived and went bankrupt, and the "public interest" is today described strictly in marketplace terms. Whatever engages the public sells ads, and therefore serves the public interest. Rich people still don't get more votes than poor people, but there is much about today's deregulated media landscape that would please free-market advocate H. L. Hunt. Assumptions about the public interest, the triumph of the marketplace, and the absurdity of liberal calls for regulation all undergird the 1/2 *Hour News Hour*'s flippant joke about Dennis Kucinich—a figure, incidentally, who is also freely mocked by the *Daily Show*.

The premiere of the 1/2 *Hour News Hour* also included a gag public-service message in which an ACLU spokesman explains, as "America the Beautiful" plays softly in the background, that

> There was a time in America when white supremacists and other hate groups had to operate in the shadows, afraid to walk the streets in the daylight, afraid to show their faces. But in 1977 the neo-Nazis sued for their *right* to march through Skokie, Illinois, a town where thousands of Holocaust survivors lived. People like me helped those neo-Nazis take their case all the way to the United States Supreme Court, and guess what? We won. *We* won. So today, vicious hate groups can march anytime they want to, anywhere they please, in these United States of America. Who did that? I did that. I'm the ACLU. [Applause, announcer intones:] The American Civil Liberties Union: twisting the Constitution since 1920.

We've already seen how suppressing the racist roots of the New Christian Right has helped today's politically engaged conservative evangelicals to spin an ersatz moderate image for themselves. As this attack on the ACLU illustrates, there's also been a concerted effort among today's secular and religious conservatives to define liberals and progressives as intolerant and bigoted. In arguing for civil liberties, then, the ACLU only helps Nazis.[18] Further, by arguing against government-sponsored religious activities, defending affirmative action, and supporting civil rights for gays and lesbians, American progressives have become the enemies of freedom. It is progressives who are racists, according to the contemporary Right. Indeed, since Martin Luther King was a Christian, revisionists like the older Dobson have explained, the civil rights movement is not the opposite of today's white-dominated Christian Right but actually the progenitor of the New Christian Right. The illogical leaps and historical elisions in play here are obviously vexing, but it is a story that has stuck. Christian right-wing broadcasters like Hargis and McIntire, who violently opposed civil rights, are the Achilles' heel of such historical revisionism.

The right's "funding father," Richard Viguerie, is another historical revisionist. As we saw in the previous chapter, Viguerie has claimed that cold war extremism did not really exist. Yes, he admits, there were a miniscule number of unwise people who advocated violence, but not because they were conservatives. The very idea that the ultras were ultras—the idea that there was an extremist superpatriot movement at all—was a smear campaign concocted by the liberal-dominated media. The ultras themselves said the same thing in the 1960s, insisting there was nothing "extreme" in their thinking. There is no doubt good reason to be wary of the way that liberals like Richard Hofstader, Seymour Lipset, and Daniel Bell understood the right-wingers of those years. The liberal intelligentsia insisted that the superpatriots were paranoid, psychotic, unbalanced, and filled with "status anxiety," and such pathologization limited the value of their analyses. At the same time, the liberals were correct to single out the superpatriot movement as an important development, and one to be wary of.

The cold war liberal intellectuals did, to some extent, *create* and not simply *describe* a coherent group identity when they discussed the ultras en masse. At the same time, there were elements uniting the ultras—or at least the ultra broadcasters—and we make a serious historical error if we take seriously Viguerie's claim that the very existence of the cold war right-wing extremists was just a liberal smear campaign. It would be just as narrow-sighted to say that the Christian Right does not exist today, even though many people active in the movement claim this to be the case. The Christian Right is not a homogeneous group, it doesn't issue membership cards, and it is made up of a wide range of people, many of whom, at the grassroots level, would not even recognize what they are doing as "politics." For true believers, blocking access to an abortion clinic or denying women their birth control prescriptions isn't "politics." It's simply that which is *right*. The organizers at the top, however, know that they are engaged in political leadership. I do believe that the secular and Christian broadcasters described in the preceding pages knew that they were engaged in a movement, if a decentralized and somewhat chaotic one. They wanted to change the world for the better. But, for the most part, they thought that such change could come through words alone, and their words were ultimately too excessive, too weird to get the job done.

\*   \*   \*

During the course of his 1966 *Firing Line* interview with Barry Goldwater, William F. Buckley was asked if those Democrats and Republicans who

branded Goldwater's platform as "extremist" rather than "truly conservative" had made a valid critique. Buckley had a rather evasive and convo-
luted answer:

> No, I consider it patently invalid. I sometimes think that people who enter-
> tained such thoughts are almost exclusively people who understood Senator
> Goldwater's campaign as it was painted by Herblock. That is to say, they began
> by misunderstanding Senator Goldwater's campaign, and then, having misun-
> derstood it, confused their misunderstanding with the reality. And for that rea-
> son [they] understand Senator Goldwater to have stood, in 1964, for a whole
> tissue of positions for which, of course, clearly he did not.

What *exactly* did voters get wrong about Goldwater? Granted, many
mainstream Democrats and Republicans only understood Goldwater as
an extremist caricature. But what about the actual extremists, people like
Smoot, Hunt, Hargis, and McIntire, who rejected both the Democratic
and Republican parties, but embraced Goldwater? Did they misread the
candidate as extremist, too? These were the "weird" Goldwater supporters referenced in the "Confessions of a Republican" ad produced by the
Johnson presidential campaign, people presumably immune to the liberal
satirical logic of a Herblock cartoon.

It seems to me that where extremism was concerned, Herblock knew
exactly what he was talking about. In 1962, four years after the founding of
the John Birch Society and a full two years before Goldwater's resounding
defeat, Herblock produced a single-panel cartoon in which Robert Welch
walked in on his wife necking with a stranger on the couch (figure 35).
The stranger was labeled "GOP right-wing" and the wife "Birchism." The
Republican interloper handed Mr. Welch his hat and explained, "Sorry,
Old Boy, but your wife and I feel you've become an embarrassment." This
epitomizes precisely what happened to the angry antiheroes of cold war
right-wing broadcasting. They built an audience eager to listen to an extremist, ultraconservative message, and, in doing so, they built a base that
could be tapped into first by Goldwater, and eventually by Reagan. But, by
the time Reagan was in the White House, no one needed embarrassments
like Hargis, Hunt, Smoot, or McIntire. It was time to unceremoniously
show them the door.

Interestingly, Viguerie himself was shown the door when he approached the American Independent Party in 1976. Offering to be their
presidential candidate, he was not only rejected but also accused of "being

FIGURE 35. Herblock perfectly summarizes the fate of the ultras. The Republican Party was happy to co-opt the ideas—and the voting base—nurtured by extremists like Robert Welch, but raw extremism was embarassing. 1962 Herblock cartoon, copyright The Herb Block Foundation.

an acquaintance of William F. Buckley, part of the Rockefeller elite." A friend of Viguerie's concluded, "They're not conservative, they're out-and-out kooks." Viguerie resigned from the party, though he had already sunk a bit of money into his ill-fated campaign. Luckily, Adolph Coors was willing to pitch in to pay off the debt.[19] With this kind of money already available to him, it should have been clear that the American Independent Party actually needed Viguerie more than the reverse. But he just couldn't get along with them. Even Dan Smoot couldn't successfully collaborate with that weird bunch. Too peculiar even for Smoot? It would appear that out-and-out kookiness is in the eye of the beholder.

# Notes

## Introduction

1. At his initial, two-day-long recruitment meeting for the society, Welch, reading straight from his notes, lectured for nearly seven hours on the first day and six hours on the second. Jonathan M. Schoenwald, *A Time for Choosing: The Rise of Modern American Conservatism* (New York: Oxford University Press, 2001), 63.

2. Ibid., 64.

3. Cited in Rick Perlstein, "In America, Crazy Is a Preexisting Condition," *Washington Post*, August 16, 2009.

4. Ibid.

5. Schoenwald, *A Time for Choosing*, 69–70.

6. Ibid., 98.

7. Many of today's conservative politicians are quite comfortable appearing on Fox News, seeing it as a viable alternative to what Sarah Palin has coined the "lamestream media." In the cold war years, though, only a handful of conservatives like Strom Thurmond and Lester Maddox were willing to associate openly with the extremist broadcasters. Though such broadcasters had little direct political efficacy, to be associated with them could only damage most politicians' images.

8. Richard Hofstadter, *The Paranoid Style in American Politics and Other Essays* (New York: Alfred A. Knopf, 1966), 3. An earlier version of "Paranoid Style" appeared in *Harper's Magazine*, November 1964, 77–86.

9. Ibid., 27.

10. Hoover and chief inspector William C. Sullivan cited by Dan Smoot, quoting FBI documents, in unmarked file containing Smoot's undated, unpublished ruminations on the FBI (quotations from pages 24 and 27). Dan Smoot Collection, Cushing Memorial Library and Archives, Texas A&M University. In his testimony before the Warren Commission, Hoover spoke negatively of the superpatriots, observing that "the extreme right is just as much a danger to the freedom of this country as the extreme left." President's Committee on the Assassination of President

Kennedy, *Hearings and Exhibits*, vol. 5 (Washington DC: US Government Printing Office, 1964), 101.

11. Technically, only McIntire was a "broadcaster" insofar as he had a license to operate a radio station. The others hosted or created their own programs. I use "broadcaster" in a general sense to refer to people who sent out their ideas on TV and radio.

12. Rick Perlstein, *Before the Storm: Barry Goldwater and the Unmaking of the American Consensus* (New York: Hill and Wang, 2001); Kevin M. Kruse, *White Flight: Atlanta and the Making of Modern Conservatism* (Princeton, NJ: Princeton University Press, 2005); Dan T. Carter, *The Politics of Rage: George Wallace, the Origins of the New Conservatism, and the Transformation of American Politics*, 2nd ed. (Baton Rouge: Louisiana State University Press, 2000); Lisa McGirr, *Suburban Warriors: The Origins of the New American Right* (Princeton, NJ: Princeton University Press, 2001); Kim Phillips-Fein, *Invisible Hands: The Making of the Conservative Movement from the New Deal to Reagan* (New York: W. W. Norton, 2009).

13. Schoenwald's book is the obvious exception, though he does not focus specifically on the extremist broadcasters, concentrating instead on the JBS, Edwin A. Walker, Barry Goldwater, William F. Buckley, and, finally, Ronald Reagan.

14. Neil Hickey, "They Call Themselves Patriots," *TV Guide*, April 15–21, 1967, 14–17. Hickey's number refers to the total number of airings, not individual shows. In other words, one show might be aired in two hundred separate markets each day or week.

15. Seymour Martin Lipset and Earl Raab, *The Politics of Unreason: Right Wing Extremism in America, 1790–1970* (New York: Harper & Row, 1970). Bell first published his book in 1955 in response to McCarthyism, then issued a revised version to take the 1960s right wing into account: *The Radical Right: The New American Right, expanded and updated* (Garden City, NY: Doubleday, 1964).

16. Elizabeth MacDonald, "The Kennedys and the IRS," *Wall Street Journal*, January 28, 1997, A-16.

17. Richard Viguerie and David Franke, *America's Right Turn: How Conservatives Used New and Alternative Media to Take Power* (Chicago: Bonus Books, 2004).

18. Bill O'Reilly, *Culture Warrior* (New York: Broadway Books, 2007).

19. Judge Henry Friendly quoted in Erwin G. Krasnow, Lawrence D. Longley, and Herbert A. Terry, *The Politics of Broadcast Regulation*, 3rd ed. (New York: St. Martin's Press, 1982), 19.

20. Alan Brinkley, *Voices of Protest: Huey Long, Father Coughlin, and the Great Depression* (New York: Vintage Books, 1983), 267. Brinkley dates the new codes to 1940. Actually, the new NAB regulations were set in motion in late 1939, but there was a proviso that 1939–40 contracts would be honored, which meant Coughlin had a short stay of execution. Donald Warren, *Radio Priest: Charles Coughlin the Father of Hate Radio* (New York: Free Press, 1996), 223.

21. Brinkley, *Voices of Protest*, 267.

22. Cited in Hugh Carter Donahue, *The Battle to Control Broadcast News: Who Owns the First Amendment?* (Cambridge, MA: MIT Press, 1989), 35. Many later defenders of the Fairness Doctrine would refer to *Mayflower* in strictly positive terms. See, for example, Senator Ernest Hollings (D., South Carolina) in *Congressional Record*, September 19, 1978, S15473.

23. Justin Miller cited in "Radio: Sinking of the Mayflower," *Time*, June 13, 1949, http://www.time.com/time/magazine/article/0,9171,800314,00.html (accessed July 6, 2009).

24. The Democratic National Committee (DNC) waged a stealth campaign against right-wing broadcasters throughout the Kennedy and Johnson years, so "citizens" sometimes meant people in cahoots with the DNC. Nonetheless, many private citizens and nongovernmental organizations did lodge fairness complaints. The superpatriots were not shut down by the DNC alone, contrary to later accounts by opponents of the doctrine.

25. On the WLBT case and the ensuing broadcast reform movement, see Kathryn C. Montgomery, *Target: Prime Time: Advocacy Groups and the Struggle over Entertainment Television* (New York: Oxford University Press, 1991), and Heather Hendershot, *Saturday Morning Censors: Television Regulation before the V-Chip* (Durham, NC: Duke University Press, 1998).

26. Curtin explains that New Frontier TV documentaries were designed to "help American citizens to see themselves as part of a global community and as playing a leadership role in the Free World. Such a sense of community was essential if the US government was going to undertake a massive increase in military and foreign aid programs." Michael Curtin, *Redeeming the Wasteland: Television Documentary and Cold War Politics* (New Brunswick, NJ: Rutgers University Press, 1995), 91. When PBS was created, "The people were not asked what they might like to see on public television, for their judgments and behaviors were implicitly held responsible for the very 'TV problem' that public broadcasting was created to solve . . . [P]ublic television was envisioned *for* the people, not *by* the people." Laurie Ouellette, *Viewers Like You? How Public TV Failed the People* (New York: Columbia University Press, 2002), 16.

27. Steven D. Classen, *Watching Jim Crow: The Struggles over Mississippi TV, 1955–1969* (Durham, NC: Duke University Press, 2004).

28. Kim Phillips-Fein, "Right On," *Nation*, September 28, 2009, 30.

29. Certainly, neoevangelicals did not turn en masse into right-wing Christians. Leaving the fundamentalist ghetto, however, was a necessary first step that enabled later political engagement. Although born-agains did not march in lockstep from fundamentalism to neoevangelicalism to the Christian Right, this is the big picture of how a subsection of believers moved from separatism to political activism.

30. Leo P. Ribuffo, *The Old Christian Right: The Protestant Far Right from the Great Depression to the Cold War* (Philadelphia: Temple University Press, 1983), xii.

31. Graham cited in ibid., 259. Jerry Falwell made a similar claim for centrism, claiming, Ribuffo reports, that "truth lies between 'radical evangelicals' drifting toward liberalism and paranoid 'hyper-fundamentalists' who quibble over trivia" (265).

32. Quoted in Phillips-Fein, *Invisible Hands*, 221.

33. Ibid.

## Chapter One

1. William F. Buckley Jr., *Execution Eve, and Other Contemporary Ballads* (New York: Putnam, 1975), 478. Here Buckley quotes himself from six years earlier.

2. Don E. Carleton, *Red Scare! Right-Wing Hysteria, Fifties Fanaticism, and Their Legacy in Texas* (Austin: Texas Monthly Press, 1985), 93.

3. On Bunker Hunt and the Wallace campaign, see Dan T. Carter, *The Politics of Rage: George Wallace, the Origins of the New Conservatism, and the Transformation of American Politics* (Baton Rouge: Louisiana State University Press, 200), 336–37, 358.

4. Harry Hurt III, *Texas Rich: The Hunt Dynasty from the Early Oil Days through the Silver Crash* (New York: W. W. Norton, 1981).

5. According to a JBS film, Welch was also a precocious child, reading at two, studying Latin and math at five, and attending the University of North Carolina at twelve years of age. Furthermore, he was skilled at chess and had "worked seriously on Fermat's Theorem." *A Visit to the John Birch Society*. Undated, but pictures a 1972 banquet. Produced by American Media. 16mm film held at MacDonald & Associates, Chicago.

6. Hurt, *Texas Rich*, 26.

7. Chad Raphael, *Investigated Reporting: Muckrakers, Regulators, and the Struggle over Television Documentary* (Urbana: University of Illinois Press, 2005), 63.

8. J. Fred MacDonald, *Television and the Red Menace: The Video Road to Vietnam* (New York: Praeger, 1985), 236.

9. "'The postwar period in international relations has ended' ('State of the World' message, February 18, 1970)," in *Richard Nixon: Speeches, Writings, Documents*, ed. Rick Perlstein (Princeton, NJ: Princeton University Press, 2008), 191.

10. Ibid., 194.

11. William F. Buckley Jr., *Flying High: Remembering Barry Goldwater* (New York: Basic Books, 2008), 69.

12. Thomas Doherty, *Cold War, Cool Medium: Television, McCarthyism, and American Culture* (New York: Columbia University Press, 2003), 260.

13. MacDonald, *Television and the Red Menace*, 56.

14. Fred W. Friendly, *Due to Circumstances beyond Our Control . . .* (New York: Times Books, 1995), 62.

15. Cited in Doherty, *Cold War, Cool Medium*, 171.

16. Just a few representative texts: Doherty, *Cold War, Cool Medium*; Friendly, *Due to Circumstances*; A. M. Sperber, *Murrow: His Life and Times* (New York: Freundlich Books, 1986); Alexander Kendrick, *Prime Time: The Life of Edward R. Murrow* (Boston: Little Brown & Company, 1969); Daniel Leab, "*See It Now*: A Legend Reassessed," in *American History/American Television*, ed. John E. O'Connor (New York: Unger, 1983); Joseph E. Persico, *Edward R. Murrrow, An American Original* (New York: McGraw-Hill, 1988); Thomas Rosteck, *"See It Now" Confronts McCarthyism: Television Documentary and the Politics of Representation* (Tuscaloosa: University of Alabama Press, 1994).

17. Sperber, *Murrow*, 445–46. See also Casey Murrow in "This Reporter," *The Edward R. Murrow Collection* DVD, disk 1.

18. Kendrick, *Prime Time*, 421.

19. Ibid.

20. Sperber, *Murrow*, 445–46.

21. *Life Lines*, October 13, 1971, 1. All *Life Lines* newsletters accessed at Melvin Munn Collection, Texas Tech, Lubbock, TX.

22. December 31, 1951, cover letter accompanying "A Prospect Inspects . . . Facts Forum Plan." 1951 pamphlet. Dan Smoot FBI file.

23. "A Prospect Inspects . . . Facts Forum Plan."

24. Donald Barthelme, "Mr. Hunt's Woolly Utopia," *Reporter* (April 14, 1960), review runs 43–46, quotation from 46.

25. H. L. Hunt, *Alpaca* (Dallas: H. L. Hunt Press, 1960), 40.

26. *Democratic Digest*, "Oil for the Lamps of Propaganda: The Facts about Facts Forum" (March 1954): 25. Group Research, box 125, "Facts Forum" folder.

27. Saul Friedman, "Richest Man Shows Zealous Concern for Politics," *Denver Post*, undated clipping. Group Research, box 170, "Hunt, H. L. and Family" folder. Friedman may only be referring here to the amount spent on Hunt's radio broadcasts. While *Facts Forum* reached its widest audience via radio, being on many more radio than TV stations, TV was more expensive than radio to produce, so he may well have sunk much more into the television enterprise.

28. *Playboy*, "Playboy Interview: H. L. Hunt" August 1966, 51. Group Research, box 170, "Hunt, H. L. and Family" folder.

29. 1954 data from the *Reporter* cited in "Facts Forum Inc," April 11, 1962. Group Research, box 434, "Group Research Directory Organizations (F–P)" folder.

30. *Facts Forum* broadcast cited in the *Reporter*, "McCarthy, Hunt, and Facts Forum, *The Reporter*," February 16, 1954, 8. Group Research, box 170, "Hunt, H. L. and Family" folder.

31. Mutual made a brief foray into television, but "never broadcast a single nationwide television program and did not exist as a television network long enough to see the completion of coast-to-coast coaxial cable construction." James

Schwoch, "A Failed Vision: The Mutual Television Network," *Velvet Light Trap* 33 (Spring 1994): 3.

32. Tona J. Hangen, *Redeeming the Dial: Radio, Religion, and Popular Culture in America* (Chapel Hill: University of North Carolina Press, 2002), 86.

33. "Manion Forum," December 23, 1965. Group Research, box 434, "Group Research Directory Organizations (F–P)" folder.

34. Note, however, that some episodes of *Facts Forum* were produced by WBAP, a Fort Worth–based NBC affiliate.

35. MacDonald, *Television and the Red Menace*, passim. On *I Led 3 Lives*, see Michael Kackman, *Citizen Spy: Television, Espionage, and Cold War Culture* (Minneapolis: University of Minnesota Press, 2005).

36. Fred J. Cook, *Nation* special issue on "The Ultras," part 2, "Home of the Locusts," June 23, 1962, 580.

37. MacDonald, *Television and the Red Menace*, 41–42.

38. Ibid., 112–13.

39. Cited in William K. Wyant Jr., "Oil Man Hunt, Other Rightists Use Radio, TV and Literature in Spreading Views over Land," *St. Louis Dispatch* (March 2, 1962), unpaginated clipping. Group Research, box 170, "Hunt, H. L. and Family" folder.

40. Hurt, *Texas Rich*, 188.

41. Ibid., 156.

42. When politicians could be procured as guests, Smoot would moderate a discussion between the politicians on two sides of an issue.

43. Robert Lasch, "I See by the Papers," *Progressive* (March 1954): 11–13. Group Research, box 125, "Facts Forum" folder.

44. Ibid., 12.

45. Bagdikian cited in ibid.

46. *Facts Forum* 50, 16mm film, MacDonald & Associates.

47. Undated *Facts Forum* episode, "Is Eisenhower Cleaning Up the Corruption in Washington DC?" 16mm film, MacDonald & Associates.

48. *Facts Forum* 45, 16mm film, MacDonald & Associates.

49. Numbers from Hurt, *Texas Rich*, 156. Combs had already had some experience in public-affairs programming, having appeared in *Through the Iron Curtain* (1953), a fifteen-minute sustaining series about censorship in the Soviet Union. The *Variety* reviewer observed that the program was marred by Combs's repeated interruption of his cohost. Herm review, *Variety*, October 28, 1953, 24.

50. No date on 16mm film, print accessioned as *Facts Forum* 57, Answers for Americans, MacDonald & Associates.

51. *Facts Forum* 35, Answers for Americans, MacDonald & Associates. Burt later headed the company US Video, which produced a weekly series entitled *Counter-challenge—Program for Victory*.

52. No date on 16mm film, print accessioned as *Facts Forum* 5, MacDonald & Associates.

53. *Facts Forum* broadcast cited in *Reporter*, "McCarthy, Hunt, and Facts Forum" February 16, 1954, 1. Group Research, box 170, "Hunt, H. L. and Family" folder.

54. Daniel Bell, *The End of Ideology: On the Exhaustion of Political Ideas in the Fifties*, 5th ed. (Glencoe, IL: Free Press, 2000), 405.

55. Hurt, *Texas Rich*, 158.

56. Quoted in *New York Times*, "McCarthy Friend on F.C.C. Queried," January 19, 1954.

57. Clayton Knowles, "Senate Backs Lee for F.C.C. by 58-25," *New York Times*, January 26, 1954.

58. Doherty, *Cold War, Cool Medium*, 93. Notably, "one of [Lee's] first acts was to join the other commissioners in approving H. L. Hunt's application for a TV channel in Corpus Christi" (Lasch, "I See by the Papers," 13).

59. Erwin G. Krasnow et al., *The Politics of Broadcast Regulation*, 3rd ed. (New York: St. Martin's Press, 1982), 253.

60. Friedman, "Richest Man Shows Zealous Concern for Politics."

61. Lasch, "I See by the Papers," 12.

62. *Playboy*, "Playboy Interview: H. L. Hunt," August 1966, 51. Group Research, box 170, "Hunt, H. L. and Family" folder.

63. *Life Line* grew quickly: 20 radio stations in 1958; 68 stations in 1959; 108 in 1960; 201 in 1961; 295 in 1962. *Life Lines*, "Life Line Anniversary Issue," November 12, 1962, 4.

64. The radio show was on daily, while the TV version aired weekly. Arnold Forster and Benjamin Epstein, *Danger on the Right* (New York: Random House, 1964), 137.

65. *Life Lines*, "Life Line to Date," July 2, 1962.

66. Hurt, *Texas Rich*, 182.

67. Ibid., 181. Evangelical Pat Boone declined to join.

68. *Life Line* radio transcript, program no. 344 (March 7, 1959), 4. All *Life Line* transcripts accessed at Melvin Munn Collection, Texas Tech, Lubbock, TX.

69. *Life Line* radio transcript, program no. 102 (December 15, 1959), 3.

70. *Life Lines*, "Essentials for Constructives," October 19, 1962, 1.

71. *Life Line* radio transcript, program no. 132 (April 11, 1959), 3.

72. Ibid., 4.

73. Hurt, *Texas Rich*, 189.

74. As recalled by June Hunt in Ardis Burst, *The Three Families of H. L. Hunt* (New York: Weidenfeld & Nicolson, 1988), 92.

75. H. L. Hunt's emphasis in Swanee Hunt, *Half-Life of a Zealot* (Durham, NC: Duke University Press, 2006), 21. Swanee further notes, "that was the only time I ever heard Dad reference the Bible" (22).

76. *Dan Smoot Report*, "Communist Invasion of America," program no. 371, 16mm film, MacDonald & Associates.

77. *Life Line* 63, 16mm film, 1963, MacDonald & Associates.

78. *Life Lines*, November 20, 1961.

79. *Dan Smoot Report*, "Race Wars, USA—Part 1," program no. 624, 1967, 16mm film, MacDonald & Associates. Smoot was also sensitive to the FCC's personal-attack rules and often quoted others making attacks, or quoted attacks from the *Congressional Record*, so that specific attacks could not be directly pegged to him.

80. *Life Line* 49, 16mm film, 1963, MacDonald & Associates.

81. *Life Line* 57, 16mm film, 1963, MacDonald & Associates.

82. *Life Line* 15, 16mm film, 1963, MacDonald & Associates.

83. *Life Line* 57, 16mm film, 1963, MacDonald & Associates.

84. *Life Line* 2, 16mm film, 1963, MacDonald & Associates.

85. *Life Line* radio transcript, program no. 93 (February 25, 1959), 2.

86. Because oil was a diminishing resource, the logic went, oilmen were entitled to a 27.5 percent tax break in 1954. "Oil for the Lamps of Propaganda," 29.

87. *Life Line* radio transcript, program no. 132 (April 11, 1959), 1.

88. October 21 and November 19, 1981, interview on audiocassettes, Oral History Collection, Melvin Munn Collection, Texas Tech, Lubbock.

89. Mutual was more a consortium of stations than an actual network. As broadcast historian Eric Barnouw puts it, by the end of World War II, competition "became a three way rivalry" between CBS, NBC, and ABC. Mutual "never achieved a truly competitive position." Eric Barnouw, *Tube of Plenty: The Evolution of American Television*, 2nd ed. (New York: Oxford University Press, 1990), 96.

90. October 21 and November 19, 1981, interview on audiocassettes, Oral History Collection, Melvin Munn Collection.

91. Sen. Maurine Neuberger cited in Saul Friedman, "Billionaire Pushes Pet Program with Fanatic Zeal," *Denver Post*, November 26, 1964. Group Research, box 170, "Hunt, H. L. and Family" folder.

92. *Dan Smoot Report*, "Communist Invasion of America," program no. 271, 16mm film, MacDonald & Associates.

93. Ibid.

94. Quoted in Friedman, "Billionaire Pushes Pet Program."

95. "The Press: Facts-Forum Facts," *Time*, January 11, 1954, http://www.time.com/time/magazine/article/0,9171,819350–1,00.html (accessed August 25, 2009).

96. Cited in Saul Friedman, "Richest Man Shows Zealous Concern for Politics."

97. Hurt, *Texas Rich*, 165.

98. *Facts Forum* broadcast cited in *Reporter*, "McCarthy, Hunt, and Facts Forum" February 16, 1954, 8. Group Research, box 170, "Hunt, H. L. and Family" folder.

99. Dan Smoot FBI file, memo to J. Edgar Hoover from SAC (special agent in charge) Omaha, April 29, 1953, 2. Oddly, the declassified documents available in Smoot's FBI file are exclusively centered on Hunt, with virtually no mention of Smoot.

100. Dan Smoot FBI File, memo to J. Edgar Hoover from SAC Dallas, June 8, 1953, 5.

101. *Life Lines*, July 13, 1962, 2, 3.

102. *Life Lines*, October 13, 1971, 1.

103. October 21 and November 19, 1981, interview on audiocassettes, Oral History Collection, Melvin Munn Collection.

104. *Anarchy, USA* (no director or date given, but includes footage from 1965), 16mm film, MacDonald & Associates. JBS is not cited directly as producer, but the film includes a plug for American Opinion bookstores and a woman who was featured in *John Birch Society Film II*.

105. Such testimonials are made, for example, in *Winter Soldier* (Winter Film Collective, 1972).

106. *Interviews with My Lai Veterans* (Joseph Strick, 1971).

107. Rick Perlstein, *Nixonland: The Rise of a President and the Fracturing of America* (New York: Scribner, 2008), 555–56.

108. Westmoreland interviewed in *Hearts and Minds* (Peter Davis, 1974).

109. Perlstein, *Nixonland*, 555.

110. Ibid., 553.

111. Daniel C. Hallin, *We Keep America on Top of the World: Television Journalism and the Public Sphere* (New York: Routledge, 1994).

112. Hurt, *Texas Rich*, 277.

113. Kim Phillips-Fein, "American Counterrevolutionary: Lemuel Ricketts Boulware and General Electric, 1950–1960," in *American Capitalism: Social Thought and Political Economy in the Twentieth Century*, ed. Nelson Lichtenstein (Philadelphia: University of Pennyslvania Press, 2006), 249–70, quotation from 265.

114. The executive producer was Raymond R. Morgan Jr. In the course of an interview with Bill Geerhart, he unequivocally stated that Frawley funded the production. Morgan added that he screened the film for Frawley onsite at Schick. E-mail communication between Geerhart and the author, August 2, 2009.

115. Information on Frawley, Knott, and Lewis all from Group Research, box 434, "Group Research Directory Organizations (S–Z) and Individuals (A–L)" folder.

116. Buckley, *Flying High*, 129. In 2008, Buckley implies that his 1962 critique had been not only of Welch but also of his entire "organization of kooks," but he actually had not declared JBS *members* to be kooks until 1965.

117. Anti-Defamation League of B'nai B'rith, "The John Birch Society—1966," *Facts Domestic Report* 17, no. 1 (February 1966): 349–84, quotation from 381. Group Research, box 434, "Group Research Directory Organizations (F–P)" folder.

118. Anti-Defamation League of B'nai B'rith, "The John Birch Society—1966," *Facts Domestic Report* 17, no. 1 (February 1966): 349–84. Buckley material on 357. Group Research, box 434, "Group Research Directory Organizations (F–P)" folder.

119. *Nation*, "Oil for the Radical Right," undated clipping, 580–89, quotation from 580. Group Research, box 170, "Hunt, H. L. and Family" folder.

120. Dan Smoot FBI file, memo to J. Edgar Hoover from SAC Dallas, June 8, 1953, 2.

121. Hurt, *Texas Rich*, 191.

122. William K. Wyant Jr., "Oil Man Hunt, Other Rightists Use Radio, TV and Literature in Spreading Views over Land," *St. Louis Dispatch*, March 2, 1962. Group Research, box 170, "Hunt, H. L. and Family" folder.

123. "Oil for the Radical Right," 585.

124. Quoted in Perlstein, *Nixonland*, 671.

125. Hurt, *Texas Rich*, 226–33.

126. Perlstein, *Before the Storm: Barry Goldwater and the Unmaking of the American Consensus* (New York: Hill and Wang, 2001), 239.

127. Alice O'Connor, "Financing the Counterrevolution," in *Rightward Bound: Making America Conservative in the 1970s*, ed. Bruce J. Schulman and Julian E. Zelizer (Cambridge, MA: Harvard University Press, 2008), 157.

128. Paul Weyrich, "Building the Moral Majority," in *The Rise of Conservatism in America, 1945–2000: A Brief History with Documents*, ed. Ronald Story and Bruce Laurie (Boston: Bedford/St. Martin's), 115.

129. Some fifty years later, the extent of Technicolor's right-wing cloak-and-dagger activities still remains largely unknown. Dr. Richard Goldberg, a Technicolor engineer and superpatriot, all but admitted in an interview with film historian Scott Higgins that he had worked on film stock especially made for surveillance use, but he insisted Higgins turn off his tape recorder. E-mail exchange between Higgins and the author, July 7, 2009.

130. Faye Ginsburg, "The Word Made Flesh: The Disembodiment of Gender in the Abortion Debate," in *Uncertain Terms: Negotiating Gender in American Culture*, ed. Faye Ginsburg and Anna Lowenhaupt Tsing (Boston: Beacon Press, 1992), 67.

## Chapter Two

1. Dan Smoot, *People Along the Way . . . The Autobiography of Dan Smoot* (Tyler, TX: Tyler Press, 1996), 88–89.

2. Dan Smoot, "Facts about Dan Smoot," informational mailing sent on request to interested TV sponsors in 1960s. Correspondence folder S, Cushing Memorial Library and Archives Texas A&M University (hereafter cited as Texas A&M).

3. Smoot, *People Along the Way*, 87–88.

4. Ibid., 165.

5. Like most news and public-affairs programs at the time, the *Report* itself ran twelve minutes, with the remaining three minutes to be used for sponsors, station identification, etc.

6. Smoot test drove the phrases "constitutional conservative" and "totalitarian liberal" while at Hunt's operation but only fully developed them later on his own. I have not found any other individuals or organizations that used these descriptive labels.

7. Like Hunt, Hargis, and many of the other cold war radio and TV ultras, anti-Semitism and, to an even greater extent, anti-Catholicism were not central components of Smoot's repertoire. When the broadcast ultras were exposed for making anti-Semitic statements, they generally denied having made them. In other words, it's not that anti-Semitic beliefs had disappeared, just that there was wider acknowledgment that such beliefs were disreputable. Father Coughlin's anti-Semitism had helped get him banned from the airwaves, marking such sentiment as particularly dangerous for extremist broadcasters. Anti-Catholicism (linked to anti-immigration sentiment) had been central to the Old Christian Right of the 1920s and '30s, but in the postwar years, descendents of Catholic immigrants had been "Americanized." Indeed, Joe McCarthy was a Catholic, as were other prominent patriotic conservatives such as Buckley and L. Brent Bozell. In sum, deep distrust of Jews and Catholics certainly did not disappear from the ranks of the right-wing in the cold war years, but it was less front and center (and more potentially embarrassing) than it had been some years earlier.

8. Smoot, *People Along the Way*, 255.

9. Ibid., 226.

10. September 19, 1955, letter from John Borden, "Letters of Congratulations" file, Texas A&M.

11. No author, *American Opinion* clipping, June 1966, MacDonald & Associates, Chicago. The forty thousand figure and the figures for numbers of broadcast outlets and numbers of states are definitive. I have not been able to ascertain how the six million and seventeen million figures were determined.

12. Smoot, *Dan Smoot Report* 7, no. 52 (broadcast 333), December 25, 1961, 409–10.

13. July 1961 *New York Times Magazine* cited in Rudiger Bernd Wersich, "Zeitgenössischer Rechtsextremismus in den Vereinigten Staaten: Organisation, Ideologie, Methoden und Einfluß, dargestellt unter besonderer Berücksichtigung der John Birch Society" (PhD diss., Ludwig-Maximilians-Univeristät München, 1977), 300.

14. *This Is the John Birch Society*, filmed December 17, 1969, narrated by G. Edward Griffin, an American Media Production. All audiovisual materials drawn on in this chapter were accessed at MacDonald & Associates, Chicago.

15. Dan Smoot ABC Broadcast no. 4, 3. "Smoot: Unused Writings" folder. Smoot explained on a note written on the ABC broadcasts folder that "I do not think any of the enclosed material was ever broadcast or published. Some agency (as best I can remember) solicited me to submit some sample broadcasts for ABC news and some columns for general syndication. The agency was unable to place

them." The ABC papers are undated but appear to be mostly from 1963. Correspondence folder S, Texas A&M.

16. For the extremists' attack on Nixon's domestic spending, see chapter 13, "The More It Changes," in Gary Allen, *Richard Nixon: The Man behind the Mask* (Belmont, MA: Western Islands, 1971). Western Islands was a JBS imprint.

17. Dan Smoot, *People Along the Way*, 277.

18. Benjamin R. Epstein and Arnold Forster, *The Radical Right: Report on the John Birch Society and Its Allies* (New York: Vintage Books, 1967), 210.

19. Janice A. Radway, *A Feeling for Books: The Book-of-the-Month Club, Literary Taste, and Middle-Class Desire* (Chapel Hill: University of North Carolina Press, 1997), 145–46.

20. E-mail correspondence with Elana Levine, June 21, 2010.

21. Michael Curtin, "News in the United States, Network," in *Encyclopedia of Television*, ed. Horace Newcomb, 2nd ed. (Chicago: Fitzroy Dearborn, 2004), 1,654. Thanks to Jeffrey P. Jones for pointing me to this reference.

22. Erik Barnouw, *The Image Empire: A History of Broadcasting in the United States from* 1953 (New York: Oxford University Press, 1970), 42–43.

23. "Speeches 1969" folder, Boston Rally, 9, Texas A&M.

24. "Smoot: Unused Writings" folder, unnumbered "Dan Smoot ABC Broadcast" Texas A&M, box 3.

25. August 17, 1955, letter from Elaine Kregeloh to Dan Smoot, "Letters of Congratulations" file, Texas A&M.

26. Smoot, *People Along the Way*, 236.

27. "Smoot, Dan: South American Tour 1963" folder. Specific date in January 1963 unknown, Texas A&M.

28. Ibid.

29. "Smoot, Dan: South American Tour 1963" folder. Dated January 12, 1963, Texas A&M.

30. Pitney-Bowes official James Turrentine, cited in the *Dan Smoot Report* 7, no. 19 (broadcast 301), May 8, 1961, 152.

31. Jason Sokol, *There Goes My Everything: White Southerners in the Age of Civil Rights, 1945–1975* (New York: Vintage Books, 2007), 54.

32. Cited in ibid.

33. Box 1, February 10, 1980, letter from Smoot to Lawrence P. McDonald, Texas A&M.

34. Box 1, February 18, 1980, letter from Lawrence P. McDonald to Dan Smoot, Texas A&M.

35. "Speeches 1970" folder, Boston Rally, 26, Texas A&M.

36. Ibid.

37. *This Is the John Birch Society*.

38. Seymore Trammell observed, "We have all the nuts in the country." Quoted in Dan T. Carter, *The Politics of Rage: George Wallace, the Origins of the New*

*Conservatism, and the Transformation of American Politics*, 2nd ed. (Baton Rouge: Louisiana State University Press, 2000), 356. See also the description of the "fringe groups" supporting Wallace on page 366.

39. Richard Viguerie and David Franke, *America's Right Turn: How Conservatives Used New and Alternative Media to Take Power* (Chicago: Bonus Books, 2004), 77.

40. Gerald Schomp, *Birchism Was My Business* (New York: Macmillan, 1970), 102.

41. The JBS created numerous front organizations in the 1960s. Schomp explains that the society "planned to hold civil rights seminars throughout the nation as a way of stopping the civil rights movement. The seminars were to be sponsored by front groups, such as Parents for Racial Harmony. Responsible civic leaders outside the Society were to be enlisted in this cause without their knowledge that the Birch Society was behind it all. The plan was kept very secret." Schomp, caption from unpaginated photo section. Schomp further explains the organization of the front organizations on page 167.

42. *Civil Rights or Black Power?* Released by The Voice of Watts, Los Angeles; distributed by American Opinion (i.e., JBS), Belmont, MA, and American Opinion, San Marino, CA. Unfortunately, I have only been able to locate the reel-to-reel tape created to go with the filmstrip, so I cannot comment on the images that originally accompanied the audio.

43. Carter, *Politics of Rage*, 306.

44. Ibid., 305–6.

45. Richard Hofstadter, *The Paranoid Style in American Politics and Other Essays* (New York: Vintage Books, 1967), 37.

46. *Dan Smoot Report* (broadcast 507), "The Voting Rights Bill," 1965. Quotation from aired program, not printed report.

47. Smoot traveled to Georgetown, in Washington DC, to film many of the programs he did for Hunt. Given Smoot's own more limited budget, it is likely that his own program was produced in Dallas. In any case, both the Hunt and Smoot shows were distributed from Dallas, and that is where their business operations were based.

48. Johnson explains, however, that ABC did nationally distribute at least two programs produced outside of Hollywood. Lawrence Welk's broadcasts originated in Santa Monica, and *Jubilee U.S.A.* (1955–60) was from Springfield, Missouri. Victoria E. Johnson, *Heartland TV: Prime Time Television and the Struggle for U.S. Identity* (New York: New York University Press, 2008), 68.

49. Dan Smoot, "An Address to the 25th Anniversary Celebration of the John Birch Society: Dan Smoot Reflects on the Right," delivered in 1983 and reproduced in *Review of the News* (January 4, 1984), 51–58, quotation from 53.

50. Christopher Anderson, *Hollywood TV: The Studio System in the Fifties* (Austin: University of Texas Press, 1994).

51. Aniko Bodroghkozy, *Groove Tube: Sixties Television and the Youth Rebellion* (Durham, NC: Duke University Press, 2001).

52. Michele Hilmes, *Radio Voices: American Broadcasting, 1922–1952* (Minneapolis: University of Minnesota Press, 1997).

53. Doug Battema, "Pictures of a Bygone Era: The Syndication of *Amos 'n' Andy*, 1954–1966," *Television & New Media* 7, no.1 (February 2006): 3–39, information from 19.

54. See, for example, Melvin Patrick Ely, *The Adventures of Amos 'n' Andy: A Social History of an American Phenomenon* (New York: Free Press, 1991); Thomas Cripps, "*Amos 'n' Andy* and the Debate over American Racial Integration," in *American History/American Television: Interpreting the Video Past*, ed. John E. O'Connor (New York: Frederick Ungar, 1983); and Marlon Brigg's groundbreaking documentary *Color Adjustment* (1991).

55. Derek Kompare, *Rerun Nation: How Repeats Invented American Television* (New York: Routledge, 2005), 66n78.

56. Initially panned, *Hillbillies* was shortly thereafter reevaluated by critics as social satire in disguise. See chapter 2 of Janet Staiger, *Blockbuster TV: Must See Sitcoms in the Network Era* (New York: New York University Press, 2000).

57. Steven D. Classen, *Watching Jim Crow: The Struggles over Mississippi TV, 1955–1969* (Durham, NC: Duke University Press, 2004), 120–21.

58. Johnson, *Heartland TV*, 56.

59. Thomas Streeter, *Selling the Air: A Critique of the Policy of Commercial Broadcasting in the United States* (Chicago: University of Chicago Press, 1996), 141.

60. See Kim A. Smith, "Why Ascertainment Failed," *Communications and the Law* 11, no. 2 (June 1989): 49–60.

61. Ibid., 50.

62. Ibid., 54.

63. Ibid., 50.

64. Ien Ang, *Desperately Seeking the Audience* (New York: Routledge, 1991), and Ien Ang, *Living Room Wars: Rethinking Media Audiences for a Postmodern World* (New York: Routledge, 1996).

65. Eileen Meehan, "Why We Don't Count: The Commodity Audience," in *Logics of Television: Essays in Cultural Criticism*, ed. Patricia Mellencamp (Bloomington: Indiana University Press, 1990), 132.

66. Michael Curtin, *Redeeming the Wasteland: Television Documentary and Cold War Politics* (New Brunswick, NJ: Rutgers University Press, 1995).

67. Kompare, *Rerun Nation*, 25.

68. Robert W. McChesney, *Telecommunications, Mass Media, and Democracy: The Battle for the Control of U.S. Broadcasting, 1928–1935* (New York: Oxford University Press, 1993).

69. Jesse Walker, *Rebels on the Air: An Alternative History of Radio in America* (New York: New York University Press, 2001).

70. Deirdre Boyle, *Subject to Change: Guerilla Television Revisited* (New York: Oxford University Press, 1997).

71. Kompare, *Rerun Nation*, xiii.

72. Michael Kackman, "Nothing on but Hoppy Badges: *Hopalong Cassidy*, William Boyd Enterprises, and Emergent Media Globalization," *Cinema Journal* 47, no. 4 (Summer 2008): 76–101.

73. Since the FCC's 1960 policy statement allowed (for the first time) for the possibility that paid programs could count as public service, effectively saying that public service would not be tainted by commercialism, some programs after 1960 were run as public service but also included ads. A sponsor might well have enjoyed a tax benefit from advertising during a public-service program.

74. In 1967, for example, the National Association of Manufacturers' (NAM) *Industry on Parade* was available "free to one station in a market," while Smoot charged stations $5.00 per film. In this year, NAM had a total of 497 episodes available for broadcasters, while Smoot offered a whopping 600. More typical of sustaining (public-service) programming were smaller packages of shows. McGraw-Hill, for example, offered 39 episodes of its *Junior Science Series*, and smalltime producer David Wade offered 13 episodes of his *Canine Comments* educational series. Broadcast Information Bureau, Inc., 1967 *Series, Serials & Packages: A TV Film Source Book* 8, no. 2 (Summer/Fall 1967), A-143. On NAM's 1950s programming, see Anna McCarthy, *The Citizen Machine: Governing by Television in 1950s America* (New York: New Press, 2010).

75. "The Fearless American" (Los Angeles: Key Records, n.d.). Smoot ends with a brief homage to his "dear friend Strom Thurmond" and an exhortation to elect Goldwater. I gather that this album is from 1963 or 1964 because of the Goldwater reference.

76. Ibid.

77. Smoot, *People Along the Way*, 244.

78. Ibid.

79. Ibid., 247.

80. *Citizens' Council Forum* was distributed as public service at least until 1965, at which point its producers claimed it was on 1,500 radio and TV stations, in every state in the union. Group Research, box 43, "Broadcasting Notes on Programs Monitored" folder, October 1965.

81. Classen, *Watching Jim Crow*, 37.

82. Smoot, *People Along the Way*, 278.

83. Rudy Villasenor, "Widow Wins More than Half: Lewis Estate Battle Settled," *Los Angeles Times*, July 31, 1967. Unpaginated clipping from "Lewis Estate File Publicity," Texas A&M.

84. Letter from Smoot to David A. Witts, April 10, 1968, correspondence folder W, Texas A&M.

85. Dan Smoot letter to Arlene and Jewell Smoot, July 28, 1960, correspondence folder S, Texas A&M.

86. Smoot letter to the Garfield family, February 23, 1971, correspondence folder G, Texas A&M.

87. Smoot, "An Address to the 25th Anniversary Celebration of the John Birch Society," 55.

88. Eric Konigsberg, "On TV, Buckley Led Urbane Debating Club," *New York Times*, February 29, 2008.

89. William Kristol, "The Indispensable Man," *New York Times*, March 3, 2008.

90. Hugh Kenner cited in Douglas Martin, "William F. Buckley Jr. Is Dead at 82," *New York Times*, February 27, 2008.

**Chapter Three**

1. Carl McIntire Papers, Princeton Theological Seminary, Special Collections, box 373, FCC files.

2. See, for example, Stewart M. Hoover, *Religion in the Media Age* (New York: Routledge, 2006); Stewart M. Hoover and Lynn Schofield Clark, eds., *Practicing Religion in the Age of the Media* (New York: Columbia University Press, 2002); and Lynn Schofield Clark, *From Angels to Aliens: Teenagers, the Media and the Supernatural* (New York: Oxford University Press, 2005).

3. I use the phrase "Old Christian Right," to describe the cold war fundamentalist Right throughout this chapter, though more often this phrase is used to describe the explicitly fascist, Brown Shirt crowd of the 1930s. See Leo P. Ribuffo, *The Old Christian Right: The Protestant Far Right from the Great Depression to the Cold War* (Philadelphia: Temple University Press, 1983).

4. Martin E. Marty, *Modern American Religion*, vol. 2, *The Noise of Conflict 1919–1941* (Chicago: University of Chicago Press, 1991), 184.

5. Ibid.

6. John Fea, "Carl McIntire: From Fundamentalist Presbyterian to Presbyterian Fundamentalist," *The American Presbyterians* 72, no. 4 (Winter 1994): 253–68, quotation from 264.

7. This moniker pays homage to Werner Herzog's documentary *God's Angry Man* (1980), about Dr. Gene Scott, an eccentric televangelist who, like McIntire, struggled endlessly with the FCC.

8. Martin E. Marty, *Modern American Religion*, vol. 3, *Under God, Indivisible, 1941–1960* (Chicago: University of Chicago Press, 1996), 98.

9. Joel Carpenter, *Revive Us Again: The Reawakening of American Fundamentalism* (New York: Oxford University Press, 1997); George M. Marsden, *Reforming Fundamentalism: Fuller Theological Seminary and the New Evangelicalism* (Grand Rapids, MI: W. B. Eerdmans, 1987).

10. Nancy Totem Ammerman, "North American Protestant Fundamentalism,"

in *Fundamentalisms Observed*, ed. Martin E. Marty and R. Scott Appleby (Chicago: University of Chicago Press, 1991), 1–65, quotation from 37.

11. Volie E. Pyles, "'Bruised, Bloodied, and Broken': Fundamentalism's Internecine Controversy in the 1960s," *Fides et historie* 18, no. 3 (1986): 45–55, quotation from 50.

12. Mel White interview, *With God on Our Side: The Rise of the Religious Right in America* (PBS Home Video, 1996).

13. See Randall Balmer, "Protestant Underworld: John F. Kennedy and 'The Religious Issue,'" in *God in the White House: A History: How Faith Shaped the Presidency from John F. Kennedy to George W. Bush* (New York: HarperCollins, 2008).

14. Susan Friend Harding, *The Book of Jerry Falwell: Fundamentalist Language and Politics* (Princeton, NJ: Princeton University Press, 2000).

15. Carl McIntire, *The Death of a Church* (Collingswood, NJ: Christian Beacon Press, 1967), 99.

16. Randall Balmer, "Fundamentalist with Flair," *Christianity Today*, May 21, 2002, 52–57, P. T. Barnum reference on 53.

17. Pyles, "'Bruised, Bloodied, and Broken,'" 46.

18. Ibid.

19. Carl McIntire, "Born-Again Vote," in "The Fundamentalist Offensive," 36. Group Research, box 212, "Rev. Carl McIntire—General 1974" folder.

20. Ibid., 34.

21. Nineteenth-century evangelicals were heavily involved in social reform, often under the banner of the "social gospel." Feeling besieged by industrialization, the influx of Catholic immigrants, and the rise of mass media, by the early twentieth century evangelicals were losing their foothold in American politics and culture. Scopes was, in many ways, simply the last nail in the coffin.

22. Randall Balmer, "'Down to the Sea in Ships': The Unsinkable Carl McIntire, Radio Free America, and the Religious Right" (paper presented at the Shelby Cullom Davis Center for Historical Studies, Princeton University, January 19, 2001).

23. Jerry Oppenheimer, "'100,000 Yippies and Freaks' Plan to Protest Ky's Visit Here," *Washington Daily News*, September 22, 1970, unpaginated clipping. Group Research, box 212, "Rev. Carl McIntire—News Clips" folder.

24. Richard Halloran, "20,000 at Washington Rally Hear Ky Message Urging Continued Aid," *New York Times*, October 4, 1970. Group Research, box 212, "Rev. Carl McIntire—News Clips" folder. A representative from the Vietnamese Embassy read an address forwarded by Ky that was apparently quite bland, not the militant call for victory that he had originally agreed to deliver in person.

25. McIntire's FBI file is currently unavailable.

26. April 10, 1972, United States March for Victory letter to supporters. Group Research, box 212, "Rev. Carl McIntire—General" folder.

27. McIntire cited in Jerry Oppenheimer, "Tableau Tennis," *Washington News*,

September 10, 1971, 3. Group Research, box 212, "McIntire, Carl News Clips 1971–" folder.

28. April 28, 1971, press release for Patriots' March for Victory. Group Research, box 212, "Rev. Carl McIntire—General" folder.

29. No author, "McIntire and Police Disagree on Victory March Numbers," *Washington Star*, May 1971, unpaginated clipping. Group Research, box 212, "McIntire, Carl News Clips 1971–" folder.

30. Nixon coined "silent majority" in a speech against the 1969 moratorium actions. David Greenberg, *Nixon's Shadow: The History of an Image* (New York: W. W. Norton, 2003), 89.

31. A limited number of such letters were accessed from the Luce Library's Special Collections at Princeton Theological Seminary. Regrettably, this collection was only completely catalogued and made open to the public on May 1, 2010, as this book was in its final stages, though the author had access to a smaller selection of McIntire's papers some years before then. With six hundred boxes of documents now available, there are certainly many more interesting discoveries to be made about Carl McIntire.

32. NAE quoted in William Martin, *With God on Our Side: The Rise of the Religious Right in America* (New York: Broadway Books, 1996), 23.

33. Allan J. Lichtman, *White Protestant Nation: The Rise of the American Conservative Movement* (New York: Grove Press, 2008), 124.

34. Martin, *With God on Our Side*, 23.

35. Erling Jorstad, *The Politics of Doomsday* (Nashville: Abingdon Press, 1970), 55–56.

36. Ibid., 43.

37. Press release authored by Dr. Donald McKnight, "Statement Concerning Dr. Carl McIntire's Attempted Take Over of the American Council of Christian Churches," undated but from late 1970, 2–3. Group Research, box 213, "Rev. Carl McIntire—American Council of Christian Churches" folder.

38. Audio recording, "ACCC McIntire Takeover," Group Research.

39. This story is a summary of events described in numerous documents. Group Research, box 213, "Rev. Carl McIntire—American Council of Christian Churches" folder.

40. December 17, 1963, letter from Arthur G. Fetzer to McIntire, reproduced in letter from Robert T. Ketchum to McIntire, March 14, 1969. Group Research, box 213, "Rev. Carl McIntire—American Council of Christian Churches" folder.

41. "Beacongram," August 14, 1975. Group Research, box 212, "Rev. Carl McIntire *Christian Beacon*" folder.

42. Millheim quoted in George Dugan, "Fundamentalist Churches Shifting Their Tactics," *New York Times*, May 10, 1969. Group Research, box 213, "Rev. Carl McIntire—American Council of Christian Churches" folder.

43. "McIntire, Council Breach," *St. Louis Post-Dispatch*, October 29, 1971.

Group Research, box 213, "Rev. Carl McIntire—American Council of Christian Churches" folder.

44. ACCC press release, Dr. Donald McKnight, "Statement Concerning Dr. Carl McIntire's Attempted Take Over of the American Council of Christian Churches," no date, 2. Group Research, box 213, "Rev. Carl McIntire—American Council of Christian Churches" folder.

45. ACCC press release, Dr. L. Duane Brown, "Shame on McIntire! Report on the American Council of Christian Churches meeting October 28–30, 1970," no date, 1. Group Research, box 213, "Rev. Carl McIntire—American Council of Christian Churches" folder.

46. Audio recording, "ACCC McIntire Takeover," Group Research.

47. Dr. Arthur G. Fetzer cited in letter from McIntire to Dr. Robert T. Ketcham, November 23, 1968, 1. Group Research, box 213, "Rev. Carl McIntire— American Council of Christian Churches" folder.

48. Dr. Paul R. Jackson, "Special Information Bulletin" reissuing "A Joint Statement by Dr. Paul R. Jackson and Dr. R. T. Ketcham," November, 1968, 4. Group Research, box 213, "Rev. Carl McIntire—American Council of Christian Churches" folder.

49. Matthew 18:15–17, King James Version: "Moreover if thy brother shall trespass against thee, go and tell him his fault between thee and him alone: if he shall hear thee, thou hast gained thy brother. But if he shall neglect to hear them, tell it unto the church: but if he neglect to hear the church, let him be unto thee as a heathen man and a publican."

50. No author given, "Millheim Explains His Pause in Attacking the McIntire Empire." Group Research, box 213, "Rev. Carl McIntire—American Council of Christian Churches" folder.

51. See also George Marsden's careful discussion of the intellectually engaged fundamentalists of the Fuller Theological Seminary. As Quentin Schultze summarizes, Marsden traces how Fuller Seminary "maintained the fundamental beliefs of the evangelical faith while largely eliminating the anti-intellectualism, cultural separatism, and rhetorical belligerency that generally characterize militant Protestant fundamentalism in the United States." Such fundamentalists were, in sum, following a neoevangelical impulse. Quentin Schultze, "The Two Faces of Fundamentalist Higher Education," in *Fundamentalisms and Society: Reclaiming the Sciences, the Family, and Education*, ed. Martin E. Marty and R. Scott Appleby (Chicago: University of Chicago Press, 1993), 491. See also Susan Rose, "Christian Fundamentalism and Education in the United States," in Marty and Appleby, *Fundamentalisms and Society*, 452–89.

52. "The FCC's Concept of the Free Press," *Virginia Law Review* 36, no. 4 (May 1950): 511. The essay gives a 1949 *Time* magazine article as its source for the ACCC number and a 1946 *Time* article as source for the Federal Council of Churches number.

53. George Dugan, "Fundamentalist Churches Shifting Their Tactics," *New York Times*, May 10, 1969. Group Research, box 213, "Rev. Carl McIntire—American Council of Christian Churches" folder.

54. Gary K. Clabaugh, *Thunder on the Right: The Protestant Fundamentalists* (Chicago: Nelson-Hall Company, 1974), 78.

55. Kevin M. Kruse, *White Flight: Atlanta and the Making of Modern Conservatism* (Princeton, NJ: Princeton University Press, 2005), 169–78.

56. Schultze, "The Two Faces of Fundamentalist Higher Education," 490.

57. Tona J. Hangen, *Redeeming the Dial: Radio, Religion, and Popular Culture in America* (Chapel Hill: University of North Carolina Press, 2002), 152–53.

58. The Mutual Network, however, was receptive to fundamentalist programming for several years; Fuller's *Old-Fashioned Revival Hour* appeared on Mutual.

59. Here we can see how politically crucial the ACCC was for McIntire. It was simply better strategy to pursue a lawsuit in the name of an organization claiming to represent a huge number of citizens than in the name of a single individual. That many individuals in the ACCC were separatists who would never dream of pursuing a lawsuit was irrelevant to McIntire.

60. "The FCC's Concept of the Free Press," *Virginia Law Review* 36, no. 4 (May 1950): 510.

61. Cited in ibid., 511–12.

62. Further, low-power FM stations were cheaper to operate than AM stations, which opened up the field, potentially, to smaller operators. In 1949, the FCC estimated that startup operating costs for low-power FM stations were less than $5,000. See ibid., 513n101.

63. In 1951 the program was known as *Frontiers of Faith*. From 1953 on, the series used three different titles: *Frontiers of Faith* for episodes on Protestants, *Catholic Hour* for Catholics, and *Eternal Light* for Jews. Hal Erickson, *Religious Radio and Television in the United States, 1921–1991* (Jefferson, NC: McFarland and Co., 1992), 44.

64. Ibid.

65. John H. Norris cited in Initial Decision of Hearing Examiner H. Gifford Irion, December 13, 1968, 39. FCC docket 17141, box 61, vol. 28, National Archives, College Park, MD.

66. Hangen, *Redeeming the Dial*, 153.

67. Michele Rosenthal, *American Protestants and TV in the 1950s: Responses to a New Medium* (New York: Palgrave Macmillan, 2007), 5.

68. Ibid., 110.

69. Rick Perlstein, *Before the Storm: Barry Goldwater and the Unmaking of the American Consensus* (New York: Hill and Wang, 2001). See also Richard Leacock and Richard E. Parmentel Jr.'s film *Campaign Manager* (1964). A parallel could also be drawn between McIntire and George Wallace, who was also an expert at staging symbolic but futile protests and getting media coverage for such events.

See Dan T. Carter, *The Politics of Rage: George Wallace, the Origins of the New Conservatism, and the Transformation of American Politics* (New York: Simon and Schuster, 1995).

70. Susan Harding, "Representing Fundamentalism: The Problem of the Repugnant Cultural Other," *Social Research* 58, no. 2 (Summer 1991): 373–93, quotation from 374.

71. Glenn Beck used the phrase "leaders in the faith community" to describe a panel of Christian guests he had on his program on July 1, 2010, to discuss the communist-socialist agenda of "social justice" and other issues. The guests, though not all political leaders, included representatives of Wall Builders, Renewing American Leadership, and the Faith and Freedom Coalition, Ralph Reed's group. While this single television program should not be taken as wholly representative of how the religious Right is portrayed in the US, the framing of this group not as "powerful Christian political leaders," but rather as "leaders in the faith community" is, I would argue, a rather typical example of how softened rhetoric is used to frame conservative evangelical activism.

72. Steven Gardiner, "Through the Looking Glass and What the Christian Right Found There," in *Media, Culture, and the Religious Right*, ed. Linda Kintz and Julia Lesage (Minneapolis: University of Minnesota Press, 1998), 141–58.

73. On the sex education controversy, see Martin, *With God on Our Side*, 100–116, and Lisa McGirr, *Suburban Warriors: The Origins of the New American Right* (Princeton, NJ: Princeton University Press, 2001), 217–61.

74. On bringing Schwarz to the US, see Lichtman, *White Protestant Nation*, 197. On Schwarz's self-distancing from McIntire, see Jorstad, *The Politics of Doomsday*, 69–70.

75. Lichtman, *White Protestant Nation*, 347.

76. Ibid.


## Chapter Four

1. Testimony of Rev. Carl McIntire before the Senate Subcommittee on Communications, April 30, 1975, transcript in Group Research, box 125, "Fairness Doctrine" folder.

2. Testimony of Rev. Everett C. Parker, director of the Office of Communication, United Church of Christ, before the Senate Subcommittee on Communications, April 30, 1975, transcript in Group Research, ibid.

3. Chad Raphael, *Investigated Reporting: Muckrakers, Regulators, and the Struggle over Television Documentary* (Urbana: University of Illinois Press, 2005), 204.

4. For a more complicated (and negative) view of the origins of the doctrine, see Hugh Carter Donahue, *The Battle to Control Network News: Who Owns the*

*First Amendment?* (Cambridge, MA: MIT Press, 1989). For a short and sweet argument in favor of the doctrine, see Nicholas Johnson, "Audience Rights," review of Stephen J. Simmons, *The Fairness Doctrine and the Media, Columbia Journalism Review* (May/June 1979): 63–66. Thanks to Brent Cunningham for procuring this review for me.

5. Matthew Lasar, *Pacifica Radio: The Rise of an Alternative Network* (Philadelphia: Temple University Press, 2000).

6. Carl McIntire, *The Death of a Church* (Collingswood, NJ: Christian Beacon Press, 1967), 79.

7. Edward E. Plowman, "McIntire's Navy," *Liberty* (January/February 1974): 2–9, quotation from 7.

8. Fred Friendly, *The Good Guys, The Bad Guys, and the First Amendment: Free Speech vs. Fairness in Broadcasting* (New York: Random House, 1985), 48.

9. In a footnote to *Brandywine*, where Cottone would also serve as McIntire's counsel, the court detailed Cottone's objectionable behavior, concluding that "perhaps Mr. Cottone's actions can be explained as 'performing' for the hometown crowd. However, the court will not mute itself to such popcorn and peanuts antics, designed to create a circus-like atmosphere . . . The attitude displayed by counsel borders on the contemptuous and we therefore refuse to let it go unnoticed." United States Court of Appeals, District of Columbia Circuit, *Brandywine-Main Line Radio, Inc. v. Federal Communications Commission, Greater Philadelphia Council of Churches et al.*, no. 71–1181, note 39.

10. H. Gifford Irion, "The Constitutional Clock: A Horological Inquiry," in *School Desegregation: Documents and Commentaries*, ed. Hubert H. Humphrey (New York: Thomas Y. Crowell Co., 1964), 49–59.

11. "Intervenors' Exceptions to Initial Decision," April 14, 1969. National Archives, box 61, vol. 29, p. 23. All National Archives material cited in this chapter comes from docket no. 17141.

12. "Intervenors' Exceptions to Initial Decision," 50. WXUR's resident socialist commentator, Martin Burak, called this poet "slime," "filthy vermin," and a racist and a Nazi. The Intervenors cited his negative comments about the racist poet to show that Burak had made a personal attack on the racist. The poet had not been able to obtain a transcript of the attack from Burak and had complained to the FCC.

13. "Exceptions of Broadcast Bureau to Initial Decision." National Archives, box 61, vol. 28, p. 20.

14. Livezey was hired by Norris, against Fulton's wishes. Norris was thrilled with Livezey and gave tapes of his shows to moderators at his other radio station, as models for how to improve the ratings of call-in shows. McIntire also had high praise for Livezey initially, but by the time Livezey was removed from the program McIntire was fed up with him. The situation seems quite different from what happened at Mississippi's WLBT, where on-air racism was more consistently fostered

by all levels of management. See Steven D. Classen, *Watching Jim Crow: The Struggles over Mississippi TV, 1955–1969* (Durham, NC: Duke University Press, 2004).

15. "Initial Decision of Hearing Examiner H. Gifford Irion," December 13, 1968. National Archives, box 61, vol. 28, p. 70.

16. Cited in Irion, "Initial Decision," 85.

17. Note, however, that from the FCC's perspective this was irrelevant. Personal-attack rules, they explained, were designed "to enable the listening public to hear expositions of the various positions taken by responsible individuals and groups on important disputed issues." Thus, "licensees have never been permitted either under the personal attack principle or the personal attack rules, to avoid their obligations merely because they anticipated that those attacked would not be sufficiently alarmed to desire reply time." Commissioner Robert E. Lee, Federal Communications Commission, "Decision," July 7, 1970, p. 14. National Archives.

18. Federal Communications Commission, public notice 46526, January 24, 1964. Group Research, box 42, "Broadcasting Clips" file. My emphasis.

19. Commissioner Robert E. Lee, Federal Communications Commission, "Decision," July 7, 1970, p. 10. National Archives.

20. *Official Report of Proceedings before the Federal Communications Commission*, McIntire testimony, December 13, 1967. National Archives, box 56, vol. 9, p. 4,282. Hereafter cited as *Official Report*.

21. Irion, "Initial Decision," 60–61.

22. *Official Report*, McIntire testimony, December 13, 1967, box 56, vol. 9, p. 4,348.

23. *Official Report*, McIntire testimony, December 13, 1967, box 56, vol. 9, p. 4,351.

24. Lee, "Decision," 13.

25. Ibid., appendix A, 2.

26. Irion, "Initial Decision," 74.

27. Ibid., 3.

28. Ibid.

29. Ibid., 7.

30. Though the FCC jumped on almost every one of Irion's rhetorical flights of fancy, they missed one strange moment when Irion described an attack by Pastor Bob on a Unitarian minister. The minister received airtime to respond and testified at the hearing that he was satisfied. Irion concluded, "The whole episode smacks of *opera bouffe* and can be dismissed by saying that neither Don Quixote nor the windmill suffered any serious casualty" (Irion, "Initial Decision," 60).

31. Lee, "Decision," 10.

32. Irion, "Initial Decision," 21.

33. *Official Report*, argument by William A. Kehoe on behalf of chief, Broadcast Bureau, National Archives, box 61, vol. 29, p. 7,838.

34. "WXUR Reply to Broadcast Bureau Exceptions and Briefs," July 1969. National Archives, box 61, vol. 29, p. 2.

35. Cited in Irion, "Initial Decision," 89.

36. John H. Norris, letter to Edward Roper, August 18, 1966. National Archives, box 54, vol. 1.

37. Ibid.

38. Ibid. McIntire made his statements about the *Protocols* when he appeared on *Freedom of Speech*, after Livezey had been removed from the program.

39. *Official Report*, argument of Benedict P. Cottone on behalf of Brandywine-Maine Line Radio, Inc., March 31, 1970. National Archives, box 61, vol. 29, p. 7,867.

40. Thomas G. Krattenmaker and L. A. Powe Jr., "Comment: The Fairness Doctrine Today: A Constitutional Curiosity and An Impossible Dream," *Duke Law Journal* 151 (February 1985): 151–76, quotation from 173–74.

41. Friendly, *The Good Guys*, 42.

42. Thomas B. Fitzpatrick, William A. Kehoe, and D. Biard MacGuineas, "Broadcast Bureau's Proposed Findings of Fact and Conclusions," September 5, 1968. National Archives, box 61, vol. 27, p. 222. My emphasis.

43. Fred Devine, letter to chairman FCC, dated as received August 4, 1966. National Archives, box 54, vol. 1.

44. Harry M. Kreider, letter to E. Wm. Henry, chairman FCC, dated as received August 8, 1966. National Archives, box 54, vol. 1.

45. WXUR was attacked for not properly ascertaining the needs of its local audience, but "ascertainment" was regarded as a joke by most broadcasters (see chapter 2). WXUR never sent out listener surveys, but it scheduled a number of programs that focused on local issues. As proof of community need for fundamentalist radio, WXUR submitted to the FCC a report on the renewal applications of other stations in the area, conclusively showing that there were no fundamentalist stations in existence in the area. WXUR's weak ascertainment record was not markedly different from the lax approach taken by most secular broadcasters.

46. The Philadelphia Council of Churches distributed programming that stations put on for free to satisfy the FCC's public-service requirements. In this way, the council was doing the same thing that the NCC did nationally. Like the NCC, the Philadelphia Council of Churches saw paid religious time as disreputable.

47. Quoted in letter from William B. Ray, Chief Complaints and Compliance Division, Federal Communications Commission reply 8330-F2. Box 373, McIntire Collection, Princeton Theological Seminary Special Collections.

48. On British pirate radio see Jesse Walker, *Rebels on the Air: An Alternative History of Radio in America* (New York: New York University Press, 2001), 175–76.

49. Raphael, *Investigated Reporting*, 212.

50. Patricia Aufderheide, "After the Fairness Doctrine: Controversial Programming and the Public Interest," *Journal of Communication* 40, no. 3 (Summer 1990): 47–72, quotation from 61.

51. Kevin S. Sandler, "Life without Friends: NBC Programming Strategies in an Age of Media Clutter, Media Conglomeration, and TiVo," in *NBC: America's Network*, ed. Michele Hilmes (Berkeley: University of California Press, 2007), 291–306, quotation from 295.

52. Walker, *Rebels on the Air*, 294n34.

53. "[W]here mainstream law professors tend to ask questions about judges' fidelity to precedent and the Constitution, Liberty professors often analyze decisions in terms of biblical principles." Adam Liptak, "Giving the Law a Religious Perspective," *New York Times*, November 22, 2004.

54. Susan Friend Harding, *The Book of Jerry Falwell: Fundamentalist Language and Politics* (Princeton, NJ: Princeton University Press, 2000).

55. Heather Hendershot, *Shaking the World for Jesus: Media and Conservative Evangelical Culture* (Chicago: University of Chicago Press, 2004).

## Chapter Five

1. Willie Morris, "Houston's Superpatriots," *Harper's Magazine*, October 1961, 48–56, quotation from 49.

2. Ronald Reagan, "Business, Ballots, and Bureaus," 1960. Reel-to-reel tape recording, MacDonald & Associates.

3. Ronald Reagan, "The Myth of the Great Society," 1966. Speech delivered at Patton Center, Bronx, New York. 16mm film, A Verity Production, MacDonald & Associates.

4. Lisa McGirr, *Suburban Warriors: The Origins of the New American Right* (Princeton, NJ: Princeton University Press, 2001), 146.

5. Cited in John Harold Redekop, *The American Far Right: A Case Study of Billy James Hargis and Christian Crusade* (Grand Rapids, MI: William B. Eerdmans, 1969), 19.

6. As in previous chapters, "Old Christian Right" here refers to the politically engaged cold war fundamentalist extremists, not to the Depression-era Christian Right that Leo P. Ribuffo describes in *The Old Christian Right: The Protestant Far Right from the Great Depression to the Cold War* (Philadelphia, PA: Temple University Press, 1983).

7. Cited in Redekop, *The American Far Right*, 70.

8. Weyrich cited in Kevin M. Kruse, *White Flight: Atlanta and the Making of Modern Conservatism* (Princeton, NJ: Princeton University Press, 2005), 9. Kruse, who concurs that Old and New Right are interconnected, cites a number of researchers, including: William C. Berman, *America's Right Turn: From Nixon to Bush* (Baltimore: Johns Hopkins University Press, 1994); Dan T. Carter, *The Politics of Rage: George Wallace, the Origins of the New Conservatism, and the Transformation of American Politics*, 2nd ed. (Baton Rouge: Louisiana State University Press, 2000); Dan T. Carter, *From George Wallace to Newt Gingrich: Race in the*

*Conservative Counterrevolution, 1963–1994* (Baton Rouge: Louisiana State University Press, 1996); and Thomas Byrne Edsall with Mary Edsall, *Chain Reaction: The Impact of Race, Rights, and Taxes on American Politics* (New York: Norton, 1992).

9. Kruse, *White Flight*, 10.

10. Prior to seeking public office, Reagan was also politically active as president of the Screen Actors Guild.

11. Rick Perlstein, *Before the Storm: Barry Goldwater and the Unmaking of the American Consensus* (New York: Hill and Wang, 2001), ix.

12. Redekop, *The American Far Right*, 83–84.

13. Kruse, *White Flight*, 6.

14. Cited in Kruse, *White Flight*, 233.

15. Richard A. Viguerie and David Franke, *America's Right Turn: How Conservatives Used New and Alternative Media to Take Power* (Chicago: Bonus Books, 2004), 51.

16. "Mutual news commentators . . . tended to be more opinionated and less neutral than their counterparts on CBS and NBC. Whether their political leanings came from the right, as in the personalities of Boake Carter and Fulton Lewis, or from the left, as was the case with Raymond Gram Swing, Mutual commentators proved lively and controversial as well as popular." James Schwoch, "A Failed Vision: The Mutual Television Network," *Velvet Light Trap* (March 3, 1994): 3–11, quotation from 5.

17. Cited in Perlstein, *Before the Storm*, 155.

18. Buckley's turn from Welch, as well as his choice to distance himself from extremists, is described in Perlstein, *Before the Storm*, 153–56.

19. Hargis in *Saturday Evening Post*, cited in "Dr. Billy James Hargis, His Christian Crusade, His Christian Echoes National Ministry and Connections with Other Groups," in Group Research Directory, box 435, "Special Reports nos. 1–9 + index" folder, 4.

20. Viguerie and Franke, *America's Right Turn*, 88.

21. Ibid., 102.

22. Cited in Angela D. Dillard, *Guess Who's Coming to Dinner Now? Multicultural Conservatism in America* (New York: New York University Press, 2001), 145.

23. Roberts was a faith healer who stuck to preaching without politics. White claimed that "he built Oral Roberts from $25 in his pocket to a multi-million dollar operation, then fell out over money." Group Research Directory, "Special Reports nos. 10–20" folder, report no. 11, 6.

24. Group Research Directory, "Special Reports nos. 10–20" folder, report no. 11, 6. The report draws this quotation from Donald Quinn, *Oklahoma Courier*, reprinted in *Congressional Record*, April 16, 1962: D6060–6061.

25. Billy James Hargis, "Vital Information Concerning the Christ-Centered Americanism Campaign," January 1, 1963. Group Research, box 65, "Christian Crusade-Ads for Books, etc." folder.

26. This exact suggestion is made in a promotional film for the public-service series "What Everyone Should Know about Communism" (1964) hosted by Garry Moore, MacDonald & Associates.

27. These figures are from Hargis. Gary K. Clabaugh gives similar numbers for 1961 in *Thunder on the Right: The Protestant Fundamentalists* (Chicago: Nelson-Hall Company, 1974), 101.

28. Robert D. McFadden, "Billy James Harigs, 79, Pastor and Anticommunist Crusader," *New York Times*, November 29, 2004. The extent of Hargis's foreign broadcasting is unclear. He used superpowered transmitters in California and Mexico to send signals across both sides of the border, and he also, at one point, had access to a station in Ottawa, Canada. He was involved in missionary work in Korea and probably had a broadcasting presence in that country, but there are no available details.

29. Hargis letter, April 26, 1972. Group Research, box 66, "Christian Crusade letters from Headquarters 1971–1973" folder.

30. Perlstein, *Before the Storm*, 11.

31. This is what Viguerie was using in 1965. Viguerie and Franke, *America's Right Turn*, 102.

32. J. Gordon Melton, Phillip Charles Lucas, and Jon R. Stone, *Prime-Time Religion: An Encyclopedia of Religious Broadcasting* (Phoenix, AZ: Oryx Press), 132.

33. Hargis letter, April 7, 1972, in Group Research, box 66, "Christian Crusade—Letters from Headquarters 1971–1973" folder.

34. William Martin, "Giving the Winds a Mighty Voice," in *Religious Television: Controversies and Conclusions*, ed. Robert Abelman and Stewart M. Hoover (Norwood, NJ: Ablex Publishing Corporation, 1990), 63–70, quotation from 66.

35. Melton, Lucas, and Stone, *Prime-Time Religion*, 150.

36. Ibid., 284.

37. Tona J. Hangen, *Redeeming the Dial: Radio, Religion, and Popular Culture in America* (Chapel Hill: University of North Carolina Press, 2002).

38. Chris Hedges, "Feeling the Hate with the National Religious Broadcasters," *Harper's Magazine*, May 2005, 57.

39. Richard Briley II cited in Fernando Penabaz, *Crusading Preacher from the West* (Tulsa, OK: Christian Crusade, 1965), 126.

40. Briley cited in ibid., 128.

41. Ibid., 147.

42. Ibid., 148.

43. Cited in Erling Jorstad, *The Politics of Doomsday: Fundamentalists of the Far Right* (Nashville, TN: Abingdon Press, 1970), 72.

44. Extracts from IRS form 990A. Group Research, box 66, "Christian Crusade Finances—Incl. Tax Exemptions" folder.

45. 1963–65 returns. Group Research, box 66, "Christian Crusade Finances—Incl. Tax Exemptions" folder.

46. Hargis letter March 1962. Group Research, box 66, "Christian Crusade, Letters from Headquarters" folder.

47. All Mortenson information from memo from Ray Denison to Wes McCune, Thursday, May 28, 1964. Group Research, box 65, "Christian Crusade—General" folder.

48. Group Research report, "Facts about Rev. Billy James Hargis." Group Research, box 65, "Christian Crusade—General" folder.

49. Memo from Ray Denison to Wes McCune, Thursday, May 28, 1964. Group Research, box 65, "Christian Crusade—General" folder.

50. Group Research report, "Facts about Rev. Billy James Hargis." Group Research, box 65, "Christian Crusade—General" folder.

51. Group Research Directory, "Special Reports nos. 10–20" folder, report no. 11, 7.

52. "Statement by Billy James Hargis, following executive meeting of Board of Advisors, Christian Crusade, at Tulsa Okla., Thursday January 31, 1962, during National Anti-Communist Leadership School." Group Research, box 65, "Christian Crusade—General" folder.

53. Ibid.

54. Jorstad, *Politics of Doomsday*, 72–73.

55. Group Research report, "Facts about Rev. Billy James Hargis." Group Research, box 65, "Christian Crusade—General" folder.

56. "Dr. Billy James Hargis, His Christian Crusade, His Christian Echoes National Ministry and Connections with Other Groups" in Group Research, box 435, "Special Reports nos. 1–9 + index" folder, 3.

57. Dr. Frederic Curtis Fowler, "The Prodigal Nation," reel-to-reel tape marked only February 10–14, 1964, MacDonald & Associates.

58. Compare this to the Christian Coalition training tapes and seminars discussed by Julia Lesage, "Christian Coalition Leadership Training," in *Media, Culture and the Religious Right*, ed. Julia Lesage and Linda Kintz (Minneapolis: University of Minnesota Press, 1998), 295–325.

59. Clabaugh, *Thunder on the Right*, 20.

60. Ibid., 22.

61. Ibid., 6.

62. The Anti-Defamation League of B'nai B'rith in particular kept a close eye on the Right and sponsored books such as Benjamin R. Epstein and Arnold Forster, *The Radical Right: Report on the John Birch Society and Its Allies* (New York: Random House, 1967), and Forster and Epstein, *Danger on the Right: The Attitudes, Personnel, and Influence of the Radical Right and Extreme Conservatives* (New York: Random House, 1964).

63. Cited in William Martin, *With God on Our Side: The Rise of the Religious Right in America* (New York: Broadway Books, 1996), 79.

64. Cited in Group Research Directory, "Special Reports nos. 10–20" folder, report no. 11, 10. The report is from 1962 or 1963; no date is given for the pamphlet.

65. Redekop writes, "In his early years Hargis wrote what might be termed a racist pamphlet but he later repudiated it" (*The American Far Right*, 37n50). Whether this means Hargis repudiated his racist sentiments or simply claimed not to have authored the pamphlet is unclear.

66. Jorstad, *Politics of Doomsday*, 94n25.

67. Billy James Hargis interview, *With God on Our Side: The Rise of the Religious Right in America* (PBS Home Video, 1996).

68. Sara Diamond, *Spiritual Warfare: The Politics of the Christian Right* (Boston: South End Press, 1989), 46–47.

69. "Religion: The Sins of Billy James," *Time*, February 16, 1976.

70. September 1984 letter. Group Research, box 65, "Christian Crusade—General" folder. Hargis did have connections with the anti-Semitic icons of the Old Christian Right of the 1930s "brown shirt scare," such as Gerald Winrod. Winrod's Defender Seminary in Puerto Rico bestowed an honorary doctor of divinity upon Hargis in 1954, according to Clabaugh (*Thunder on the Right*, 87). However, anti-Semitism (or anti-Catholicism, for that matter) never became a focal point of Hargis's public persona. Describing McIntire and Hargis, Ribuffo notes that "Jew-baiters sometimes joined their respective organizations . . . but neither supposed that Zionist Elders ran international Communism" (Ribuffo, *The Old Christian Right*, 260).

71. February 20, 1981, letter. Group Research, box 65, "Christian Crusade—General" folder.

72. McGirr, *Suburban Warriors*, 240.

73. Dillard, *Guess Who's Coming to Dinner Now?*, 155.

74. Heather Hendershot, *Shaking the World for Jesus: Media and Conservative Evangelical Culture* (Chicago: University of Chicago Press, 2004), chap. 1.

75. Ann Burlein, *Lift High the Cross: Where White Supremacy and the Christian Right Converge* (Durham, NC: Duke University Press, 2002), 143.

76. Ibid., 148.

77. Dillard, *Guess Who's Coming to Dinner Now?*, 56.

78. Cited in ibid., 59.

79. As Hunt was less willing to take a public stand against civil rights and preferred to center his efforts on free market economics, he would have been of less interest to Thurmond. Publicly, Hunt seemed tone deaf to the social issues that most inflamed Thurmond, although the *Life Line* program and *Life Lines* newsletter would, in its later years after Hunt had drifted away, gravitate more toward the social issues ("permissiveness," etc.) that also inflamed Thurmond.

## Conclusion

1. Demographic details from *New York Times* poll. Kate Zernike and Megan Thee-Brenan, "Discontent's Demography: Who Backs the Tea Party," *New York Times*, April 15, 2010.

2. Ibid.

3. Rick Perlstein, "In America, Crazy Is a Preexisting Condition," *Washington Post*, August 16, 2009.

4. Kate Zernike, "At Tea Party Meeting, Looking to Forge a Full-Fledged Movement," *New York Times*, February 7, 2010.

5. Judson Phillip cited in ibid.

6. Zernike and Thee-Brenan, "Discontent's Demography." See also http://www .cbsnews.com/8301–503544_162–20002534–503544.html?tag=contentMain; contentBody (accessed June 28, 2010).

7. Mark Lilla speculates that "being ideologically allergic to hierarchy of any kind, they still have no identifiable leadership" and that "after tasting a few symbolic victories they will likely dissolve." Lilla, "The Tea Party Jacobins," *New York Review of Books* (May 27, 2010). It seems early, at this point, to make such predictions.

8. David Barstow, "The Party Lights Fuse for Rebellion on the Right," *New York Times*, February 16, 2010.

9. Ibid.

10. Jonathan Raban, "At the Tea Party," *New York Review of Books* (March 25, 2010): 8.

11. The Family, an elite fundamentalist group serving as a right-wing network for highly placed politicians, works behind the scenes to support "biblical economics" and upholds Stalin, Mao, and Hitler as evil men who, nonetheless, offer a great model for understanding how power works. Founded in 1935, the group only went low profile ("underground") in the late sixties. Their major "aboveground" activity is the Presidential Prayer Breakfast. Jeff Sharlet, *The Family: The Secret Fundamentalism at the Heart of American Power* (New York: HarperCollins, 2008).

12. Laurie Goodstein, "Radio Show for Focus on the Family Founder," *New York Times*, January 16, 2010.

13. http://www.icareaboutorphans.org (accessed February 11, 2010).

14. Chris Hedges, "Feeling the Hate with the National Religious Broadcasters," *Harper's Magazine*, May 2005, 58.

15. Mark Leibovich, "Being Glenn Beck," *New York Times Magazine*, October 3, 2010, 54. Leibovich notes that in late 2010, there were 296 advertisers who refused to be shown during Beck's program, even though it had great ratings. A certain kind of extremist rhetoric may draw viewers, but it is "toxic for ad sales."

16. After his hearing, the FCC resolved, based in large part upon fairness violations, to take away McIntire's license. The appeals court that later upheld the decision, however, focused on misrepresentation in McIntire's application. Though it is technically accurate to say that this court decision is responsible for McIntire's final defeat, liberal supporters of the doctrine are kidding themselves when they claim that no one ever lost a station because of the doctrine. A fairness complaint was the foundation of the FCC's epic McIntire hearing, a hearing that he finally lost.

17. Chad Raphael, *Investigated Reporting: Muckrakers, Regulators, and the Struggle over Television Documentary* (Urbana: University of Illinois Press, 2005), 203.

18. A second spot aired during the premiere explains that the ACLU has helped fight for consent to drug testing, with the express purpose of enabling pregnant women to snort cocaine.

19. Kim Phillips-Fein, *Invisible Hands: The Making of the Conservative Movement from the New Deal to Reagan* (New York: W. W. Norton, 2009), 220.

# Index